This book series is dedicated to the radical love and actions of Paulo Freire, Jesus "Pato" Gomez, and Joe L. Kincheloe.

TRANSGRESSIONS: CULTURAL STUDIES AND EDUCATION

Cultural studies provides an analytical toolbox for both making sense of educational practice and extending the insights of educational professionals into their labors. In this context *Transgressions: Cultural Studies and Education* provides a collection of books in the domain that specify this assertion. Crafted for an audience of teachers, teacher educators, scholars and students of cultural studies and others interested in cultural studies and pedagogy, the series documents both the possibilities of and the controversies surrounding the intersection of cultural studies and education. The editors and the authors of this series do not assume that the interaction of cultural studies and education devalues other types of knowledge and analytical forms. Rather the intersection of these knowledge disciplines offers a rejuvenating, optimistic, and positive perspective on education and educational institutions. Some might describe its contribution as democratic, emancipatory, and transformative. The editors and authors maintain that cultural studies helps free educators from sterile, monolithic analyses that have for too long undermined efforts to think of educational practices by providing other words, new languages, and fresh metaphors. Operating in an interdisciplinary cosmos, Transgressions: Cultural Studies and Education is dedicated to exploring the ways cultural studies enhances the study and practice of education. With this in mind the series focuses in a non-exclusive way on popular culture as well as other dimensions of cultural studies including social theory, social justice and positionality, cultural dimensions of technological innovation, new media and media literacy, new forms of oppression emerging in an electronic hyperreality, and postcolonial global concerns. With these concerns in mind cultural studies scholars often argue that the realm of popular culture is the most powerful educational force in contemporary culture. Indeed, in the twenty-first century this pedagogical dynamic is sweeping through the entire world. Educators, they believe, must understand these emerging realities in order to gain an important voice in the pedagogical conversation.

Without an understanding of cultural pedagogy's (education that takes place outside of formal schooling) role in the shaping of individual identity–youth identity in particular–the role educators play in the lives of their students will continue to fade. Why do so many of our students feel that life is incomprehensible and devoid of meaning? What does it mean, teachers wonder, when young people are unable to describe their moods, their affective affiliation to the society around them. Meanings provided young people by mainstream institutions often do little to help them deal with their affective complexity, their difficulty negotiating the rift between meaning and affect. School knowledge and educational expectations seem as anachronistic as a ditto machine, not that learning ways of rational thought and making sense of the world are unimportant.

But school knowledge and educational expectations often have little to offer students about making sense of the way they feel, the way their affective lives are shaped. In no way do we argue that analysis of the production of youth in an electronic mediated world demands some "touchy-feely" educational superficiality. What is needed in this context is a rigorous analysis of the interrelationship between pedagogy, popular culture, meaning making, and youth subjectivity. In an era marked by youth depression, violence, and suicide such insights become extremely important, even life saving. Pessimism about the future is the common sense of many contemporary youth with its concomitant feeling that no one can make a difference.

If affective production can be shaped to reflect these perspectives, then it can be reshaped to lay the groundwork for optimism, passionate commitment, and transformative educational and political activity. In these ways cultural studies adds a dimension to the work of education unfilled by any other sub-discipline. This is what Transgressions: Cultural Studies and Education seeks to produce—literature on these issues that makes a difference. It seeks to publish studies that help those who work with young people, those individuals involved in the disciplines that study children and youth, and young people themselves improve their lives in these bizarre times.

Writing the Family

Women, Auto-Ethnography, and Family work

Kathleen Skott-Myhre
Korinne Weima
Helen Gibbs

SENSE PUBLISHERS
ROTTERDAM/BOSTON/TAIPEI

A C.I.P. record for this book is available from the Library of Congress.

ISBN: 978-94-6091-747-9 (paperback)
ISBN: 978-94-6091-748-6 (hardback)
ISBN: 978-94-6091-749-3 (e-book)

Published by: Sense Publishers,
P.O. Box 21858,
3001 AW Rotterdam,
The Netherlands
https://www.sensepublishers.com/

Printed on acid-free paper

TABLE OF CONTENTS

INTRODUCTION

WRITING THE FAMILY: THREE STORIES

This is a book about the family. In a very important way, it is a book about being a woman in relation to the current form of family under the current regime of post-modern capitalism in North America. The authors are three women whose interest in the family stems from their own unique and varied experience with its force and substance as a social form. The text is comprised of three auto-ethnographies. Each section looks at the family from a radically distinct perspective rooted in the author's own life experience, both personal and professional. All three women are involved in working with young people and each section reflects a desire to find a way in which an understanding the family might enrich and benefit this work.

In the first auto-ethnography, Korinne Weima provides a writing of the family as an insider. She explores family in two parallel realms of her own lived experience, external and internal. She explains that the inspiration for exploring these two realms of experience arose from the following quotation:

We all have two families, one that we live *with* and another we live *by*. (Gillis, 1996, p. xv)

She argues that for two key reasons, the quotation immediately had a profound effect on her. First, she had never considered the thought of having two families at the same time: the external that one lives *with,* that has evolved in composition over the course of time, and another internal family that one lives *by*, that represents one's personal ideal notions of the family construct. Second, and most importantly, the quotation prompted the realization that the internal lived *by* family ideal continually informs perceptions about the external lived *with* family.

Overall, Gillis's (1996) quotation, then, provides the (under)tone for Weima's auto-ethnography, dividing her lived experience into two separate, but related, realms: (1) the external (lived *with* family); and (2) the internal (lived *by* family). As she explores these two realms of lived experience, she addresses the hegemony of the nuclear family as the idealized lived *by* family structure both internally and in our dominant culture. Weima notes that what presents the greatest challenge to writing about the family is the fact that it is a ubiquitous phenomenon. Certainly, one could write at length about instances of nuclear family idealization that are immediately apparent. What Weima is concerned about, however, are the instances of nuclear family idealization that remain unrecognized. To explore and deconstruct these family idealizations, Weima uses postmodern theory and alternative histories of the family that challenge our common beliefs about its structure and purpose. In particular, Weima maps the way that the evolving field of psychology constructed the family as a site of discipline for the emerging capitalist society. Unpacking this history in both contemporary pop-culture forms, such as Dr. Laura Schlessinger and Dr. Phil McGraw, and through the historical appropriation of parenting as a form of social control, Weima explores the ways in which our family life is written through our social experience.

In the second auto-ethnography, Kathleen Skott-Myhre examines the family from the perspective of gender, race, class, and culture. Specifically, she explores the ways in which the relationships between mothers and daughters are shaped by family patterns developed under colonial and patriarchal regimes of power and force. Using her own experience as a woman of Irish descent raised in North America, Skott-Myhre engages a postmodern feminist analysis to explicate the manner in which power comes into play across generations of women living within patriarchal family systems. Utilizing the power analytics of Foucault, critical race theory, feminist psychoanalysis, theories of cultural hybridity, and Deleuze and Guattari's concept of the rhizome, she argues against traditional psychological tracings of the family. She makes a case that such tracings obscure important elements of female experience and limit the creative possibilities inherent in mother-daughter relationships. As a counselling psychologist, she argues for a new mapping of the family based on the contingent and creative possibilities of the family as an open-ended system of creative force across generations.

She concludes with a proposal for a new approach to family therapy with young women and their mothers based on her alternative mapping of the family.

In the final auto-ethnography, Helen Gibbs extends the analysis of the family as a site of disciplinary power through an examination of her own work as a child protection social worker. In this final self-study, Gibbs offers us a perspective from outside the family. Unlike the first two, whose focus is on the experience of women within the family, Gibbs focuses on the role of the social worker that engages the family on behalf of the system.

Gibbs's chapter takes some steps in examining the child protection system from a position that is rarely discussed. Specifically, Gibbs explores how Foucault's concept of disciplinary power can be used to demonstrate how power operates within the client/worker relationship. This relationship is shown to be complex with power flowing bi-directionally, rather than hierarchically. Instead of viewing power imbalances as a function of state control, she shows how the client/worker relationship is constituted by the worker, the client, the organization and the social body. She utilizes auto-ethnography to document her personal encounters with youth and families as she exposes the disciplinary practices and instruments to which she was subject as a worker and used with the families she encountered.

Given that the child protection system is constantly shifting and changing in order to improve its ability to safeguard children, a greater emphasis is required to examine how workers operate within this complex, overwhelming, and multi-dimensional world. Gibbs demonstrates that by engaging in a reflexive examination of her position of power, different approaches to making intervention beneficial to all involved become available. This is important if child protection work aims to work *with* clients rather than *on* clients.

WRITING THE FAMILY: THEORY AND AUTO-ETHNOGRAPHY

Each of the authors in this volume has chosen to interrogate the family as a kind of social structure founded in relations of power and force. Although each author engages the family from a unique position and perspective, the authors share certain theoretical affinities and an interest in postmodern research approaches such as those articulated in the work of Michel Foucault, as well as Gilles Deleuze and Felix Guattari. That is to say, they hold an interest in the ways in which power functions as both an instrument of discipline and control while simultaneously offering new creative possibilities for flight and liberation. In this sense they see the family as

> [n]ot only a product of the larger society, but also its producer and reproducer. Any adequate historical understanding of family must acknowledge its central role in social and political as well as personal relationships, in societal as well as biological reproduction. 'The family' may be classified as a 'natural' or biological unit, a 'traditional,' divinely ordained, and universal entity, but it also very much a social construction. It is whatever we need it to be, at once the source of all good and of all evil. (Comacchio, 1999, p.6)

A Government Machine?

The family then for each of the authors of this volume operates in some sense as an instrument of the dominant regimes of power. It is interesting to note that while the family has maintained a relation of mutual self-interest with the prevailing regime of power, it was not until the period of modernity that the family, as a unit, became of interest to the state. In other words, as Marx (1987) has pointed out in *The German Ideology*, the division of labor between men and women prescribed by the earliest forms of patriarchal society sets the template for discipline and domination. However, it is only with the advent of the modern state with its proliferation of disciplinary mechanisms that the family reaches its full force as a site of discipline on behalf of forces outside itself.

This shift begins at the end of the Feudal period. Foucault (1978) indicates that until this time the sovereign was not concerned about the state of affairs within families or their health and well-being.

This is not to say that there was no relation between the sovereign and the patriarchal head of household. Rather, that relation allowed for a relative autonomous sphere of influence for the head of household separate from the obligation to the state. As the newly instituted state form develops, the "art of government," which involved making the head of the household responsible for all aspects of the family's life, begins to become increasingly seen as an avenue through which the needs of the sovereign could be achieved (Tait, 2000). Over time, therefore, the family's designation as a governing unit became emphasized.

Similar to Foucault, Aries (1967) argued that in the fourteenth century, the modern family began to take shape. The system of power changed from the sovereign as overseer of the population to that of patriarchy, where males were identified as the dominant force within each family. Therefore, "a value was attributed to the family which had previously been attributed to the line. It became the social cell, the basis of the State, the foundation of the monarchy" (Aries, 1967, p. 367).

The significant piece here is that the family served a specific function for the sovereign that elevated the importance of families and precipitated the beginning of its manipulation by outside forces. Donzelot, in his book *The Policing of Families* (1979), argued that the central role of the family became the production and government of good children. This production was overseen by "medical, educational, and psychological experts who successfully bridged the gap between the inner workings of the family unit and the broadest objectives of government" (Tait, 2000, p. 69).

Comacchio (1999) identifies how the concept of family has become so encompassing and enduring when she says:

> Much of the family's symbolic power comes from the religious, moral and ideological forces that have sustained it in the face of continued threats, real and imagined. Add to these the power of law, education, science and the state, and it is clear why the family's institutional basis is so durable. A pervasive ideology of 'familism' has left few social relations untouched. (p. 147)

Comacchio highlights a number of key points. The family has been subjected to religious and political forces that have strengthened its purpose and argued its usefulness. Any “attack” on the “ideal” family is often matched with activism from people or groups who promote religious ideology. Significantly, the family has also functioned as a means to teach appropriate conduct to future generations (Tait, 2000). Middle class norms have been promoted and perpetuated, either through families incorporating these norms into their daily lives or by its use as a baseline to judge families who do things differently. Those families who fail to meet the “norms” are often labelled as deviant or dysfunctional. Obviously, all three of the auto-ethnographies in this volume are centrally interested in the ways in which dysfunction and deviance operate within the family as a disciplinary machine of the state.

AUTO-ETHNOGRAPHY: METHOD AND METHODOLOGY

We have used the term auto-ethnography to describe each author’s contribution to this volume. However, what is this methodology exactly and why is it used here? Certainly, one reason that auto-ethnography even begins to be an option for researchers such as the authors here is that over the past few decades, methods used to conduct research have broadened. Arguments launched by postmodernists about our ability to “know” others, group people according to characteristics, and be objective, have brought forth the inconsistencies and limitations of scientific research (see Tierney, 2001). Postmodernists have suggested that knowledge is not something “hidden” within individuals waiting to be “discovered.” Rather, knowledge is created by and between individuals and groups. Knowledge, then, is not unitary but shifting, based on social, cultural, and political contexts. This is different from the modernist model that suggests that knowledge is cumulative and linear and could be obtained value-free within the research process. Post-modernist researchers acknowledge that there are limitations to knowledge being described because language is not neutral. Over the years, philosophers have pointed out that the “facts” scientists saw were inextricably linked to the vocabulary they used to express or represent them (see Rorty, 1982; Toulmin, 1969).

The recognition, especially within the qualitative field, that completely objective research is not attainable has led to new approaches to conducting, and writing up, research. One approach shifted the focus of the research onto "observing the observer" and writing more directly, from the source of one's own experience (Ellis & Bochner, 2000, p.747). This style of research and writing is commonly referred to as auto-ethnography.

WHAT IS AUTO-ETHNOGRAPHY?

Ellis and Bochner (2000) defined auto-ethnography as "an autobiographical genre of writing and research that displays multiple layers of consciousness, connecting the personal to the cultural" (p. 739). Usually written in first person accounts, the researcher's personal experience is used to illuminate a particular culture, event and/or institution. Often starting with the exploration of a social experience, the researcher reflects back on self and looks deeply at *self-other interactions* (Ellis & Bochner, 2000). Through this process of examination and reflection, the researcher comes to know him/herself in deeper ways. As Ellis and Bochner (2000) argue, "by understanding yourself comes understanding of others" (p. 738).

Over the years, the use of auto-ethnography has evolved in a manner that makes exact definition and application difficult. Historically, the earliest transcription, as provided by Heider focused on ethnography to describe one person's account of what others do (as cited in Reed-Danahay, 1997). Conversely, Hayano interpreted auto-ethnography in the more literal sense, as a study in which anthropologists study their own peoples (as cited in Reed-Danahay, 1997). In the early 1980s, Brandes was the first author to focus on the importance of telling autobiographic life histories within the broad ethnographic description of cultural phenomena (as cited in Reed-Danahay, 1997).

In the late 1980s, Denzin enhanced the former interpretation by explicitly avoiding any notion of the researcher as an outsider capable of objectivity in his or her ethnographic writing (as cited in Reed-Danahay, 1997). He made this distinction by explicitly stating that the autobiographic life history of the researcher is textually melded, and inseparable from, the ethnographic writing about others (as cited in Reed-Danahay, 1997).

In the mid-1990s, Pratt went beyond the focus on autobiographical life histories within ethnographic writing, and recognized the unavoidable engagement between dominant discourse and autobiographical representations (as cited in Reed-Danahay, 1997). Pratt interprets auto-ethnography, therefore, as the opportunity to write about alternatives to the dominant meanings that infiltrate life histories and cultural understandings (as cited in Reed-Danahay, 1997).

Recent interpretations of auto-ethnography recognize the inevitable infiltration of the author's surrounding dominant culture. Reed-Danahay (1997) defines auto-ethnography as "a form of self-narrative that places the self within a social context" (p. 9). Similarly, Atkinson, Coffey, and Delamont (2003) state that, "[a]utoethnography intimately and categorically relates the research process to both the social world and the self" (p. 65). Ellis and Bochner (2000) suggest that it is now appropriate to incorporate under the broad rubric of auto-ethnography studies that have been referred to by other similarly situated terms, such as personal narratives, narrative ethnography, and critical autobiography.

Auto-ethnographic studies vary in their emphases, some focus on the research process (graphy), on culture (ethno), and on self (auto). According to Carolyn Ellis (in Denzin & Lincoln, 2000), what they have in common is an autobiographical genre of writing that displays multiple layers of consciousness, connecting the personal to the cultural. Auto-ethnographers gaze back and forth, first through an ethnographic wide-angle lens, focusing outward on social and cultural aspects of their personal experience; then, they look inward, exposing a vulnerable self that is moved by and may move through, refract, and resist cultural interpretations.

Auto-ethnography is the giving of attention to personal feeling thoughts and emotions and "…by exploring a particular life . . . [I] hope to understand a way of life" (Ellis, 1991 p. 737); it is a way to research sensitive topics that might not be accessible through other means (Philaretou & Allen, 2006; Ronai and Ellis, 1992), a way to better understand the data of research participants through engaging similar personal experiences (Clarke/Keefe, 2006), and a way to contextualize the self in his and/or her social and cultural surroundings (Reed-Danahay, 1997). Auto-ethnography can be conceptualized as a version of ethnography in which the subject is the self (Anderson, 2000; Philaretou & Allen, 2006); an act of resistance performed by subordinated people against dominant cultures in colonial or post-colonial environments (Pratt, 1992, 1994); or as "evocatory" performance art designed to provoke the reader into analytical thought (Ellis, 2004; Ellis & Bochner, 2000).

The telling of one's experience is not to attempt to explain or to seek the singular truth but rather to bring attention to the complexities of lived experiences. Auto-ethnography acknowledges that recollections of one's experiences are always stories, in that they are never fully complete in recalling the past. Instead of trying to analyze the past it provides a story so that readers decide for themselves what meaning it has for them in their lives. Ellis and Bochner (2000) suggest that these texts "long to be used rather than analyzed, to be told and retold rather than theorized and settled; to offer lessons for further conversation rather than undebatable conclusions" (p. 744).

Bochner (2000) described why he turned to auto-ethnography as a research method:

I wanted a more personal, collaborative and interactive relationship, one that

> centred on the question of how human experience is endowed with meaning and on the moral and ethical choices we face as human beings who live in an uncertain and changing world. I also wanted to understand the conventions that constrain which stories we can tell and how we can tell them and to show how people can and do resist the forms of social control that

> marginalize or silence counternarratives, stories that deviate from or transgress the canonical ones. (p.744)

Here, Bochner addresses that auto-ethnography is an effective means to document one person's experience of examining relationships within the world. Similar to the intent of this project, Bochner used auto-ethnography to examine how we are faced with conventions that attempt to constrain us but also how we find ways to resist and create new ways of being (see Ellis & Bochner in Ellis & Flaherty, 1992).

There are two further reasons that this research method fits with the methodology of the present project. First, because auto-ethnography situates the researcher as the subject, the issue of positioning is dealt with in detail. Not only does the critical role that researchers play in selecting and conducting research get identified but it is continually addressed throughout the process. This is important, as identifying one's position in relation to the project and to the participants has become a crucial element of good qualitative research (see Acker, 2000; Gabriel, 2000).

Second, auto-ethnography acknowledges that the researcher is an "active agent" who will be impacted by listening to, and writing about, other people's stories and allows for documentation of this "transformation." The authors in this collection were drawn to the idea that auto-ethnography "stresses the journey over the destination" (Ellis & Bochner, 2000, p. 744). This is important because it identifies that there is so much more to research than just the final results. It is a process that is personal, convoluted, agonizing, and transformational. Stressing the journey also resists the standard practice of portraying social life and relationships as a "snap shot" (p. 744). Ellis and Bochner (2000) argue that researchers have been trained into this monologic style of reporting but this style of reporting has left some researchers dissatisfied with the product as it is not representative of their lived experiences. Rather than aiming to report truths, auto-ethnography promotes dialogue (Ellis & Bochner, 1999). Readers are engaged with the text on an emotional level, thinking along with the researcher about their own personal experiences (Ellis & Bochner, 2000).

From this perspective, auto-ethnographers are seen as "boundary-crosser[s]" and "can be characterized as that of a dual identity" (Reed-Danahay, 1997, p. 3). Therefore, the usefulness of the method can be extended to include the ability to "question the binary conventions of a self/society split, as well as the boundary between the objective and the subjective" (Reed-Danahay, 1997, p. 2).

Forms of auto-ethnography vary and may include one, or a combination, of the following: first-person texts, "short stories, poetry, fiction, novels, photographic essays, scripts, personal essays, journals, fragmented and layered writing, and social science prose" (Ellis, 2004, p. 38). Atkinson, Coffey, and Delamont (2003) supplement this list of auto-ethnographic forms by adding: "dialogues", "diaries", and "biographical reflections" (p. 65). The freedom in auto-ethnographic form is extended to the acceptable range of author expression. Gergen cited in Bochner and Ellis (2000) argues that:

> In using oneself as an ethnographic exemplar, the researcher is freed from the traditional conventions of writing. One's unique voicing—complete with colloquialisms, reverberations from multiple relationships, and emotional expressiveness—is honoured. In this way the reader gains a sense of the writer as a full human being. (p. 14)

AUTO-ETHNOGRAPHY: ADDRESSING CREDIBILITY.

Writers of auto-ethnography are not interested in developing a specified framework for others to follow. This is too much like other formalized methods of inquiry which in many ways limit and constrain ways of collecting information. However, this has left auto-ethnography open to criticism, as it does not provide clear guidelines, especially for those who judge qualitative inquiries (Holt, 2003). Rather than providing a framework, Ellis and Bochner (2000) discuss how issues that are often questioned in qualitative research such as validity, reliability, and accountability can be addressed.

One aspect of promoting credibility in qualitative research is describing the history/experiences of the researcher such that he or she is viewed as a capable researcher. In contrast to some other research methods, using auto-ethnography allowed for the personal life histories, professional practices, and lived experiences of the authors to provide critical context to this collection.

A level of accountability is therefore extremely important. Accountability involves documenting who the person is who is collecting and analyzing the evidence. Auto-ethnography recognizes that as researchers we are not only central to the selection of the topic but also how the research will be analyzed and reported. Rather than attempting to control for researcher bias, auto-ethnography uses the researcher's lived experience and relationships as a topic of investigation (Noy, 2003). For the authors of this collection, then, research becomes a way in which they can take personal accountability and make obvious the fact that all research is biased by the researcher's history, values, beliefs, life experiences, and so forth. Auto-ethnography allows the researcher to show the importance of the researcher's own experiences in their own right. It removes the false impression that one is able to keep personal experience out of research.

Validity or credibility of qualitative research can be addressed through instituting practices that promote rigor. However, an acceptance within the field of what these practices are has remained hotly debated (Caelli, Ray, & Mill, 2003). In response to arguments around inconsistencies of practices within qualitative research, Sandelowski and Barroso (2002) argue that due to the wide range of methodologies that fall within the rubric of qualitative research, no singular set of procedures can exist. Rather, each qualitative approach needs to be evaluated in a manner that is congruent with the intentions set out in the beginning of the research process. Therefore, it is the responsibility of the researcher to explain how validity will be addressed. For this, we turn to Ellis and Bochner's (2000) explanation on how auto-ethnography can address issues of validity. They said, "validity means that our work seeks verisimilitude: it evokes in readers a feeling that the experience described is lifelike, believable, and possible" (p. 751). Therefore, this collection aims to create a document that will resonate with, and hopefully inspire, other people in their work with families or in their own personal experience of their family.

One of the main differences in post-modern research is the move away from establishing findings that generalize across the population. Rather, through the use of the researcher's case, the reader creates the generalizations for themselves, given their own experiences. There is a shift from "generalization across cases to generalization from within a case" (Ellis & Bochner, 2000, p. 744).

Michel Foucault (1980) poses a question with which the authors in this volume have wrestled while determining how to approach academic writing: "What types of knowledge do you want to disqualify in the very instance of your demand—is it science" (p. 85)? Implicit in this question is the idea that being scientific in one's approach has the capacity to disqualify other ways of knowing. As authors who are specifically interested in non-dominant discourses as a both feminists and anti-oppressive researchers, each author in this volume has taken Foucault's challenge seriously. In what ways does the scientific approach keep us from hearing other voices?

Each of the authors here is rooted in the field of counselling and psychology. Without exception, they have found the dominant paradigms of modernist psychology inadequate to their needs as researchers and practitioners. Auto-ethnography as a kind of writing against the grain is an underutilized methodological process in the field of psychology. Auto-ethnography as a method of self-examination, reflexivity, and actualization allows for what Magnet (2006) calls deconstructing the implications for counselling of the privileged position that the therapist/researcher holds. At the same time, it facilitates the pointing out of various struggles and inconsistencies that each author faces in her multiple subject positions as woman, as family member, as instrument of state power, as raced, gendered and classed subject, and as an academic of working class background. Each of the authors here also takes note of the work of Mary Louise Pratt and her use of auto-ethnography as a tool of resistance in the representation of subordinated people by the dominant culture. It is the intention of the authors in this volume to create a text that will resist both the dominant configurations of women within families as well as traditional research methods.

Ellis and Bochner (2006) describe auto-ethnography as "unruly, dangerous, vulnerable, rebellious, and creative," as a genre of writing that "shows struggle, passion, embodied life, and the collaborative creation of sense-making in situations in which people have to cope with dire circumstances and loss of meaning" (p. 433). Skott-Myhre notes that this is where she struggled with the more traditional approach to qualitative research and auto-ethnography when attempting to use a more systematic and detached approach. She reflects that she wants this project to be much more compelling, "I want people to feel the story in their guts, not just know the 'facts' in their heads" (Ellis & Bochner, 2006, p. 435). She aligns herself with Ellis and Bochner (2006) when they say, "our goal is to open up conversations about how people live, rather than close down with a definitive description and analytic statements about the world as it 'truly' exists outside the contingencies of language and culture" (p. 435). This sentiment deeply resonates with the way that all three authors in this collection approach the way they work with people in therapy and social work.

In using auto-ethnography, the authors will be investigating their experiences as both therapists and academics from their various perspectives with the hope of contributing to an ongoing exchange of ideas filled with multiple voices from diverse backgrounds. In speaking as women, they are attempting to open up a space to valorize other women's voices. Each will be focusing on the covert language of those they have encountered in their families and workplaces in an attempt to "explode" this hidden language in public so that other women can know it is possible.

This approach comes with a cautionary note. As explicated by Joan Scott (1992), the experiences or stories shared here are not to be used as irreducible evidence nor should it be assumed that what is proposed is generalizable to a specific population. Rather, the reader is encouraged to think *with* the story instead of *about* it (Bochner and Ellis, 2002).

WHAT IS GOOD AUTO-ETHNOGRAPHY?

Bochner (2000) offer six ways to judge auto-ethnography in terms of how effective it is in helping the reader to "understand and feel the phenomena under scrutiny" (p. 270):

1. The use of concrete detail to describe "not only facts but also feelings" from the commonplace triviality of everyday to the raw "flesh and blood emotions" felt as people cope with life's contingencies.
2. The incorporation of structural complexity "that rotates between past and present reflecting the nonlinear process of memory work."
3. The display of "emotional credibility, vulnerability, and honesty" on the page while digging at and exploring beneath one's actions, "limitations", "cultural scripts", "contradictory feelings", "ambivalence", and "layers of subjectivity."
4. The believable expression of "two selves" as historically transformed from "who I was to who I am."
5. The standard of "ethical self-consciousness" that shows sensitivity for how other people are represented, as well as "for the kind of person one becomes" through the process of storytelling (i.e., "moral commitments and convictions that underlie the story").
6. The ability to move the reader's "heart and belly" as well as his/her mind by acting out the subjective life in ways that shows the reader what "life feels like now and what it can mean."

It is with this last admonition that we conclude our introduction. It is our hope as auto-ethnographers that we can move the reader to reflect upon his/her own life, identity and practices. In investigating a social phenomenon as ubiquitous and deeply rooted in our central psyche as the family, we hope we can unsettle some of the disciplinary overlays that hide what Weima calls the *lived with* family from view.

As women, we hope to introduce a feminist/womanist perspective to our reading of the family that emphasizes relationship over structure, creative becoming over disciplined behavioral shaping, and mutual reciprocity over hierarchical force. To this end we share our lives, experience, research and reflections. We hope this will be a beginning that opens new lines of inquiry and reflections that shake the world to come.

Part I

My Two Families: An Auto-ethnographic Exploration ofthe Internalized Lived By and the Externalized Lived With Family Experience

Korinne Weima

CHAPTER 1

WE ALL HAVE TWO FAMILIES

Taken in totality, the following auto-ethnographic piece explores family in two parallel realms of my lived experience: external and internal. The inspiration for exploring these two realms of experience arose from the following quotation:

> ...we all have two families, one that we live *with* and another we live *by* (Gillis, 1996, p. xv).

For two key reasons, it immediately had a profound effect on me. First, I had never considered the thought of having two families at the same time! My external that I live *with,* that has evolved in composition over the course of time. And my other internal family that I live *by*, that represents my personal ideal notions of the family construct. Second, and most importantly, the quotation prompted the realization that my internal lived *by* family ideal has continually informed my perceptions about my external lived *with* family.

Overall, Gillis' (1996) statement provides the (under)tone for my auto-ethnography, dividing my lived experience in two separate, but related, realms: (1) the external (lived *with* family); and (2) the internal (lived *by* family). As I explore these two realms of my lived experience, I address the hegemony of the nuclear family as the idealized lived *by* family structure both internally and in our dominant culture. I must admit that writing a parallel analysis of these two experiences (inner and outer) of the family has been no small feat.

What presents the greatest challenge to writing about the family is the fact that it is a ubiquitous phenomenon. Certainly, I could write at length about instances of nuclear family idealization that are immediately apparent. What I am concerned about, however, are the instances of nuclear family idealization that remain unrecognized: hidden in the nothing. Let me try to explain what I mean.

*   *   *

WORLD – PERCEPTIONS = NOTHING

Recently, I attended a symposium wherein the speaker discussed how an art canvas must represent nothing before it can mean something. In other words, an art canvas—in itself—represents nothing until it acquires meaning through the perceptions of an observer.

Upon hearing this statement, I understood why it has been a challenge to write about a phenomenon that is so ubiquitous. After all, if I apply the same logic to my auto-ethnography and conceptualize the world as an art canvas, nullified of meaning without my own perceptions, then a formulaic reduction would be as follows:

World – Perceptions = Nothing

Reduced/deduced from this formula is nothing—my nothing. And so I ask, what is left in my nothing? Post-modern thinking suggests is that what remains invisible (in my nothing) are my taken-for-granted truths. They remain invisible because they are so deeply intertwined into my being.

CRISIS? WHAT CRISIS?

Certainly, you could say that I am in a crisis of sorts.
After all, I am confronting the hegemony of my internal lived *by* family and how it affect(s) the feelings I have about my actual lived *with* family. Of course this awkward experience forces me (in) to the unfamiliar.

Crisis (present state) + Return to the "Commonsense World"
(to occur, arguably)

=

Therapeutic effect (to be determined)

It is curious how, once again, I've minimized my lived experience into a formulaic abstraction…

*   *   *

MY LIVED *WITH* FAMILY

I return to the statement made by Gillis (1996) that inspired the division of my lived experience of family into two separate realms:

> ...we all have two families, one that we live *with* and another we live *by* (Gillis, 1996, p. xv).

My lived *with* family formation has evolved four times over the last three decades. I have experienced the transition from the traditional nuclear family, to a single-parent family, to a common-law family, and now, to its present form as a step-parent family. Regardless of the changes in formation (as a result of different constituent members), I *feel* I have been a part of the same one lived *with* family—perhaps as a result of what Laing (1969) refers to as perceiving a shared "family synthesis", as will be discussed in Chapter One of this auto-ethnography. That is, despite its variability and sudden changes in lived expression, I've considered it as being the same lived with family.

On the other hand, my internal lived *by* family evolved slowly, in response to sudden, traumatic changes in my lived *with* family circumstances. Thus, my internalized thoughts about the lived *by* family (what I thought was considered socially acceptable) were in a constant state of "catch-up" to what was transpiring around me.

I believe that my internal lived *by* notions of an ideal family continually informed my perceptions about my lived *with* family. And because my internal lived *by* notions of family evolved more gradually, in response to my lived *with* family circumstances, differences have always existed between them. I explore the differences between my internalized lived *by* family and the one I actually lived *with*.

* * *

CRISIS MEANS TO THERAPEUTIC EFFECTS

To engage in such an exploration, I will revisit my previous internalized notions of the ideal family (my lived *by* family), how it became internalized through modern psychological discourse, and how its normalizing gaze may have been harmful to the perceptions I had about my lived *with* family. Such a nonlinear exploration requires a non-traditional methodology, such as an auto-ethnography.

It is my contention, and hope, that auto-ethnography can be therapeutic. The therapeutic (re)turn/effect/growth can only be revealed, however, upon my return from the process of crisis/abstraction, after I have deconstructed my lived by family ideal. As Tyler (1986) argues, it is only upon my return to the "commonsense world," that the product/auto-ethnography (the process in documentation form) may reveal a renewed outlook on my lived *with* family. I am hopeful that I can reveal what could be different within the everyday experience of my lived *with* family, within my lived *with* commonsense world.

Alas, I (re)align my auto-ethnography intentions to fit Tyler's (1986) therapeutic context, to produce a space wherein my internalized family ideal (influenced by society's hegemonic image) is thrown into crisis/abstraction. By placing my internalized lived *by* family ideal into a space for questioning, I am deconstructing it. By deconstructing my internalized lived *by*, I am putting into movement different possibilities of thinking about my lived *with* family. Within this space of crisis, things get messy as many voices get thrown into the mix. The braided exploration that best describes this process is a parallel recursive analysis. Let me explain what I mean.

PARALLEL RECURSIVE ANALYSIS

Imagine my auto-ethnography like a long braid of hair. Following one fragment of hair with your eyes, notice how it weaves in and out—appearing recursively—yet remains parallel to the others. Similarly, I pull fragments of writing forward, and push others back, allowing them to appear and retract recursively, but always remaining parallel to the others. In other words, no fragment is ever forgotten, nor does it ever appear in exactly in the same way. Instead, fragments are recursively brought forward—imploded into the next—to produce continually thickening parallel analysis.

In this way, format and methodology are intimately related because my writing format *is* the methodology. Overall, what is created is an unconventional, uniquely textured, and what may be conceptualized as a recursive parallel analysis.

Each recursion can arise from one of two main areas: my personal voice(s) and those of the outside academic and socially constructed world of dominant psychological discourse. As such, each area is potentiated with a multiplicity of voices. The imported voices range from the refined academic and hegemonic ideals, to the raw popularized and satirized constructions of the family ideal. I purposely unfold the refined, and then raw, to shadow how the ideal family tracing is first internalized through dominant psychological discourse, and then, percolated throughout popularized venues of indoctrination. Taken together, they provide the objects/code from which I recursively reflect and respond, unbridled by the linearity of temporal and spatial restrictions.

In the first recursion in Chapter Two, I explore the hegemonic definitions of the ideal family from outside sources, only to implode these objects into my own internalized ideal definition of family through personal reflection. I begin with the literature of Gilles Deleuze and Felix Guattari (1987) because their theoretical concepts of mapping and tracing provide the basis from which the rest of the crisis/abstraction oscillates. Mapping and tracing are not dichotomous concepts, but instead, the tracing is one representation off the map of infinitely lived realities. In the personal reflection that follows, I implode these theoretical concepts to demonstrate how the idealized nuclear family structure is but one tracing of family on the infinite map of lived expressions of family. I will reflect how the hegemony of this nuclear family tracing is harmful to the remaining expressions of family structure.

In Chapter Three, I continue the discussion of the idealized nuclear family tracing by introducing R.D. Laing's (1969) notion of internalization. I will use this code to reflect upon the notion of a shared family auto-ethnography, and how it is maintained to the degree the nuclear family tracing is internalized in each family member. I will also reflect on how family members engage in transpersonal defenses, acts on the other, in an effort to maintain the shared family auto-ethnography when it is threatened. More specifically, I will explore the most common transpersonal defense, the act of mystification (a complex process of subtle coercions that may or may not be recognized by the other).

In the second recursion, I carry forward what has been imploded, deconstructed, and analyzed within the first chapter and introduce new objects for reflection. In this way, each recursion enhances the parallel analysis, thickens the braided exploration, and provides more depth to my crisis/abstraction and deconstruction of the ideal lived *by* family.

Thus, in Chapter Four, I pull forward the theoretical concepts of mapping and tracing (Deleuze & Guattari, 1987) and internalization (Laing, 1961; 1965; 1969), along with the personal reflections I have made, and implode them into the next recursion of codified literature. More specifically, I pull forward the notion of the internalized family tracing and implode it, by exploring its ethological formations.

I use the outside voice of Ian Parker (1995; 1997; 2005; 2007) to discuss how the nuclear family tracing is internalized through the process of psychologization. Psychologization is the term used to describe how dominant psychological discourse imports ideas from other dominant discourses, in order to bolster theoretical pronouncements. Thus, psychological discourse uses other dominant discourses (e.g., biology, medical, anthropology, and so on) effectually to idealize the nuclear family structure as the normalized template, against which all other forms of family are compared and contrasted. The psy-complex is the network of psychological venues that effectually produces the notion of family normality and abnormality on the basis of compositional structure.

Also in Chapter Four, I carry forward the previous theoretical concepts and introduce the concrete lived experience of Canadian families using the outside voice of Mona Gleason (1999). More specifically, Gleason (1999) provides the historical context of how psychologists gain access to families, and then exercise their "technologies of normalcy" (p. 9). Extending from Foucault's notion of technologies of the self, Gleason (1999) speaks of the "technologies of normalcy" that make families self-regulating and self-deprecating units (p. 9).

Within this chapter, I will also dissect the popularized venues of family indoctrination and offer the voices of dominant psychological proponents Dr. Laura Schlessinger and Dr. Phil McGraw. I chose these two public figures because they personify the current state of popular psychology, and because their popularity in the Western culture reflects how we have normalized and accepted the language and techniques of psychology into the everyday lives of the family.

In the third and final recursion, I carry forward what has been imploded, deconstructed, and analyzed within the third and fourth chapter, and introduce new objects for reflection. The recursive parallel analysis has grown into a thick and in-depth braided exploration, and this is the last recursion for crisis/abstraction and deconstruction of the ideal lived *by* family, prior to my (to be determined) return to the commonsense world.

Thus far, in my recursive parallel analysis, I have pulled forward: the theoretical concepts of mapping and tracing (Deleuze & Guattari, 1987), internalization (Laing, 1961; 1965; 1969), the process of psychologization through the psy-complex network (Parker, 1995; 1997; 2005; 2007), the normalization of the ideal family (Gleason, 1999), the popularized ministrations of the ideal family (McGraw, 2004), and finally, the reflections from the third and fourth chapter which include the raw satirized conceptualization of the ideal family.

In Chapter Five, I talk about how the redundancy of the tracing obstructs infinitely lived expressions of family conceptualized on the map. I bring forth the outside voices of Deleuze and Guattari (1987), this time to help implode the tracing of the nuclear family back onto the map of infinitely lived expressions of family.

I propose the format of my auto-ethnography to be a nonlinear interwoven piece of personal reflections, modernist psychological discourse, and various theoretical frameworks. My overall aim is not to redefine family, nor is it to provide definitive answers about how to resolve the inevitable differences between the family we live *by* and the family we live *with*. Rather, my intention is to invite the reader to join me in exploring and experiencing the two notions of the family (lived *by* ideal and lived *with* reality). In hopes of opening up new ways of thinking about the concept of the family, I will evoke more questions than answers. This is in line with Ellis and Bochner's (2000) suggestion to auto-ethnographers to resist the impulse to find "undisputable conclusions" (p. 745). Instead, I offer the reader an opportunity to explore my continuous open dialogue, and perhaps they will engage in their own. In the end, Tyler (1986) suggests, the therapeutic effect of my auto-ethnography will come when I return to the commonsense world with a renewed sense of my own lived *with* family.

In my auto-ethnographic exploration, my goal is not to find a new definition of "the family" that better suits today's postmodern world of multiple selves, and as many conceivable realities. As Gergen, Lightfoot, and Sydow (2004) suggest in the following quotation, to establish a new definition or truth would be antithetical to my path onto postmodern thought:

> [T]o establish a final truth, a foundational logic, a code of values, or a slate of practices would be antithetical to the very unfolding of understanding championed by the [postmodern] movement. (p. 389)

Therefore, because I value the postmodern notion of a multiplicity of truths and realities, I will not redefine or establish as "True" any new vision of the family construct. This is not to say that I reject the notion of having an "ideal" or some "thing" that one holds in one's mind's-eye as flawless, pure, or the epitome of perfection. After all, if the world does not lack, then all to which one has ever aspired, wanted, hoped, dreamed, or "needed" is hidden in plain sight. When an ideal is held in mind to inspire and explore endless possibilities and avenues, it can be helpful.

On the other hand, I am critical of the belief that any ideal may be universally authenticated and ontologically "True". In other words, I am deeply suspicious of rigid, binary, idealized thought processes that serve to produce (unrealistic/harmful) universalized definitions of the family construct as ideal versus non-ideal.

To reiterate, I do not intend to redefine the family. Instead, I deconstruct how society effectively constructs and locates the notion of an ideal family *exclusively* within the nuclear family structure. In doing this, I join with the reader to open up a multiplicity of new ways of thinking and talking about the family.

Let's start the journey.

CHAPTER 2

THE IDEAL FAMILY: A TRACING INTERNALIZED

DELEUZE AND GUATTARI: THE MAP AND TRACING

Deleuze and Guattari's (1987) theoretical concepts of the map and tracing offer a helpful framework in understanding how the infinite lived expressions of the family are covered over by the one dominant nuclear family structure.

Imagine the infinite expressions of the lived *with* family on a *map*, existing despite of the dominant *tracing* of the lived *by* nuclear family ideal that dominates Westernized culture, and permeates our internal unconscious. As you imagine a "map" in your mind, you may see a two-dimensional folded piece of paper, for instance, a map of Canada. But by the end of this section, I hope to convince you that a map of Canada is not a map at all!

INFINITE EXPRESSIONS OF THE LIVED WITH FAMILY ON THE MAP.

Deleuze and Guattari (1987) describe a rhizome as a "subterranean stem" system made up only of lines as its dimensions: while lines of segmentarity break the rhizome, making it "stratified, territorialized, organized, signified, attributed" (Deleuze & Guattari, 1987, p. 9), lines of flight deterritorialize the rhizome by exploding the lines of segmentarity, freeing the rhizome through their rupture. Indeed, Deleuze and Guattari (1987) suggest that we "[a]lways follow the rhizome by rupture; lengthen, prolong, and relay the line of flight; make it vary, until [we] have produced the most abstract and tortuous of lines of n dimensions and broken directions. Conjugate deterritorialized flows" (p. 11). In an infinite process of territorialization and deterritorialization, the rhizome always "start(s) up again on one of its old lines, or on new lines" (p. 9). This is because it is "not amendable to any structural or generative model" (p. 12). To illustrate this process of territorialization and deterritorialization,

Deleuze and Guattari (1987) use the example of ants, and how we can never get rid of them because “they form an animal rhizome that can rebound time and again after most of it has been destroyed” (p. 9).

The rhizome is a map, and the map is “part of the rhizome” (Deleuze & Guattari, 1987, p. 12). In other words, “the rhizome pertains to a map that must be produced, constructed, a map that is always detachable, connectable, reversible, modifiable, and has multiple entryways and exits and its own lines of flight” (p. 21). The map is “entirely oriented toward an experimentation in contact with the real” because it is:

> open and connectable in all of its dimensions; it is detachable, reversible, susceptible to constant modification. It can be torn, reversed, adapted to any kind of mounting, reworked by an individual, group or social formation. It can be drawn on a wall, conceived of as a work of art, constructed as a political action or as a meditation. (Deleuze & Guattari, 1987, p. 12)

As part of the rhizome, the map fosters infinite possibilities, connections, and performative capacities (Deleuze & Guattari, 1987, p. 12). The map removes blockages on “bodies without organs[1]”, allowing “the maximum opening of bodies without organs onto a plane of consistency[2]” (Deleuze & Guattari, 1987, p. 12). Finally, the map “has to do with performance” in all its potential for multiplicity and unbridled desire[3] (Deleuze & Guattari, 1987, p. 12). But what does all this abstract language mean for the family construct?

Essentially, Deleuze and Guattari’s (1987) concept of the map is fully potentiated with endless desire and a multiplicity of performative assemblages (where an assemblage is an “increase in the dimensions of a multiplicity that necessarily changes in nature as it expands its connections” [Deleuze & Guattari, 1987, p. 8]). On their notion of the map, therefore, there is no pre-traced family destiny, ready-made family definition, but rather, we can imagine all the infinite performative capacities of the family flowing free of/from dominant ideals, definitions, or professional restrictions.

Like so many of so many of Deleuze and Guattari's abstract concepts, their conceptualization of the map does not lend itself easily to concrete thought, especially because it lacks a sense of temporal restriction. That is, there are no blockages to inhibit the infinite performative capacities of the family, including those existing in the past, present and future. As such, a concrete conception of the map, in the Deleuzo-Guattarian sense of the word, is confounded by our inability to conceive of all previous, present and future performed expressions of the family. Even if we cast past and future "realities" aside, an attempt to conceive of all the present infinite lived realities of the family could never be accurate, because the family as a construct is never stable and constantly evolves.

To take one picture of "the family", freeze it, and use it to represent "the family" of the past, present, and future; is not unlike taking a picture of a glacier and claiming it has *always* existed in that spot, *presently* remains in existence in that exact spot, and *will forever* remain there in that location, completely unchanged by the course of time and the force of the elements. Indeed, Basaglia (1987) eloquently warns of the dangers of freezing reality: "the reality of today will differ from the reality of tomorrow, and in trying to freeze it, it either becomes distorted or irrelevant" (p. 4).

In many ways, we have not heeded Basaglia's warning against freezing the reality of today. One very common way that we have attempted to freeze reality is in our construction of geographical maps. As such, we have run the risk of distorting our lived realities.

DELEUZE AND GUATTARI'S CONCEPT OF THE MAP AND CANADA.

Parallel Deleuze and Guattari's notion of the map to a geographical map of Canada, and it should encompass the infinite performative capacities (past, present, and future) of the Canadian landscape. This is not the case, however, because the two-dimensional constructed maps of Canada are a prime example of an attempt to freeze reality. Two-dimensional paper versions of maps, therefore, are very different from the notion of the map inspired by Deleuze and Guattari.

On the other hand, the paper map of Canada is not unlike our constructed definition of “the family” in the way that they both claim to provide an accurate representation of infinite and constantly evolving landscapes.

A “MAP” OF CANADA

On the exquisitely colourful map of Canada spread before me, I see each of the Canadian provinces from coast-to-coast, their carefully labelled capitals, cities, and towns. Each labelled location is connected directly, or indirectly, by a web of highways, roads, and streets. Lakes, rivers, and other waterways, expand like blue venous capillaries across the page. As I look at the map, it appears to be an accurate representation of the lived Canadian landscape. Appearance, as “they” say, is not all that it may seem.

The University of Wisconsin’s Cartography Laboratory (UWCL) (2006) states that maps are limited by their general purpose; that is, to gain an overall picture on one piece of paper using ink, colour, shadows, lines, and text. The map of Canada, therefore, is limited by its ability to capture all the complexity of the Canadian landscape. Instead, all the variable aspects of the land are reduced “down to just a few important attributes” (UWCL, 2006, par. 5). This is because “an attempt to plot each feature true to scale would result in a product impossible to read even with the aid of a magnifying glass” (Map Navigation, n.d., par. 2). Unavoidably, therefore, the map of Canada is a limited expression of actual lived Canadian landscape.

As previously forewarned by Basaglia (1987), another factor that limits the ability of a map to represent the Canadian landscape accurately has to do with the passage of time. The map of Canada is subject to temporal expiration due to, for instance, constant and unpredictable modifications in borders, deterioration and construction of established routes, alterations in city limits, and so on.

Finally, we cannot forget that geographical maps have been constructed by someone. As such, a map of Canada is also limited to the perspective of its creator, that of the cartographer (Norman B. Leventhal Map Centre, n.d.). The cartographer forcibly organizes the vast and varied landscape of Canada, onto a two-dimensional paper representation. Perhaps this cartographer has drawn this map with the help of previously created maps, but that map was also limited by the perspective of that cartographer, and so on. Inevitably, the cartographer creates a version of Canada that drastically differs from, and distorts, the actual lived realities and expressions of the Canadian landscape.

Dare I ask: Is a map of Canada really a "map" in the Deleuzo-Guattarian rhizomorphic sense of the term? I would argue that the two-dimensional map of Canada is not a map but is rather a tracing!

(FALSE) SENSE OF CERTAINTY

My patient reader, you may wonder where I am headed with all of this and what it all has to do with the family. I ask that you stick with me, and consider the following scenario.

What if we decided to stop making new tracings (maps) of Canada to account for changes in the Canadian landscape? With no new map to account for the demolition and/or creation of manmade roadways, or the natural erosions and burgeoning of the land, we would be ignoring the inevitable and continual propensity of the changing landscape, and forcing an image of stability where it does not exist. We would become stuck on one version of Canada.

So why have maps (tracings) of Canada at all? In one word: certainty. Setting out on the road, we feel certain and secure in knowing that when in doubt of our location, we can consult a map of Canada. The map will remind us of where we were (past), where we are (present), and where we will be (future).

But as Basaglia (1987) warned us, the reality of today differs from the reality of tomorrow, and freezing it only leads to distortion and irrelevancy. Thus, a map (tracing) of Canada is outdated the day after its creation. It no longer represents an accurate reality of Canada, but a distorted version that may no longer be relevant.

We may even suggest that the map of Canada had never been accurate, that we are being guided by a false sense of certainty and security, or a false sense of stability. The question then becomes: Have we always been guided by a false sense of certainty or security in an instable and ever-evolving geography? Moreover, have we not been gathering our certainty and security through the limited perspective of the (one) cartographer?

* * *

HOW DOES THIS RELATE TO THE FAMILY CONSTRUCT?

In a similar way, our perceptions of the family are limited to the perspective of the family cartographer of our dominant culture. In other words, I suggest that the forcible organization and freezing of reality of the vast and varied landscape of Canada, is not unlike the way Statistics Canada confines the vast and varied lived expressions of the family into a census family definition.

Just as the map of Canada is very different from the reality it represents, I argue that the census family definition differs drastically from, and distorts the actual lived realities of, the family.

DEFINING THE FAMILY

Currently, the family is defined into a limited representation of its lived expression, as both national and international forces aim to align it into a static and definable representation. The most recent definition of the census family by Statistics Canada, is heavily influenced by the international force of the United Nations. This is because the United Nations Statistical Division (UNSD) is at present, undertaking a massive scale coordination of various aspects of census collection internationally. Why are they doing this?

STATISTICS CANADA'S CENSUS DEFINITION OF THE FAMILY.

Overall, the purpose of a national census questionnaire is to collect pertinent data about a country's population, including information about the family. In order for the questionnaire to be implemented with consistency across the nation, a standardization of definitions and concepts must be delineated. Baker (1995) offers two reasons that explicit definitions of family are important:

> Government policies need to be based on explicit definitions of family, since the way in which the institution is defined establishes who will be eligible for government benefits such as family allowance, social assistance, or child tax credits. For the purpose of gathering census data and producing statistics on family life, the term 'family' needs to be defined consistently in order to enable long-term comparisons. (p. 9)

In other words, the census family definition allows countries to do two things. First, it gives the government the control to provide and restrict allowances and assistance to the family by way of their alignment toward what is socially acceptable. Second, the standard definition of the family allows for long-term comparative research about family life across a nation.

Earlier, I had asked why the United Nations is pushing for an international standard definition of the family. Their intention is to be able to conduct long-term comparative research about the family on an international scale. This requires a massive coordination effort, in order to standardize all of the definitional and conceptual qualities of all the United Nations census definitions of the family. This large-scale concerted effort is currently underway by the United Nations Statistics Division (UNSD), and Statistics Canada has been influenced by this UNSD effort in their most recent definition of the census family.

UNITED NATIONS STATISTICS DIVISION FAMILY NUCLEUS PROTOCOL.

The UNSD (2007a) is currently facilitating the 2010 World Population and Housing Census Programme. The primary aim of the 2010 World Programme is to ensure that "each Member State conducts a population and housing census at least once in the period from 2005 to 2014 and disseminates the results" (UNSD, 2007a, par. 3). In order to guide each country, the UNSD (2007b) has developed governing principles specifically for international statistical activities with the aim to "enhance the functioning of the international statistical system" (UNSD, 2007b, par. 1). Immediately relevant to the present discussion on coordinating a standardized census definition of the family, are the fourth and ninth principles governing international statistical activities.

The fourth principle states that concepts and definitions used in international statistics should be "made transparent for the users" (UNSD, 2007b, par. 12). As such, good practice entails "documenting the concepts, definitions and classifications" and "making this information publicly accessible" (UNSD, 2007b, par. 14). The ninth principle addresses the "coordination of international statistical programmes" and states that good practice entails "working systematically towards agreements about common concepts, classifications, standards and methods" (UNSD, 2007b, par. 29).

In regards to this agreement process, the UNSD (2001) acknowledges that "arrangements within a given country will naturally depend on the administrative structure existing in that country, [however] centralized coordination of statistical activities is desirable in order to ensure that the structure functions efficiently in producing statistics which are based on standard concepts, definitions and classifications" (p. 12). As such, the UNSD (2001) insists that civil registration officers "familiarize themselves with the census procedures in their countries and globally" (p. 91).

In addition to the governing principles, The UNSD (1998) provides a handbook called *Principles and Recommendations for Population and Housing Censuses: Revision 1,* to help international coordination efforts. This handbook provides "guidance on census operations and the content of censuses, including illustrative tabulations and definitions of concepts and terms used" (p. 91). The UNSD (1998) recognizes that "family composition can be examined from different points of view [however] for census purposes it is recommended that the primary aspect considered should be that of the family nucleus" (p. 67, par. 2.77). The UNSD (1998) family nucleus protocol reads as follows:

> A family nucleus is of one of the following types (each of which must consist of persons living in the same household):
> (a) A married couple without children,
> (b) A married couple with one or more unmarried children,
> (c) A father with one or more unmarried children or
> (d) A mother with one or more unmarried children.
> Couples living in consensual unions should be regarded as married couples. (p. 67, par. 2.78)

Acknowledging that this family nucleus protocol does not provide "information on all types of families", the UNSD (1998) recommends that each country extend their family definitions "in accordance with their own [country's] interests" (p. 67, 2.81).

STATISTICS CANADA CENSUS FAMILY.

Statistics Canada (2006a) has verified that it conformed to the UNSD internationally recognized standard by implementing a census family definition that is "compatible with the definition of family nucleus" (par. 3). As such, Statistics Canada (2006a) most recently defines the census family as:

> a married couple and the children, if any, of either or both spouses; a couple living common law and the children, if any, of either or both partners; or, a lone parent of any marital status with at least one child living in the same dwelling and that child or those children. All members of a particular census family live in the same dwelling. A couple may be of opposite or same sex. Children may be children by birth, marriage or adoption regardless of their age or marital status as long as they live in the dwelling and do not have their own spouse or child living in the dwelling. Grandchildren living with their grandparent(s) but with no parents present also constitute a census family. (par. 1-2)

To summarize, Statistics Canada complies with the UNSD (1998) family nucleus protocol and has taken up the invitation by the UNSD to extend their definition "in accordance with their own interests" (p. 67, par. 2.81). Thus, for the first time since the Canadian census inception in 1871 (Canadian Broadcasting Company [CBC], 2007), Statistics Canada (2006a) has extended the census family definition to include: (1) "same sex" couples; and (2) families comprised of "grandchildren living with their grandparent(s) but with no parents". In addition, Statistics Canada (2006a) has also acknowledged that children are children "regardless of their age or marital status as long as they live in the dwelling and do not have their own spouse or child living in the dwelling".

To get a better perspective on how this census family definition translates into the actual two-dimensional paper questionnaire, I present a snapshot from the most recent Statistics Canada (2006b) census form. (NOTE: only the section relevant to this discussion, where the responder is to enter family information, is shown.)

Evidently, Statistics Canada does not provide the census family definition directly on the census questionnaire form. As such, I am inclined to ask: Did Statistics Canada violate the UNSD (2007b) guiding principle number four, which states that concepts and definitions used in international statistics should be "made transparent for the users" and good practice entails "documenting the concepts, definitions and classifications" and "making this information publicly accessible" (UNSD, 2007b)?

What if Statistics Canada *did* print the census family definition directly on the form? It would have been evident to the responder that same-sex married spouses are "now" accepted as part of the census family definition. The responding public would have been aware, and possibly questioned: "Why are same-sex married spouses still categorized as "other"?

Further adding to the omission of a same-sex union category, the form is also devoid of any extraneous details indicating how the respondent's family will be categorized in post-hoc data analyses.

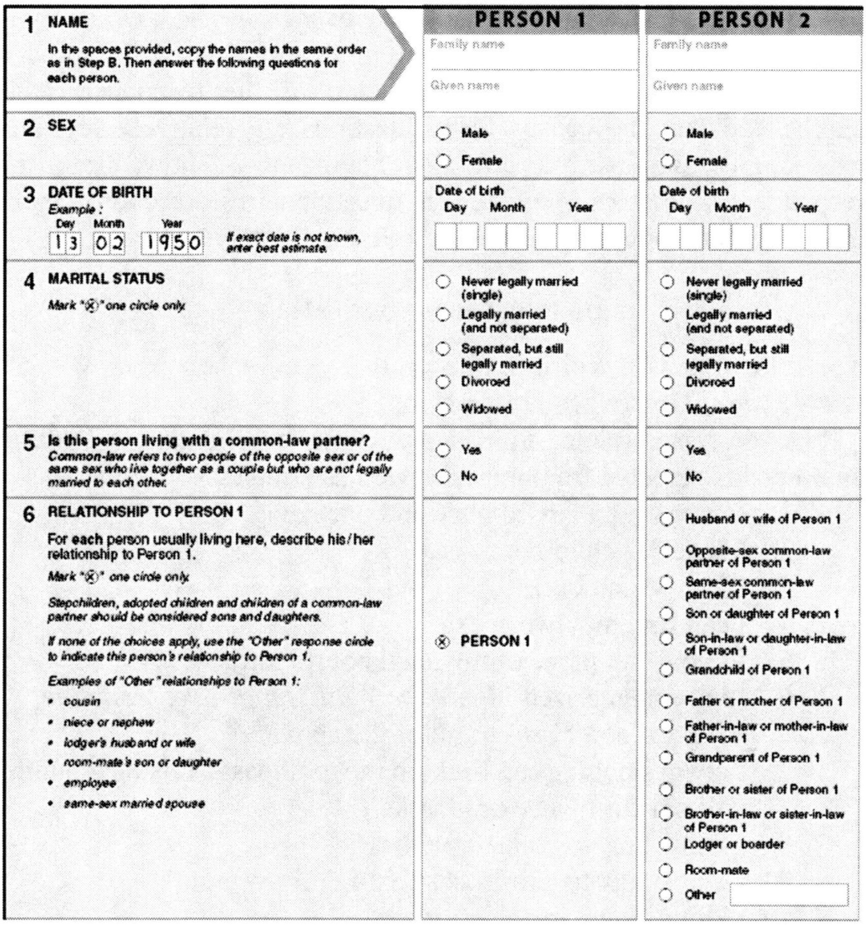

		PERSON 1	PERSON 2
1	**NAME** In the spaces provided, copy the names in the same order as in Step B. Then answer the following questions for each person.	Family name Given name	Family name Given name
2	**SEX**	○ Male ○ Female	○ Male ○ Female
3	**DATE OF BIRTH** *Example :* Day 13 Month 02 Year 1950 *If exact date is not known, enter best estimate.*	Date of birth Day Month Year	Date of birth Day Month Year
4	**MARITAL STATUS** *Mark "⊗" one circle only.*	○ Never legally married (single) ○ Legally married (and not separated) ○ Separated, but still legally married ○ Divorced ○ Widowed	○ Never legally married (single) ○ Legally married (and not separated) ○ Separated, but still legally married ○ Divorced ○ Widowed
5	**Is this person living with a common-law partner?** *Common-law refers to two people of the opposite sex or of the same sex who live together as a couple but who are not legally married to each other.*	○ Yes ○ No	○ Yes ○ No
6	**RELATIONSHIP TO PERSON 1** For each person usually living here, describe his/her relationship to Person 1. *Mark "⊗" one circle only.* *Stepchildren, adopted children and children of a common-law partner should be considered sons and daughters.* *If none of the choices apply, use the "Other" response circle to indicate this person's relationship to Person 1.* *Examples of "Other" relationships to Person 1:* • *cousin* • *niece or nephew* • *lodger's husband or wife* • *room-mate's son or daughter* • *employee* • *same-sex married spouse*	⊗ PERSON 1	○ Husband or wife of Person 1 ○ Opposite-sex common-law partner of Person 1 ○ Same-sex common-law partner of Person 1 ○ Son or daughter of Person 1 ○ Son-in-law or daughter-in-law of Person 1 ○ Grandchild of Person 1 ○ Father or mother of Person 1 ○ Father-in-law or mother-in-law of Person 1 ○ Grandparent of Person 1 ○ Brother or sister of Person 1 ○ Brother-in-law or sister-in-law of Person 1 ○ Lodger or boarder ○ Room-mate ○ Other

Somehow, in post-hoc data analysis, Statistics Canada produced data indicating how many same-sex unions there are across the nation. So, I am eager to know: How were same-sex married couple data extracted from the "other" category in post-analyses? How did they produce such detail from the vaguest of all categories, the "other"?

The average Canadian does not take a deeper look at how family is defined by the nation. Indeed, it may not even cross his/her mind. I acknowledge that, from the perspective of the responder, it is appreciated that the census form questions are relatively few and exceedingly simplistic. I am also cognizant of how, from the respondent's point of view, census questionnaires are one of those governmental obligatory tasks that seem completely harmless.

HOW NUCLEAR IS YOUR FAMILY?

The following is a satirical true or false quiz taken from Wylie's (1997) book, *Family: An exploration*:

True or false. (Note: this is a generic questionnaire. Truthful answers are expected from males as well as females.)

1. I have been married once and once only.
2. I have 1.7 children.
3. I like peanut butter.
4. I can find my own socks.
5. I know that name of my neighbour's turtle.
6. I have memorized *Where the Wild Things Are*, *Madeline*, *I'll Love You Forever*, all of the above.
7. I always put the cap back on the toothpaste. (Using a pump will not earn you extra marks.)
8. I know how to make brownies.
9. I know how to darn socks (but I don't want to).
10. I know where my children are.

(Wylie, 1997, p. 221)

Although this true and false questionnaire is in jest, I detect a hint of cynicism. A mini-social commentary, if you will, on how a number of seemingly harmless questions can have serious social implications for the family.

I draw a similar parallel between this excerpt and the Statistics Canada census form. That is, I suggest that the social implications of the questionnaire far surpass the little time and effort it took to fill out.

STATISTICS CANADA'S HISTORICAL ACTION.

I acknowledge the progressive and historical step that Statistics Canada took by expanding their census family definition to acknowledge *some of* those families who were previously ignored and allocated to the "other" categorization (with the marked exception of same-sex married couples). Simultaneously, I cannot help but see the omission of the census family definition (and details about the post-hoc categorization of different family structures) from the census form as a pre-meditated and strategic move on the part of the Canadian government.

I am inclined to wonder: Was changing the census family definition a purely aesthetic or ostensive move by the Canadian government to appear inclusive of other lived expressions of family?

The census family definition, therefore, is not a map of infinite performative capacities of family because it excludes many "other" families from existing governmental provisions. I suggest the census definition of the family is a tracing, the governmental representation of the ultimately favoured nuclear family form. Evidence of this favoured tracing of family is in our family policies, which are created by white, middle-class, males in the Canadian Parliament.

CANADIAN FAMILY POLICY.

Gaps exist between how Statistics Canada (2006a) currently defines the census family, and how the Canadian family is categorically defined and treated by the Canadian government, and this is evident in our family policies.

Baker (1995) defines family policies as "a coherent set of principles about the state's role in family life which is implemented through legislation" (p. 5) and "social programs" (p. 8). Social programs will inevitably be steeped in the "implicit values about equality and justice" of the dominant political party representations (Baker, 1995, p. 12). What this means is that legislation and social programming is ultimately decided and delivered in direct accordance to the “political ideology of the government in power” (p. 9). For instance, on December 16, 2004, Prime Minister Stephen Harper was confronted with the issue of changing the Canadian census’s traditional definition of marriage, to which he responded, “It’s a question for Parliament to decide: Does it want the traditional definition of marriage, or does it want to change that definition?” (CBC, 2005).

Ideally, legislators elected to represent the “public” are unbiased by their own world-views, but the opposite is actually true. As Baker (1995) points out, it is inevitable that government legislators will be “influenced by their background and personal characteristics, especially their gender, social class, cultural background, and political world-view” (Baker, 1995, p. 14). Having said that, it is pertinent to note that the majority of “legislators are middle-class or upper-middle-class men with occupational backgrounds in business, agriculture, or law” (Baker, 1995, p. 14). Overall, she continues to state, white male legislators will not only personally defend their own views through overt or covert means, they will also “protect their own world-view when selecting their advisers, amending existing legislation, or creating new policies” (Baker, 1995, p. 14).

A case in point: On February 16, 2005, Prime Minister Stephen Harper was, once again, confronted with the issue of changing the government’s view on traditional marriage and family. He replied, “Fundamental human rights are not a magician's hat from which new rabbits can constantly be pulled ... Same-sex marriage is not a human right” (CBC, 2005).

This statement does not reflect an unbiased world-view. As an elected official representing the Canadian public, it is abundantly clear from what world-view Prime Minister Stephen Harper operates. Undoubtedly, his personal views about the (rights of) family influence and inform the legislated family policy while he remains in office. But wait a second—what about those damned pain-in-the-ass human rights people? How does he deal with them?

CANADIAN HUMAN RIGHTS COMMISSION: DEFINITION OF FAMILY.

The Canadian Human Rights Commission (CHRC) (2004) states that human rights cannot be limited with "no bona fide justification", adding that, "the burden of proof shifts to the party seeking to limit the human right in question to prove that it can be justified" (par. 20). As such, although the current government in power made arguments against same-sex unions (based on their traditional definition of marriage), they ultimately failed to provide the burden of proof needed to "justify barring same-sex couples from civil marriage" (CHRC, 2004, No Bona Fide Justification for Barring Same-Sex Marriages).

A CLOSETED PROPONENT OF THE TRADITIONAL FAMILY?

Thus, I am inclined to ask: Did/Could Prime Minister Stephen Harper's traditional/Conservative/fundamental(ist) opinion on same-sex marriage change since 1995? Did he sit his Conservative party leaders down to discuss the way traditional/Conservative/fundamental(ist) constructions of the family alienate the majority of Canadian families? Had he convinced the current dominant Conservative party to change their world-view, thereby, influence the governmental alteration of the census definition of the family? Or, was it the failure to justify a ban on same-sex unions that ultimately prompted the governmental change of Statistics Canada's census family definition? Is it possible that the Canadian government could not "hold back" from altering the census family definition any longer (but that their internal fundamental(ist) world-views have not faltered)?

As such, has Prime Minister Stephen Harper become one of many traditional, Conservative, fundamental(ist)s who are left little choice but to be *closeted proponents* of the traditional nuclear family form?

ULTIMATE FAVOURITISM OF NUCLEAR FAMILY FORM

Despite the overt alteration to the Canadian government's definition of the family, there are still overt *and* covert instances of family form discrimination, which effectually undermine these inclusive efforts. Until very recently, only minimal analysis or research attention has been dedicated to instances of overt and covert family form discrimination (Ontario Human Rights Commission [OHRC], 2007). In March 2007, however, the OHRC released a report on family form discrimination that discusses a wide range of overt instances, and touches on the notion of covert examples.

OVERT DISCRIMINATION.

Overt instances of family form discrimination "generally arise from negative attitudes and biases" that are "deeply embedded in our society" and may "affect an individual's access to services, employment and housing" (OHRC, 2007, p. 17). The most relevant example to the present discussion is related to the Canadian government's census definition of family. The OHRC (2007) recognizes the government's omission of a "full range of relationships that most would consider familial" from the census family definition (p. 9). Indeed, the OHRC (2007) explicitly states that the Canadian government ignores certain non-traditional families, "including relationships with siblings, or with members of the extended family, such as grandparents and grandchildren, aunts and uncles, nieces and nephews, and cousins… as well as the diverse forms of support networks developed by persons with disabilities" (p. 9). The government considers these unrecognized family relations to be "chosen families", and therefore, they negate the ability to file complaints of family form discrimination. The following example taken directly from the report reveals a real-life scenario of overt family form discrimination:

> When a single mother has difficulty caring for her two young children because of her economic circumstances, her cousins offer to take them until she is back on her feet. When that couple attempts to find rental housing that will accommodate these two young children, a landlord turns them away on the basis that this is an "adult-oriented building". (OHRC, 2007, p. 10)

Other overt instances of family form discrimination revealed by the OHRC (2007) are direct manifestations of negative attitudes, stereotypes and biases. The attitudes regarding various family forms, for instance, spawn "disapproval of lone parent families, foster families, families with large numbers of children, or families headed by LGBT [Lesbian, Gay, Bisexual, Trans] persons [which] may result in negative treatment" (OHRC, 2007, p. 18). Moreover, the stereotypes about "persons with disabilities, or about individuals who are LGBT may dictate that these persons do not have the capacity to parent well, and should not be responsible for children" (OHRC, 2007, p. 18). Overall, the above examples are seen as overt instances of family form discrimination based on a bias toward the nuclear family form.

COVERT DISCRIMINATION.

On the other hand, covert instances of family form discrimination are extremely difficult to detect, because "individual acts themselves may be ambiguous or explained away" by the perpetrators (OHRC, 2007, p. 19). Another reason that covert is difficult to identify is because "it is not necessary for language or comments related to family status to be present in the interactions between the parties to demonstrate that discrimination has occurred" (OHRC, 2007, p. 19). The OHRC (2007) Report illustrates a real-life scenario that may be indicative of covert family form discrimination:

> When a woman returns to work after the birth of her first child, she notices that her career, which had seemed to be on a "fast-track", now appears to have stalled. She is given smaller and less important projects to manage, and is passed over for several training opportunities. When she asks about a promotional opportunity, her manager tries to discourage her, stating that the job requires "super-dedication" and "killer-hours". (OHRC, 2007, p. 19)

The OHRC (2007) goes on to state, without conducting a more thorough examination of all the surrounding circumstances, "it can be difficult to determine whether subtle discrimination is indeed a factor in such situations" (p. 19). Such an investigation would have to involve an "analysis that examines the context, including the presence of comparative evidence contrasting how others were treated, or evidence that a pattern of behaviour exists" (OHRC, 2007, p. 19). Difficulty in identifying and investigating covert instances of family form discrimination leads to a deep and unrecognized entrenchment of family form discrimination in the social body. To begin remediating this entrenchment, the OHRC (2007) proposes an amendment to the Human Rights Code to "recognize the broad spectrum of family types", which would alter the discriminatory practices of *some* "employers, housing providers, and service providers" (OHRC, 2007, p. 9).

Overall, the discussion of the above report is relevant to this auto-ethnography for two reasons. First, it signifies a positive step toward an acceptance of previously unrecognized family forms, because it is the "the first time that human rights issues related to family status have been explored in depth" (OHRC, 2007, p. 5). Second, the report reveals what I suspected, that despite positive steps toward the acceptance of all family forms, overt and covert discrimination against non-traditional family forms *does* persist. In other words, this OHRC report indicates that society still favours the nuclear family forms as the normal and traditional ideal.

In order to help break apart the inconsistencies between how the Canadian government and the grand social body defines and actually treats the family (as seemingly more inclusive and accepting), I return to the theoretical perspective(s) of Deleuze and Guattari. More specifically, I revisit their theoretical notions of mapping and tracing, but here, I pay careful attention to the tracing.

DELEUZE AND GUATTARI'S CONCEPT OF TRACING

Although Deleuze and Guattari's (1987) concepts of the map and the tracing are related, it would be a misconception to say that the "tracing reproduces the map" (p. 13). Instead, the authors liken the tracing to "a photograph or X ray that begins by selecting or isolating, by artificial means such as colourations or other restrictive procedures, what it intends to reproduce [from the map]." (Deleuze & Guattari, 1987, p.13)

In other words, the tracing is lifted selectively from the map, in a way that produces something very specific, stable, and organised. The tracing can be one of any number of specific translations that can be extracted from the map. In fact, Deleuze and Guattari (1987) continue to describe the tracing as some "thing" that has, "already translated the map into an image… It has organized, stabilized, neutralized the multiplicities according to the axes of significance and subjectification belonging to it." (p.13)

Overall, Deleuze and Guattari's notion of tracing can be likened to ready-made concepts of "the family", in particular, the notion of the nuclear family as the ideal tracing/image of the family. As a tracing extracted from the map of "the family", the nuclear structure is specifically isolated by a certain set of restrictive conditions that are not modifiable; that is, it must be two biological parents and their offspring. In other words, it is exclusive—either you are in a nuclear family form, or you are not.

THE FAMILY TRACING I LIVE *BY*?

Although I can't be absolutely sure—I can say that the tracing I lived *by* was probably the family I found myself born into: the nuclear family form.

I was the first born of my biological parents, who welcomed me to a big, warm, brick house in Sarnia, Ontario, in late March 1978. I certainly was born into what society deemed the natural, normal, and ideal family structure.

My earliest memories—firmly embedded with(in) this family structure—are images of my mother, father, and eventually my new baby brother who arrived in early October, 1980. By all accounts, I was living with(in) the lived by "dream", at least for the first seven years of my life.

Tracings, Deleuze and Guattari (1987) explain, are associated with a level of competence. As such, tracings can be harmful because they tend to dominate and negate all other possible tracings from the map (Deleuze & Guattari, 1987). Relating this to the concept of family, idealizing the nuclear family tracing is harmful because it defaults all other notions of what a family can be as "less ideal".

A family's competence is, therefore, measured by alignment to the ideal tracing. Either the tracing is matched perfectly and competency is confirmed, or there is no match, and competency is questioned. For instance, OHRC (2007) discussed stereotypes about non-traditional family forms and the notion that they "do not have the capacity to parent well, and should not be responsible for children" (p. 18).

Deleuze and Guattari (1987) point out the dangerousness of such redundancy, wherein one tracing of a map continually reproduces itself, and obstructs all other possible expressions on that map. To illustrate, Deleuze and Guattari (1987) liken a teacher's language to a tracing because it is possesses a dominating competence. As such, the language a teacher uses can "upset the local balance of power", thereby over-throwing a child's own set of existing semiotic systems (such as, "gestural, memetic, ludic") (Deleuze & Guattari, 1987, p. 15). In other words, the language of the teacher negates the child's own language processes through the sheer dominance of its tracing and related competency.

In the context of the family, the nuclear family ideal is the tracing that is perpetuated by the dominant discourses of our time (e.g., psychological discourse) and the "competent" language of their undaunted/relentless proponents (Deleuze & Guattari, 1987). Thus, as long as dominant discourses are deemed competent and authoritative in our opinions of the family, the tracing of the nuclear family as ideal will also continue to upset the balance of power and negate all other forms of family.

Put in Deleuze and Guattari (1987) terms, if we allow tracings of dominant competence (for example, psychology as an "arborescent culture") to grow into "trees, roots, and radicles" in our brains, we are disallowing our brains to be adventitious or rhizomorphous in thought. "Thought," Deleuze and Guattari affirm, "is not [meant to be] arborescent" (Deleuze & Guattari, 1987, p. 15). That is, despite what we have been told, our brains are not a continuous neuronic and dendritic fabric, or "rooted or ramified matter"; rather, the brain is naturally discontinuous/uncertain as a nervous system as messages make leaps across fissures in a probablistic manner (Deleuze & Guattari, 1987, p. 15).

The brain, however, is meant to be a "multiplicity immersed in its plane of consistency or neurolgia", or in arborescent terms, the brain is naturally "much more a grass than a tree" (Deleuze & Guattari, 1987, p. 15). As Deleuze and Guattari (1987) point out, however, most "people have a tree growing in their heads". Sadly, this indicates their inclination for arborescent hierarchical structures of power, which subjects them to pre-established destinies.

Upon first reading this, however, I thought that the notion of the brain growing tiny grass, as opposed to a large tree, seemed to be a negative alternative. But what Deleuze and Guattari (1987) are actually suggesting is that the brain is capable of much more than we allow. When they illustrate our brains as growing grass, they are describing freedom of thought; that is, a multiplicity of thought.

When they illustrate our brain as growing a tree, they are describing how many people chose to prescribe to the homogeneity of dominant thought. Thus, Deleuze and Guattari (1987) exclaim, "We're tired of trees. We should stop believing in trees, roots, and radicles. They've made us suffer too much. All of arborescent culture is founded on them" (p.15).

Therefore, to believe in the nuclear family as the ideal family tracing is to allow dominant arborescent culture to take root, and proliferate into a harmful tree in the brain. Ultimately, to allow this to occur is to go against the brain's natural propensity to multiplicity in thought. In other words, to allow the nuclear family tracing to pervade our minds, is not unlike treating our brains like a frozen Etch-A-Sketch—a "thick, flat gray screen in a plastic frame, and is equipped with two knobs on the front of the frame in the lower corners. The knobs move a stylus that displaces aluminium powder on the back of the screen, leaving a dark line as the stylus is moved. The knobs can thus be used to create lineographic images. One knob moves the stylus horizontally, and the other vertically" (Etch-A-Sketch, 2008).

A LIMB SEPARATED FROM THE INTERNAL FAMILY TREE

Deleuze and Guattari's analogy of the tracing growing a tree in our brains, suits the discussion of family. If we imagine the tracing as an ideal "family tree" in our mind, then each limb represents the ideal family relations of mother, father, and their growing offspring.

Just as the human body has an ideal pre-destined form, that is, to have four limbs (two arms and two legs), the pre-traced family ideal also comprises of an ideal and normative set of biological elements. As such, what really happened inside of me was an internal loss/injury. I had lost a limb from my internalized family tree.

When people lose a physical limb from their body, we marvel at how they ever bore the excruciating pain of the injury. Then we're told of the body's natural defense to place the person into a state of shock—essentially dulling the bodily sensation of pain for a period of time. I suggest that a similar dulling process happens for children after post-traumatic severances of internalized family tree limbs.

Don't get me wrong, I certainly felt like a limb had been ripped off. But I was in shock. I didn't feel the effects of the loss right away. Of course, the limb to which I am referring to was my real father. And the remaining family tree was no longer a whole representation of the ideal family tracing. But I gripped its after-image so tightly in my mind's eye—I could not let go of it.

I wonder if it is the same for other children whose internal family tracing is no longer whole because of a parent's choice to leave. I wonder how I, or any other child in the same situation, could renegotiate their internalized family tracing. And by renegotiate, I mean let go of the ready-made tracing to accommodate the new mappings of family more readily?

To conclude this section on Deleuze and Guattari's theoretical notions of mapping and tracing, I offer the following arguments. I contend that Statistic Canada's census family definition is not a map, but is one tracing of family. It cannot be considered a map of family, because it does not capture the multiplicity of family and its past, present and future realities. At best, I contend that Statistics Canada's census family definition is more of an *attempted* map of family because it does encompass multiple lived expressions or performances of family.

Statistics Canada's definition can be considered a tracing, however, because it represents what Canada deems the ready-made family definition linked intimately to a level of competence. The Statistics Canada's family tracing, however, does not represent the family we *ultimately* favour as the ideal family tracing, as evident through overt and covert family form discrimination. As such, despite the Canadian government's *attempt* at mapping a more inclusive definition of family, I argue that a family's competency is still determined solely by its structure. More specifically, a family's competency is judged on the basis of the extent of its match to the ideal tracing of the nuclear family form.

Recall Gillis's (1996) differentiation between the family we live *with* (our own lived family) and the family we live *by* (the family we think we *should* be living). Deleuze and Guattari's (1987) concepts of mapping and tracing infer a similar distinction between how we would *like-to-think-that-we-think* about families (that is, accepting of the map of infinite lived expressions of the family), and how we actually *do* think and treat families (ultimately, living *by* the tracing of nuclear family ideal and penalizing those who do not fit). Additionally, this is not unlike Parker's (1997) notion of the dominant family *image* which exists in our mind regardless of whether we have lived it or not (i.e., the nuclear family exists as an image in our minds as the ideal structure).

There is a pre-traced destiny to which we all ascribe, despite the kind of family into which we're born. Similar to the pre-traced destiny of our physical body to have four limbs (that is, two perfectly formed legs and a proportionate pair of arms), we are equally surrounded by a pre-traced image of a perfectly formed family (in the form of two biological parents and their jointly formed offspring).

Thus, I do not believe that I could have consciously chosen the pre-traced family I lived by, any more than I could have chosen the pre-traced destiny of my physical body. It was chosen for me by the surrounding socio-historical/cultural nexus/world. Although I was born into the normative ideal family structure, I believe it would have been chosen for me regardless. Overall, the pre-traced family ideal became two-fold a part of my being: first, by being born into it, and second, by living in a world that favoured it.

The family I lived by was intimately synchronized with what was considered "normal" in the world around me. It infested my neighbourhood, grocery store, library, school, church, and plastered its image throughout my reading materials and on the television that permeated my young mind.

Any exceptions to the rule were regarded as the unfortunate, the abnormal, or the family who lacks. Similar to when a physical body lacks a limb and it no longer fits the pre-traced normative ideal, a family that lacks an integral limb from its pre-traced family tree is also considered abnormal. Feelings of lack breed a need for assimilation.

We want to fit in, we dream of, we ache for, phantom limbs...

Overall, what the theorists discussed in this chapter are trying to convey is that we all live *by* the nuclear family ideal, which forms a *tracing* (Deleuze & Guattari, 1987), or alternatively, a dominant *image* (Parker, 1997) in our internal mind's eye. To understand the ramifications of internalizing this tracing or image within families, I turn to the clinical perspectives of R.D. Laing.

CHAPTER 3

R.D. LAING: THE INTERNALIZED FAMILY

Similar to the Deleuze and Guattari, Laing notes a distinction between our lived *with* family and the internalized lived *by* family. What distinguishes Laing from the other theorists, however, is his closer position as a psychiatrist to the realm of family therapeutic practice. From this practical viewpoint, Laing witnessed and wrote about the collusion and ramifications of these two families and their distinct sets of relations. Each notion of family, internalized and lived, has sets of relations comprised of "elements and relations between elements" (Laing, 1969, p. 117). Elements are the "persons, things, or part-objects" (Laing, 1969, p. 4). Therefore, Laing's perspective addresses what can happen to a family's sense of auto-ethnography or integrity when there are discrepancies between the relational set of the internal family they live *by* (i.e., *tracing* or *image*), and that expressed in the family they live *with*.

FAMILY AS INTERNALIZED SYSTEM

Laing (1969) states that "the family as a system is internalized" (p. 4). In this sense, the internalized family is made up of "[r]elations and operations between elements and sets of elements" (Laing, 1969, p. 4). Elements are "persons, things, or part-objects" and internalized are the relations and operations that occur between them (Laing, 1969, p. 4). For instance, "[p]arents are internalized as close or apart, together or separate, near or distant, loving, fighting, etc., each other and self" (Laing, 1969, p. 4). Overall, Laing (1969) points out that "what is internalized are not objects as such but patterns of relationship by internal operations upon which a person develops an incarnate group structure" (p. 8). This incarnate group structure is the lived *with* family.

Tell me, how do you feel about your father leaving? As a seven year old, what words could I have possibly articulated that would represent my anguish? I question, even to this day, whether such trauma can ever be adequately captured in words alone.

What is conjured are bodily sensations—what feels like aches behind my eyes, drawing them down to my feet; and pangs in my heart, lurching it back into my spine. Unnatural feelings.

On the other hand, art seemed to have been an outlet for me. Through my childhood drawings, I found evidence that I was acutely aware of formational changes occurring in my lived *with* family. But, what do my childhood art pieces say about the state of my internal lived *by* family tracing? I had not yet let go.

Laing used various synonyms to refer to the internalized family, for instance, in his second book *Self and Others* (1961), he refers to the internalized family as a shared social phantasy. By using this different, yet synonymous, language, Laing (1961) effectually highlights the transcendental "need [of family members] to find [a shared] pseudo-real experience…found only through the modality of phantasy" (p. 24). Moreover, he continues to state that "the *normal* state of affairs is to be so immersed in one's immersion in social phantasy systems that one takes them to be real" (1961, p. 23). As such, he concludes that "the family is not experienced as the modality of phantasy but as 'reality'" (Laing, 1961, p. 24). In fact, Laing (1961) contends that we never realize we are part of a social phantasy system, nor do we ever think of "extricating ourselves" (p. 24). On the other hand, we do "tolerate, punish, or treat as harmless, bad, or mad those who [do] try to extricate themselves [from the shared internal lived *by* family], and tell us that we should also" (1961, p. 25). Before I directly address disruptions in family auto-ethnography more deeply, however, I ask: How is family auto-ethnography felt and maintained?

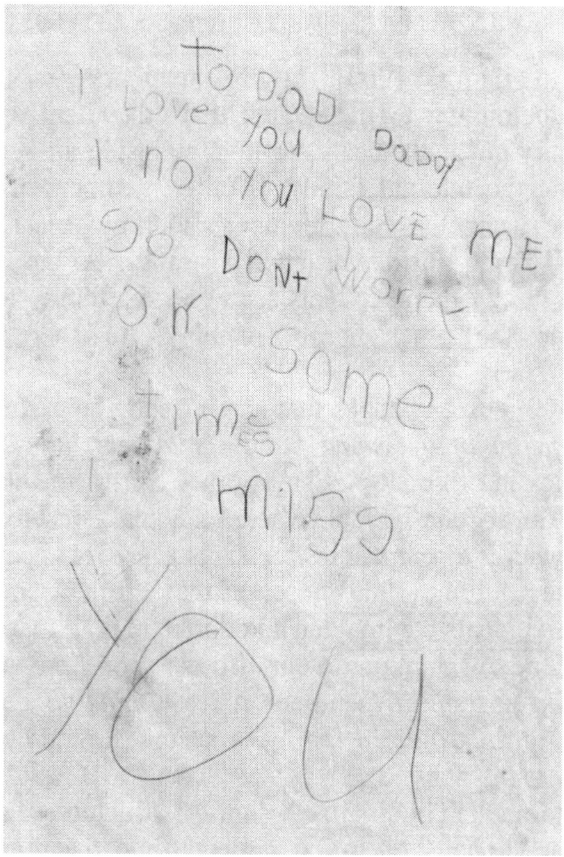

To Dad Daddy
I love you
I no [know] you love me
So don't worry
Oh some
times
I miss
YOU

FAMILY MEMBERSHIP/BELONGING AS A FEELING

According to Laing (1969), family members *feel* a sense of membership/belonging to the degree that "they feel themselves to have the family inside themselves and to be inside the set of relations characterizing the internal family of other members of the family" (p. 4). More succinctly, each member's identity "rests on a shared [internalized] family inside the others" (Laing, 1969, p. 13). In other words, each family member feels secure in the family to the degree they imagine the other family members to share their same internalized family.

Laing (1969) acknowledges that sharing may be real or imagined, because "*[t]o be in the same family is to feel the same 'family' inside*" (italics in original, p. 13). In other words, the sharing of the internalized family can be real (where an actual consensus exists) or imagined (where discrepancies exist but are not perceived). In another context, Laing (1969) observes that, "[b]etween truth and lie are images and ideals we imagine and think are real, that paralyse our imagination and our thinking in our efforts to conserve them" (p. 77). Thus, as long as family members at least *think/imagine* that they share the same *internalized* family, a secure structure is perceived and integrity is maintained.

To maintain the internalized family structure, Laing (1969) observes that "[e]ach generation projects onto the next" what had been "*projected* onto it by prior generations", "*induced* in it by prior generations", and finally, "its response to this projection and induction" (p. 77). Whereas the process of internalization means "to map 'outer' onto 'inner'" (idealizing, psychologizing, and thus internalizing the "outer" nuclear family onto the "inner"), re-projection involves the opposite transaction (that is, idealizing, psychologizing, and thus internalizing the "inner" onto the "outer") (Laing, 1969, p. x). Laing (1969) observes that when we re-project, we are superimposing "one set of relations" (for example, the *internalized* lived *by* family) "onto another" (for instance, our lived *with* family) and "the two sets may match more or less" (p. 9). As such, we re-project our internalized family (the idealized Western nuclear family form) and its prescriptive sets of relations onto our own lived *with* family, and the feeling of belongingness relates to the degree they match.

WHEN YOU CAN'T FAKE IT…

When I lived *with*(in) it, I never questioned my lived *by* socio-historical/cultural normative tracing of family. Nor did I start to question it when I no longer lived *with*(in) it.

By this, I am not surprised; after all, it is rare enough that an adult questions inborn tracings of socio-historical and cultural norms and prescribed societal expectations. These norms are more often than not subscribed to unconsciously, and without any further rumination.

Perhaps questioning the ideal family tracing may have been helpful for me to renegotiate new mappings of family? Could I have felt less alienated and alone if I were made aware of my unoriginal situation (that others were also experiencing the same transition)?

Instead, I fully accepted and played my role in the part of a broken family. Part of a family that was considered "lesser than" by the dominant social body.

It was 1985, and ~~most of my friends~~—no, scratch that—*all* of my friends remained "blessedly" part of the ideal family: two biological parents who still lived together! My immediate surroundings dictated that normalcy was *the* nuclear family.

Had I been attending a school with a less biased representation/sampling of the world's families, a school other than the Cambridge Christian School, I may have felt like less of a freak.

Certainly, the historical time (mid 1980s) was not devoid of family divorce. Yet, by a stroke of (bad)luck, I happened to be immersed within a bubble of family form homogeneity, wherein all my fellow peers were part of families uniformly nuclear in structure.

For most children, it is important to fit in with your peers, at every level. And so, my aim was to fit in with my fellow peers, the very best I could.

Sharing with friends the same tastes in clothing and music was relatively important to me, but if I didn't completely meld to their tastes in music, I knew I could always fake it. For instance, outwardly, I told my friends, “I love Debbie Gibson!” But inwardly, I felt that Tiffany held more clout and touted considerably more talent.

The point is that if one hopes or wishes to fit in, there are aspects that one can fake. I had a level of control over this aspect/realm of assimilation. On the other hand, sharing the same family structure is something over and above that which children have any control. Family structure is something that a child cannot fake. Indeed, sharing the same family structure as the majority of my fellow peers was a lost cause for me.

Sure, I could have lied to my fellow peers about my family’s “state of affairs” (pardon the pun). However, given the particularly prominent, and not to mention visual, presence that one’s family members have over the course of childhood, a lie of this magnitude would require nothing short of an epic theatrical production!

* * *

WANTED: AN ACTOR TO PLAY THE PART OF MY FATHER

WANTED: an actor to play the part of my biological father (must be a Tom Selleck doppelganger) to counteract the lived reality that I am part of a single-parent family structure, headed by my biological mother.

Your role as my fake actor Dad is needed immediately, in order for me to appear part of a “normal” and “ideal” family. You must be available to fulfill a number of duties that I see my friend’s fathers fulfilling. First, you should be present at the most crucial social events such as parent-teacher nights, birthday parties, and choir assemblies. Second, your signature (or in this case, your autograph?) must accompany my mother’s on various childhood records, such as assignments and report cards. Third, on occasion, your presence is needed to drop me off (or pick me up) from school or a friend’s house. Finally, it is imperative that you come to my apartment and to answer the door (perhaps wearing something totally embarrassing?), and—of course—to answer the occasional phone call from my friends.

Overall, your valuable appearances as my actor father will afford me, at very least, the same appearance of family normalcy *afforded to* my peers.

* * *

AUTO(BIOLOGICAL) NORMALCY

I was tempted to write "*enjoyed*" by my peers, but then reconsidered. I thought about whether or not they are actually aware of their so-called ideological family position. When I look back to when I was part of a nuclear family, I do not recall "*enjoying*" a feeling normalcy. Nor do I think I was cognizant of the automatic degree of social acceptance I was afforded as part of a biologically complete set of family members. Why would I?

What I am trying to convey is that the ideal family tracing does not require additional actors to fill in the gaps. It is a biological whole. And despite of functionality, the nuclear family will always be considered "more normal" and "more ideal" when compared with any other family structure. Consider, for instance, that a nuclear family struggling *privately* with abuse, for example, will always *appear* more "ideal" and "normal", versus a non-nuclear family who is not struggling with abuse.

It remains to be addressed, however, if Laing was referring to the Western nuclear family ideal when he discussed the notion of an internalized family. In other words, as he wrote about the shared social phantasy, was he implying a shared social internalization of the nuclear family structure?

LAING AND THE FAMILY IDEAL

In his book called *R.D. Laing: The Philosophy and Politics of Psychotherapy,* Andrew Collier (1977) provides a brief analysis regarding Laing's implicit critique on the nuclear family structure. The key observation that Collier (1977) makes about Laing is that he was first and foremost a practitioner, not a politician—although others, such as Claude Steiner (1974), describe Laing as radical in his politics but conservative in his psychiatric practice. Having described Laing as practitioner, Collier contends that although Laing recognized that the nuclear family effectively "frustrates people's desires and limits their possibilities", it was not his priority to change capitalist society's dependence upon or propensity for it (Collier, 1977, p. 125). In the following quotation, Collier (1977) illustrates Laing's dilemma as a practitioner in the therapeutic context:

> If *discrepancies* between familial and societal norms are, in many cases, involved in the production of schizophrenia, it will not be a simple matter of taking sides with the patient against all comers, but possibly of taking sides with those elements in the patient which would make for a satisfying life in the wider world, against those elements in the patient which would keep him or her trapped within the confines of the family. (Collier, 1977, p. 130, italics in original)

In other words, as a practitioner, Laing often faced the dilemma of either taking the side of the patient no matter what, encouraging a patient to submit to the expectations of the family, or promoting those elements in the patient that would encourage a happier life in the world. Hence, Collier (1977) proposes that Laing did recognize the harm in investing all normality within the nuclear family ideal, because he was first and foremost "a psychoanalyst, [and] not a political leader", which suggests that his approach to strained families does not involve political action (p. 137).

Given the state of dominant culture and the expectations of the family, Laing was often forced to place the "burden of responsibility squarely on the shoulders of individuals" in the name of his client's best interests (p. 123). Collier (1977) describes how Laing may have determined the best course of practice:

> If the kind of family best suited to our civilization is destructive of the happiness of individuals, it is the individual that must adapt, not civilization that must be changed, and hence that the

requisite reform of the family must consist in individuals adapting to their roles of mother, father and child. (Collier, 1977, p. 123)

Overall, Laing was not entirely explicit about his feelings regarding how political change could help the family. Laing, then, differs greatly from Franco Basaglia who, in his work, set forth boldly "wedding psychiatry to a political praxis" in order to de-stigmatize and de-institutionalize patients in Italy (Lovell & Scheper-Hughes, 1987, p. 3). But this is not to imply that Laing negated "the possibility that human beings have far greater potentialities than are allowed to develop by the conditioning process imposed by the contemporary society" (Collier, 1977, p. 137). In fact, Collier (1977) does indicate that Laing felt the study of "ill effects of the social structures on the individual should remain open toward the politics which could transform these structures" (p. 137).

I have chosen to add Laing's perspective to this writing because he extracts the role of the individual (as members of the family) in the dominant culture's propensity and idealism of the nuclear family structure. In other words, Laing highlights attended to the way individual members of the family can be just as (if not more) harmful to each other, than the dominant culture. Overall, Laing focused more heavily internal family processes of domination, than on external societal processes, bringing to light how disruptions in family auto-ethnography, can lead to the transpersonal defense process called mystification.

DISRUPTION IN FAMILY AUTO-ETHNOGRAPHY

Laing (1969) describes how the shared family auto-ethnography, among and between family members, is constantly undergoing an unconscious comparative process. My question concerning Laing in this auto-ethnography is: What happens when two sets of relational expectations do not match among, or between, family members?

Overall, he states that a mismatch of the shared family synthesis among or between family members only becomes problematic when members actually perceive a mismatch (Laing, 1969). To put this phenomenon into the terms of this auto-ethnography, Laing is essentially describing a mismatch among and/or between the family members internalized lived *by* notions of the family. For example, my internalized lived by notion of our family is different from my brother's internalized lived by notion of our family. Moreover, Laing suggests that problems will arise only when a mismatch of internal family conceptualizations is *felt* by the members of the family. For instance, I may not feel any indication that my conceptions of the internal lived *by* family differs from that of my brother's, and vice versa.

A COMMON, BUT DIFFERENT, LOSS OF LIMB

When my stepfather was seven years old, his "real" father was killed instantly in an industrial accident. He did not talk about this event—but on this day—he did.

In my early teenage years, I was struggling to come to terms with my real father's distance in location and emotions. His continued existence in my life was maintained primarily through random gifts and telephone calls. Of course I was grateful for his efforts, but I simultaneously longed for remnants of the previous existing relationship. I was longing for the family synthesis we once shared, despite knowing that it was no longer possible.

Sharing these confusing feelings with my stepfather, I intended to (by comparison) convey that I appreciated his more substantial presence in my life. I think he already knew of his positive contribution to my life, and consequently changed the course of the conversation by opening up himself.

He said something like, "We have something in common you know..."

I remember that his voice became different as he changed his manner of speaking. It was slow, deliberate, and quiet.

He then continued to say, "We both lost our fathers when we were seven years old".

It was uncharacteristic for him to open up and speak so sensitively; not to mention that he had never talked to me about his father's death. I appreciated it, but the unfamiliarity of the conversation took me by surprise.

Still a little stunned, I was unsure of how to react. All I could muster was, "I know…" with my eyes looking straight ahead.

He stopped the car and continued to say something like, "I heard somewhere that the death of a parent is easier for a child to recover from, than a divorce or separation—and I think that's true. When my father died, I was sad but I was able to move on. For you, your father is still out there, and it has probably made it harder for you to move on."

And there it was, what I had felt deep inside, vocalized out loud. But all I could say was, "Yeah, you could be right."

I was ashamed. How could I admit something so horrible? That there was a part of me that wanted the limb to have fallen away forever!

Instead I am haunted by the dull ache of a distant limb: an offshoot from the original family tree tracing that is still connected by energy-sucking roots.

Laing (1969) states that the internalized family "becomes a medium to link its members, whose links with one another may otherwise be very attenuated" (pp. 13–14). Moreover, the lived *with* family may *feel* the shared internalized lived *by* family as "the whole world" (Laing, 1969, p. 14). As such, any notion of a family member wanting to break away is distressing to the remaining family members.

To illustrate the thought-processes behind the distress, Laing (1969) refers to some parents who "cannot allow children to break the [internalized lived *by*] 'family' down within themselves, if that is what they want to do, because this is felt as the breakup of the family, and then where will it end?" (p. 13). In other words, "[t]o destroy the [internalized lived *by*] 'family' may be experienced as worse than murder, or more selfish than suicide. 'It would be to destroy my parents' world,' and felt as such by the parents. And what the parents do may be experienced by the children as shattering if it breaks up the [internalized lived *by*] 'family' as well as the [lived *with*] family" (Laing 1969, p. 14).

GONE BY CHOICE

Looking back, there were early clues that he was pulling away from the family tracing. But on that day—after what we saw, and the words that she spoke as she frantically opened and closed the kitchen cupboards—I knew it would not be long now…

Some call it precociousness—I attribute it up to first hand observation—but I understood. I knew that he was leaving by choice, and once he left, he would be gone for good.

I remember his presence, the smell of his cologne, his cheerful voice, his silly laugh, his big hands holding mine, his arms swinging me around as we danced, his eyes watching proudly as I read my books and rode my bike with two wheels for the first time…

Would it have been easier to remember just *these* things—had they remained untouched by the events that followed his tearing away?

When I close my eyes, would his after-image appear more like my father and as opposed to an off-shooting limb whose intermittent appearances effectually remind me of what I lost.

What I lost not from death, but by virtue of choice, his choice.

Was it that he left by choice that was so difficult to accept? Is the death of a parent really easier for children in the long run?

Given the distress felt, it is not surprising that these perceptions of family destruction are held, despite whether or not the intent, or motivation, of a dissenting family member was malicious (Laing, 1969). Consequently, what are the options for a family member who becomes so dissatisfied with the shared internalized lived *by* family that they see no alternative to leaving or dissolving *it* within themselves?

Laing (1969) observes that the dissenting family member is faced with several dilemmas: "If I do not destroy the [internalized lived *by*] 'family', the [internalized lived *by*] 'family' will destroy me. I cannot destroy the [internalized lived *by*] 'family' in myself without destroying 'it' in them. Feeling themselves endangered, will they destroy me?" (Laing, 1969, p. 14). As such, the preservation of the internalized lived *by* family is "equated with the preservation of the self and world" whilst "the dissolution of the [internalized lived *by*] 'family' inside *another* is equated with death of self and world-collapse" (Laing, 1969, p. 14). As such, self-sacrifice for the preservation of the shared internalized lived *by* family is seen as an essential (unspoken/non-selfish?) expectation.

MYSTIFICATION: A TRANSPERSONAL DEFENSE

In order to maintain a level of perceived family synthesis, it is common for members to engage in what Laing refers to as transpersonal defense processes. Transpersonal defenses differ from the (more well-known) psychoanalytic intrapersonal defense mechanisms such as introjection, denial, and repression (Laing, 1969). Whereas intrapersonal defenses are "*what a person does to himself*", transpersonal defenses are instances where the "self attempts *to regulate the inner life of the other in order to preserve his own*" (Laing, 1969, pp. 12–13, italics in original). That is to say, "I act not only on myself, I can act upon you. And you act not only on yourself, you act upon me" (Laing, 1967, p. 18). In other words, family members "act on the 'inner' worlds of others to preserve their own inner worlds" (Laing, 1969, p. 13).

Laing (1969) recognizes these attempts to "*regulate the inner life of the other*" as nothing short of persecution (p. 13, italics in original), adding further that "[p]eople are doing such things to each other all the time" and it "is not unusual" (Laing, 1967, p. 19). But how do these attempts manifest? Laing (1967) observes that "in order for transpersonal invalidation to work…it is advisable to overlay it with a thick patina of mystification" (p. 19).

Mystification, as Laing (1965) defines it, is "both the act of mystifying and the state of being mystified" (par. 5) and its "prime function…appears to be to maintain the status quo" when,

> one or more members of the family nexus threaten, or are felt to threaten, the status quo of the nexus by the way they are

> experiencing, and acting in, the situation they share with the other members of the family. (Laing, 1965, par 46)

What does it look like when one attempts transpersonal manipulation on another?

To mystify, Laing (1965) says, "is to befuddle, cloud, obscure, mask whatever is going on, whether this be experience, action, or process, or whatever is 'the issue'" (par. 6). Successful mystification "induces confusion in the sense that there is a failure to see what is 'really' being experienced, or being done, or going on, and failure to distinguish or discriminate the actual issues" (par. 6).

For instance, mystification may be attempted to "maintain stereotyped roles…and to fit other people into a preset mold" (par. 47). In such a case, "[p]arents may struggle to preserve their own integration by maintaining their rigid preconceptions about who they ought to be, who their children are and ought to be, and the nature of the situation that characterizes family life" (par. 47). Laing (1965) further describes that mystification can be used to befuddle "what rights and obligations each person in the family has in respect of the others" through the following scenario:

> A boy of fourteen tells his parents he is unhappy, and they reply:
>
> But you can't be unhappy. Haven't we given you everything you want? How can you be so ungrateful as to say you are unhappy after all that has been done for you, after all the sacrifices that have been made for you? (par. 18-19)

In this illustration, mystification is used "in such a way that one person [the boy] is under an obligation to the others [the parents] to experience, or not to experience, himself, them, his world or any aspect of it, in a particular way", and the question then becomes, "has the boy a right to be unhappy, or must he be happy because if he is not he is being ungrateful?" (Laing, 1965, par. 20).

The state of mystification is difficult to explain because it "is possibly, though not necessarily, a feeling of being muddled or confused" (Laing, 1965, 7). In other words, one is mystified, but may not actually feel the confusion because one has been mystified from perceiving the act of mystification (Laing, 1965, par. 8). Moreover, the act of mystification (detected or undetected) induces a state of confusion only if it is not otherwise neutralized in the counteraction of secondary conflicts (Laing, 1965). When mystification is detected, "we are alerted to the presence of a conflict of some kind that is being evaded" and,

> [a]lthough one of the functions of mystification is to avoid authentic conflict, it is quite common for open conflict to occur in mystifying and mystified families. The masking effect of mystification may not avoid conflict, although it will cloud over what the conflict is about. (par. 7)

Mystification is only one of many transpersonal actions that "serves the defenses, the security, of the own person" (1965, par. 36). In fact, Laing (1965) points out that "[t]here are many kinds of persuasion, coercion, deterrence, whereby the one person seeks to control, direct, exploit, manipulate the behaviour of the other" (par. 37). In an effort to maintain his/her "interiorization of the group unchanged", other coercive ways include "by sympathy, blackmail, indebtedness, guilt, gratitude, or naked violence" (Laing, 1967, p. 58). All of these acts on the other have one element in common, which is to promote the denial of personal vindication for the betterment of the family synthesis.

Denial of personal un-satisfaction in order to maintain family synthesis is what Laing (1969) calls the "transpersonal system of collusion" (p. 99). The following illustration describes how this system of collusion transpires internally.

> I am unhappy. I deny I am to myself; I deny I am denying anything to myself and to the others. They must do the same. I must collude with their denial and collusion, and they must collude with mine. (Laing, 1969, p. 99)

It is this transpersonal cycle of self-denial that Laing (1969) emphasizes is required in order to play the game of "Happy Families" (p. 99). Here are the rules:

> So we are a happy family and we have no secrets from one another. If we are unhappy/we have to keep it a secret/ and we are unhappy that we have to keep it a secret and unhappy that we have to keep secret/the fact/that we have to keep it a secret and that we are keeping all that a secret. But since we are a happy family you can see this difficulty does not arise.

WHAT WOULD BE DIFFERENT? PART I

What if my father had chosen not to leave? What if he had engaged in the transpersonal act of collusion to play the game of happy families? What would be different?

I could not stop my Dad from leaving, and I was not under the impression that I could mystify him otherwise. I somehow understood that some things cannot be amended by sheer determination/mystification.

When mystification fails to hold the family synthesis together and the tracing lived by can no longer be materialized in the lived with, what is the alternative?

CHAPTER 4

PSYCHOLOGIZATION OF THE (NUCLEAR/IDEAL) FAMILY

The family is an unstable construct that is capable of a multiplicity of lived *with* expressions over time. Yet, we tend to impose the stability of the lived *by* nuclear family form upon our lived *with* family. As the internalized social ideal, there is a need to attain, maintain, assimilate, or at the very least, strive for the nuclear family form. But where does this internalization originate?

It is my contention that the internalized family is imposed upon us through the dispersal of discourse(s) across the social, necessitating our conformity. Of the many discourses defining the nuclear family as ideal, I focus on the power of psychological discourse to disperse its particular knowledge about the family, and how it has a profound effect on how we feel about our lived *with* family. My aim in this chapter, therefore, is to delineate the effects of the psychological complex to disperse particular definitions and expectations of the family through its discourse. Key to understanding this process is a discussion on discourse, and the ways in which it attains dominance.

A DEFINITION OF DISCOURSE?

Psychology contributes to the construction and maintenance of the nuclear family form as the ideal through its discourse. But what exactly is meant by discourse? It is my aim to read Foucault, determine his definition of discourse, and relate it to the construction of the ideal family. As simple as that! No, not "as simple as that."

Oh, without explorations gone asunder, where would I be? I have discovered that it is in a space of sheer confusion and disillusionment, that I eventually experience the (inter)connections once evading my perception. Until that moment, however, blasts of information surround me on all angles keeping me in a state of imbalance by the brute force of their messages. I am engaged in a constant struggle to remain (semi)standing. In the face of these awkward blasts, my strength could go on indefinitely, and I delight in the thought…

On the other hand, I long for the occasional instances where blasts occur simultaneously. Their force presenting evenly to my body (either below and above, front and back, left and right, and so on). As they collide, they intersect through me, and connect to my thoughts as an assemblage. It is then/here, previous experiences of imbalance and limited scope subside, and I can focus my gaze upon the whole picture.

Eventually the occasion arose where two blasts of thought collided, intersected, and assembled in me. In a moment of clarity, I realized that Foucault and I analyze our individual objects of study in a similar way. Just as Foucault tends to oscillate frequently between describing what is the "reality of discourse" (that is, as a proliferation of rich and uncontrollable elements), and how society actually treats discourse (in general, as organized and constrained), I also recognize the reality of "the family" (as a constellation of people capable of a multiplicity of lived expressions), and how it is actually treated in society (as either ideal or non-ideal according to its alignment with the nuclear family form). As such, we both acknowledge the indefinable "true" nature of discourse and the family, and are both concerned about how the social world uses force to constrain them.

All in all, I ceased my quest to find a clear definition of discourse. After all, why should I impose upon Foucault a (re)definition of discourse, when I myself have never intended to (re)define the family? On the other hand, I do offer various descriptions of "the family", and Foucault (1972) also offers various descriptions of discourse.

DISCOURSE: DESCRIBED

In *Archaeology of Knowledge*, Foucault (1972) *describes* discourse as "a group of statements that belong to a single system of formation" (p. 107). This *description* of discourse, although concise, captures how society limits discourse into a "finite and temporally limited" ensemble of statements belonging to the same discursive formation (Foucault, 1994, p. 400). Discursive formations are the systems of dispersion, that define regularities "between objects, types of statement, concepts, or thematic choices" in a given historical and cultural period (Foucault, 1972, p. 38).

Limit yourself to this *description* of discourse, however, and there is a danger of misreading Foucault as an invitation to analyze discourse based purely on language and textual level (Hook, 2001). Instead, discourse should be approached more as "an active 'occurring', as something that implements power and action, and that also *is* power and action" (Hook, 2001, p. 532).

Hook's perspective on discourse converges nicely with what Foucault (1980) stated as his main concern, that is, with the *how* of power (p. 31). Foucault (1980) stresses the intimate, indivisible, and co-dependent relationship between power and discourse in the following statement:

> [I]n a society such as ours…there are manifold relations of power which permeate, characterize, and constitute the social body, and these relations of power cannot themselves be established, consolidated, nor implemented without the production, accumulation, circulation, and functioning of a discourse. (p. 31)

Thus, by relating the force of the social body to exercise power through discourse, Foucault (1972) is essentially saying that it is a "violence that we do to things" or "as a practice we impose upon them" (p. 158). How is discourse then *done*? Foucault insists that, at their base, discourses are the *forms of practice* imposed on people (as cited by Hook, 2001, p. 538). As such, discourses are implemented through the power of discursive practices.

Discursive practices are "rules, systems, and procedures" that provide "the order of discourse", and there-under, the "conceptual terrain in which knowledge is formed and produced" (Hook, 2001, p. 522). Power, therefore, is exercised through the *rules* of discursive *practices*, which constitute and reproduce the *social system*, by way of their carefully executed *procedures* (Hook, 2001). Discursive practices are additionally thought of as the “sites in institutions like prisons and schools where patterns of meaning are embedded in techniques of discipline, where we are made to act and be in certain ways” (Parker, 1997, p. 7). It is through discursive practices, therefore, that discourse exercises the power simultaneously to form, constrain, produce, and exclude that which can be written, spoken, or thought (Foucault, as cited by Hook, 2001). Indeed, the “effect of discursive practices is to make it virtually impossible to think outside of them; to be outside of them is, by definition, to be mad, to be beyond comprehension and therefore reason” (Hook, 2001, p. 522).

Once again, there is a risk of misreading Foucault, but in this instance, as an invitation to identify discourse as either an *effect of power* translated through text, or alternatively, as an *instrument of power* for systems of domination (Hook, 2001). Neither conceptualization, according to Foucault (as cited by Hook, 2001), captures how discourse is the “thing for which and by which there is a struggle” (p. 539). Power is neither fixed, nor “apprehended in the meanings and significations of texts”, rather, it can only be “grasped and traced through the analysis of tactical and material relations of force” (Hook, 2001, p. 530). As such, Foucault seems to be stating that a discourse’s very existence is a *becoming,* an endless process of struggle for dominance.

Taking pause to recollect my thoughts about power and discourse as the “thing for which and by which there is a struggle” (Hook, 2001, p. 539), I experience another moment of clarity. A thought assemblage linked to (my) notions of mapping and tracing, as inspired by the abstract writings of Deleuze and Guattari’s *A Thousand Plateaus* (1987). In particular, I consider how dominant discourse can be likened to the tracing of the nuclear family. Both are extracted, brought forth by the social body from the map of infinite expression, and each is subsequently engaged in a struggle to attain or maintain a position of dominance.

In a similar mode of thought, Hook (2001) states, “[t]o engage critically with discourse…one needs…to map discourse, to trace its outline and its relations of force across a variety of discursive forms and objects" (p. 541). Here, Hook (2001) is not referring to *map* in the Deleuze and Guattari (1987) sense of the term which suggests infinite expression. Rather, he is suggesting the opposite, that is, a finite boundary of discourse. It is also helpful to realize that discourse often appears in a variety of forms, for instance, as "both [an] *instrument* and *result* of power, as both its antecedent and its offshoot" (Hook, 2001, p. 540). In this way, one could conceive that the nuclear family ideal appears as both an *instrument* and a *result* of power. One could even speculate that the nuclear family would not exist as an idealistic instrument, without the power of discourse.

I base this contention on Foucault's observations that the notions of "madness, disease, delinquency, sexuality, et cetera" are brought/willed into existence by dominant "regimes of truth" (Foucault, 2008, p. 19). That is, through their governance of "realities", dominant regimes of truth make "something that does not exist able to become something" (Foucault, 2008, p. 19). Can we conclude, therefore, that the nuclear family as ideal is something of a "wicked illusion" (Foucault, 2008)? On the contrary, Foucault (2008) clarifies that "the something" that dominant regimes of truth make, is *not* an illusion at all; rather, "*it* is precisely a set of practices, real practices, which established it and thus imperiously marks it out in reality" (p. 19, emphasis in original).

The power of these regimes of truth, therefore, cannot be underestimated. After all, a discourse subsists within them and makes it difficult for individuals to challenge the "realities" that are constructed around them (Parker, 1997). As such, the various categories of "the family", (including the nuclear family ideal and those forms classified as non-ideal), are not illusions, but exist as "reality" through the governance of a regime of truth. With the power to form, constrain, produce, and exclude what can be written, spoken, or thought, discursive practices reinforce classifications of the family through the meanings embedded in techniques of discipline (Hook, 2001; Parker, 1997).

Overall, Foucault (2008) observes that "the coupling of a set of practices and a regime of truth form an apparatus of knowledge-power that effectively *marks out in reality that which does not exist*" (p. 19). Using the term conceptual apparatus (instead of Foucault's term, apparatus of knowledge-power) to describe particular disciplines of knowledge, Parker (2008) observes how conceptual apparatus, such as psychology or psychoanalysis, [h]ave a peculiar power in modern society to *produce what they find*, and to do so within particular institutions and cultural practices such that they are able to incite, mobilize and recruit human subjects who will testify to the 'truth' of their investigative procedures and there determinate knowledge. (p. 149)

This leads to a discussion on how psychology, as a conceptual apparatus, gains authority over the "conceptual terrain in which knowledge is formed and produced" through its particular set of discursive practice and regimes of truth (Hook, 2001, p. 522). That is, how psychology as a discipline of knowledge, constructs the nuclear structure as the natural and normative ideal form of family.

PSYCHOLOGIZATION

Central to understanding how psychological discourse exerts its power and authority over the social body is through a process called psychologization. Parker (2008) describes psychologization as a process "by which academic and cultural questions are transformed into questions about the nature of individual psychology" (p. 158). Recall, however, that Foucault discouraged approaching discourse dualistically, that is, as either an *effect of power* translated through text, or as an *instrument of power* for systems of domination. Rather, Foucault *describes* discourse as "the violence…which we do to things" through *forms of practice*, or as the thing "for which and by which there *is* a struggle" for domination (as cited in Hook, 2001, p. 538). On the other hand, it is necessary to speak of discourse dualistically, as it appears in texts and practices, because they provide the evidence of the violence and struggle.

In either case, the overall aim of psychology and its proponents is to transform the knowledge of other conceptual apparatuses (e.g., biology, sociology, anthropology, and religiosity) into something that reflects a psychological epistemology (Parker, 2007; 2008). The *violence*, therefore, "which we do to things" is in the (re)construction of reality that is not questioned. The *struggle*, moreover, is to turn what is/was not psychological, into something psychological, or alternatively, into something that can be psychologized. Nothing, in this process, is safe/sacred, not even the family.

PSYCHOLOGIZATION OF THE FAMILY.

Psychological discourse has heralded a particular *kind* of family as the natural and normal ideal in Western society, and this family is none other than the patriarchal nuclear family form. In this way, psychology has "set itself the task of examining what a happy family really is like and repairing it when things go wrong" (Parker, 2007, p. 66). The family is psychologized, by psychological discourse, to fit a particular form in order to meet the categorization of ideal. From the psychological perspective, therefore, families are categorized based on *form* or *structure* alone (i.e., nuclear family ideal versus all other non-nuclear family forms) while other contextual aspects, such as a family's stability, duration, or quality, are ignored (Erera, 2002).

Erera (2002) confirms that the "normalizing gaze" of professional knowledge is particularly fixated upon the *structure* of a family regardless of the family's history of "stability, duration, or quality" (p 15). Consequently, with the template of normality based on the idealized nuclear family structure, all other non-nuclear forms are diverted into one of "two broad stereotypical categories: the deviant and the variant" (Erera, 2002, p. 13).

The *deviant* stereotype is attached to families that "seem much too different to be regarded as a variation of the first-married, heterosexual [ideal] family" (e.g., single-parent families, gay and lesbian families, childless families, and so on) (Erera, 2002, p. 13). Therefore deviant families are considered "bad or wrong in some way" and in need of proving their legitimacy (Erera, 2002, p. 14).

The *variant* stereotype is attached to families that are more similar to the ideal family structure because they "usually have two parents of the opposite sex who reside with children in the same household," but they still differ in biological underpinnings (for instance, families falling under the adoptive or stepfamily categories) (Erera, 2002, p. 14). "Characterized as falling short of the ideal or as lacking legitimacy leads to feelings of intense failure, therefore, there is an 'appeal of assimilation' that is attractive (Erera, 2002, p. 14).

Although the *variant* stereotype is considered more desirable than the deviant stereotype (because of greater similarity to the nuclear family form), both of the non-ideal categorizations of family are subjected to "unrealistic expectations based on the model of the traditional nuclear family" (Erera, 2002, p. 14). The fact that family categorizations and unrealistic expectations are accepted as "reality" reflects the way dominant discourse is "the violence…which we do to things" (Foucault as cited and quoted in Hook, 2001, p. 538). As tension is created between the "actual [lived *with*] and idealized [lived *by*] lifestyles of family members," feelings of "failure, shame, and identity confusion" create an overall feeling of lack (Erera, 2002, p. 14).

THE PSY-COMPLEX

According to Parker (2007), "an intricate network of theories and practices" are in place which govern "what abnormal emotional and correct mental functioning looks and feels like, and how child-care and family processes should be described and relayed to mothers and fathers" (Parker, 1997, pp. 3–4). This network is called the psy-complex and includes "psychology, psychiatry, psychoanalysis, social work, governmental agencies" (Parker, 1997, p. 7), all of which are "concerned with how we should look after our children, and [produce] advice columns in newspapers and magazines concerning how we should manage our emotions and relationships" (Parker, 1997, p. 7).

The psy-complex network, Parker (1997) suggests, has not always been in a position to define what an ideal family is, nor has it always been granted the kind of access to the family home that it enjoys today. Instead, the family was gradually inundated by emerging social disciplines. Whereas Parker (1997) specifically situates the psychologization process in England, Donzelot (1979) discusses in-depth how the psy-complex gradually took possession of "the family" in France.

JACQUES DONZELOT: THE POLICING OF FAMILIES.

In his book, *The Policing of Families,* Donzelot (1979) highlights how the psy-complex network effectively dissolved family resistance to the oppressive regimes of state control through the implementation of normalizing practices. Under the grip of the old state and judicial systems, families were required to fulfill strict family life expectations in exchange for access to critical support services and survival. For example, families depended on the state for "access to a profession," "the obtaining of housing," and "social benefits" (Donzelot, 1979, p. 167). Within this time period, the state placed the bulk of the responsibility on the head of the family, who "received aid and protection for maintaining his power over his own…insofar as this power was in keeping with the requirements of the public order" (Donzelot, 1979, p. xx).

As the old state and judiciary systems broke down, however, families started to demonstrate acts of resistance to outer intervention and state expectations. As the previous oppressive state and judicial discourse was no longer effective in exacting control over families, a massive reframing of control techniques was needed. As such, the social body was a space "ripe for psychologism"; that is, it became a climate eager for the emergence of social science disciplines and their "aptitude for relaying juridical authority in the coordination of normalization activities" (Donzelot, 1979, p. 167).

With their expertise on human thought and behaviour, the psy-complex network of professionals set themselves the task of dissolving family resistance to the previous oppressive practices of the judicial system. The psychologists and other social scientists, then, set out to transform oppressive practices into normalizing activities that *seemed* less repressive, *appeared* to be necessary, and most importantly, were deemed *acceptable* to the general public.

Important to reframing the previous oppressive language and practice was the social sciences discipline's ability to convey educative instructions for a proper family life and child rearing practices as *advice*. As Donzelot (1979) recognized, advice is the most effective tool for exacting influence over families, because it persuades them "that they are entirely free to refuse what [is asked] of them" (p. 65). Overall, he continues, "[a]dvice is the act that evinces the most equality since it follows at the same time from the desire to influence in the one who gives it and from the perfect freedom of the one who receives it" (Donzelot, 1979, p. 65).

MONA GLEASON: NORMALIZING THE FAMILY IDEAL.

In Canada, key historical developments and circumstances allowed the family to become a target for the *advice* of psy-complex experts. Gleason (1999) addresses how, in the decades pre-post Second World War (late 1920s to 1945), Canadian psychologists were in a prime position to penetrate the home environment, due to two key historical developments occurring external to the family. These two key historical developments were the creation of the Canadian National Committee on Mental Hygiene (CNCMH) and its shift to a focus on prevention and treatment, and the expansion of social agencies in the form of child guidance clinics.

Together, these developments provided psychologists with the opportunity to solidify their ostensible authoritative status as professionals, and perfect their specialized *advice* as expert problem solvers. This specialized status made them (trust) worthy enough to gain intimate/unquestioned access to the homes and lived experiences of Canadian families. In this way, the evolution of the psychological profession in pre-post-war Canada was thoroughly involved with the normalization of the nuclear family ideal.

CNCMH Needed The Social Science Disciplines.

The first significant historical development that helped social science disciplines, in particular psychology and psychologists as professionals, to gain expert status and authority was the creation and enhancement of the Canadian National Committee on Mental Hygiene. Formed in 1918, the CNCMH was the first committee to educate the public about the "dangers of inherited mental deficiency" and promote the eugenics movement: a concerted "effort to rid the country of 'defectives' and 'social misfits' by preaching the primacy of the inheritability of inferior character traits" (Gleason, 1999, p. 22). Gleason (1999) notes that inferior and feeble-minded people were lumped together into a "catch-all category" of undesirables, who shared common characteristics, such as "laziness, alcoholism, crime, venereal disease, and/or mental breakdown" (p. 22). Interestingly, Donzelot (1979) similarly addressed the ways in which medical authorities in France ordered "all children having reached the biological age of reproduction (fifteen to seventeen years old) to appear before the court and undergo an individual examination" wherein "[t]he doctor may then decide to issue a 'voucher for social service,' which will give them permission to effect temporary or permanent sexual unions, or he may defer the individual to the following year, or order his sterilization" (p. 182).

The CNCMH relied heavily on the research of Canadian psychological researchers/proponents, such as Charles K. Clarke (first Canadian editor of the American *Journal of Insanity*); Helen MacMurchy (key spokesperson for mental hygiene in public health and Ontario's appointed "inspector of the feeble-minded"), and Clarence Hincks (key financial contributor to the CNCMH and fighter "against mental defects") (Gleason, 1999, pp. 22–23) for the statistical and scientific proof that mental deficiency was biologically inherited. Foucault (1961) notes a similar link between medical authority and the confinement of the derelict members of the social body. He specifically pinpoints the creation of the general hospital in Paris, with the founding of mental illness, or madness. In short, then, the work of psychologists helped to rationalize the eugenics movement, while the eugenics movement brought "psychology out of the laboratory and into public spaces" in pre-war Canada (Gleason, 1999, p. 19). Eventually, however, both the CNCMH and its psychological proponents realized that by pinpointing *heredity* as the "culprit of mental illness", they were precluding the enhancement of the psychological profession to move beyond the ability to test, diagnose, and label (p. 23).

With this realization, the influential work of psychologists, such as William Blatz and Samuel Laycock, whose re-educational programs promoted the influence of the *environment* in determining mental deficiency, could no longer be ignored. With the work of these two key Canadian psychologists in this historical period, the focus on heritable mental deficiency and the need for eugenics eventually "fell out of favour" (p. 24). Instead, the environmental influences of mental deficiency became of focus, and the family became the target for a *preventative* movement (Gleason, 1999). Donzelot (1979) noted the similar trend in France, as eugenics was eventually replaced—rationalized by the medical authorities who drew causal links between heredity and delinquency—in favour of family intervention, spearheaded by the psy-complex that located the origin of delinquency in family relationships and parenting skills.

This reorientation toward the notion of environmental influence and the prevention movement allowed psychology and its practitioners to gain the power to construct, promote, and legitimize not only "certain models of mental health as superior to others", but also the normalization of "psychological intervention into [the] private lives" of Canadian families (Gleason, 1999, p. 24). Overall, the shift to *environmental* influences and the notion of prevention secured the "future of psychology as a vibrant and viable social science" by highlighting its strength to reframe normalizing activities into language that appears as harmless advice (Gleason, 1999, p. 24).

William Blatz and Samual Laycock, two prominent Canadian psychologists, both argued that the common factor underlying children's behavioural issues was the family home, more particular, the improper child-rearing practices of parents (Gleason, 1999).

With the contention that prevention and treatment efforts at school were useless if "the child's home life did not conform to their expectations," they led the insurgency of psychological advice into the home of Canadian families (Gleason, 1999, p. 30). In this way, psychological advice became accepted as a necessary aid to all Canadian parents who struggled with the unruly behaviour of their children.

Although both Blatz and Laycock led the psychological insurgency into the lived experiences of Canadian families, they did so through two independent paths: Blatz through the psychologization of parenting practices, and Laycock through the development of child guidance clinics.

Psychologization of parenting.

William Blatz, the head of the St. George's Nursery School for Child Study in Toronto Ontario in 1925, was a significant contributor to the "psychologizing of parenting" in Canada. In fact, he was the first in Canada to provide parents (mostly mothers) with the opportunity to learn valuable parenting skills through the completion of reports and assignments. Urging parents (mostly mothers) to go beyond simply tending the home, he encouraged them to "become amateur scientists in their own right" (Gleason, 1999, p. 26).

The school's clientele (primarily white, educated, middle-class mothers coming from single-income families) was largely unrepresentative of Canadian families in the late 1920s. Despite the biased misrepresentation of the school's research population, it was their "circumstances and priorities [that] determined the school's research agenda", and informed "parent education leadership" training that was offered exclusively to social agency workers (Gleason, 1999, p. 26). Family normality in Blatz's research literature and parent education classes, therefore, was constructed around a population of "full-time mothers [and] the predominance of a white, middle-class orientation" (Gleason, 1999, p. 26).

William Blatz was particularly influential in promoting the intrusion/insertion of psychological intervention practices within the child-rearing practices of Canadian parents. Not only did he convince parents that they could implement the preventative psychological measures on their own, but that this psychological advice and procedures were *crucial* for a normal family life. Overall, Blatz helped perpetuate the spread of "psychological approaches [to parenting] ever outward" and characterized "much of the popular psychological discourse on parenting and the family for decades to come" (Gleason, 1999, p. 26).

Similar to Blatz, Laycock stressed the importance of psychological intervention/intrusion within the home environment in order for progress in child behaviour to occur successfully, both at school and in the family home. In fact, he was quoted as stating that "every child brings his home to school, [therefore], normal progress and behaviour at school depended on normalcy at home" (Gleason, 1999, p. 51). With this stance on child behaviour, he encouraged the development of "child guidance clinics in every community in the country…to complement family welfare agencies and family counselling" (Gleason, 1999, p. 28).

Child guidance clinics.

The first child guidance clinic opened in 1919, and from the date of this opening, they proliferated across Canada well into the 1930s. All clinics operated with the common mandate of "shaping and changing the behaviour of both children and their parents" (Gleason, 1999 p. 28). Donzelot (1979) notes a similar trend in France, where the first cluster of Parents' Schools opened in the 1930s with the following four primary objectives in their mandate:

> (a) to teach parents to education and instruct one another in order to make their children into future social and moral assets; (b) to work toward a reawakening of the familial spirit in France; (c) to safeguard the rights of the family over the child: (d) to achieve a sacred union through the family. (Parents' School mandate as quoted in Donzelot, 1979, p. 190)

Overall, the expansion of child guidance clinics in Canada and France helped psychology as a discipline, and psychologists as professionals, to gain expert status and authority. In both locations, psy-experts depended upon the same rationalization for the widespread inundation of child guidance clinics and specialized advice. That is, the dependence on the "familial etiology of delinquency and character disorders to raise [their] level of intervention from the simple educative relation to a treatment of the general problem of family life" (Donzelot, 1979, pp. 192–193). In this way, both Canada and France led the psychological insurgency into the lived experiences of families by promoting the importance of good child-rearing practices in the prevention and treatment of delinquent children.

To uncover exactly how psychologists "facilitated psychology's various techniques of normalcy" (Gleason, 1999, p. 31) in Canadian families, Gleason (1999) examined the details of individual cases from a child guidance clinic in Vancouver (p. 30). Not surprisingly, this exploration reveals that it was common for psychologists to blame poor parenting skills (particularly those of the mother) for children's undesirable behaviour. By placing the blame on poor parenting, psychologists had the ability to reorient their "therapeutic energies from the process of diagnosing [socially unacceptable children] to ultimately correcting and preventing further transgressions" in their "socially unacceptable families" (Gleason, 1999, p. 31).

The most poignant finding from the examination of referral sheets reveals what Donzelot (1979) had already discussed—that is, that the psy-complex exacts its power on "the social" in such a way that those dominated are unaware/oblivious of their domination. Moreover, the finding also solidifies that the psy-complex has an ability to create conditions similar to those produced by the panopticon, the model prison described by Foucault (1977, p. 201) in *Discipline and Punish* as "inducing in its inmates a state of conscious and permanent visibility that ensures the automatic functioning of power." Inmates of the panopticon, become inflicted by a state of self-surveillance and self-discipline. However, "the influence of psychology's technologies of normalcy on Canadian parents was not exclusively one-directional" (Gleason, 1999, p. 31); that is, parents began referring themselves, their *own* family, to the child guidance clinics. According to Gleason (1999), this increase in voluntary parental referral was indicative of an increase in societal acceptance of psychology's technologies of normalcy, and the interference of psychological advice within the family.

Not only was this finding in line with Donzelot and Foucault, it also confirms Ian Parker's (1997) notion that the "psy-complex" is a network that is highly effective in regulating "how people behave and think" by turning "them into self-monitoring, self-regulating subjects" (p. 123). In fact, by the time the Second World War began, psychologists and other social science disciplinary experts of the psy-complex had effectively constructed their dominant definition of family normalcy around the nuclear family form, and normalized their expert advice within the private lives of Canadian families.

As time went on, the continual spread of advice from the psy-complex required the development of a reciprocal relationship between modern psychological discourse and popular culture (Parker, Georgaca, Harper, McLaughlin, & Stowell-Smith., 1995). In fact, Parker (1997) has determined that the psy-complex "is most dense in the urban interior of the modern West, where it informs day-time television discussions, and 'step' programmes for self-improvement" (p. 4). There is no doubt that the Western world has borne witness to an increase in popular psychotherapists on mass media television talk shows such as Oprah Winfrey and Phil Donahue (Parker et al., 1995), and more recently Dr. Laura Schlessinger and Dr. Phil McGraw (as I will discuss shortly).

Overall, Parker (1999) observes the increasing popularity of psychological advice as both a symptom and response to the process of psychologization of the social body, and its experts' desire to diagnose and treat forms of unhappiness through their use of ostensibly non-oppressive language of advice. Donzelot (1979) similarly notes the same popularization trend in France, where the

Parents' School disseminated its prescriptive knowledge about the family and proper parenting skills "via radio broadcasts and the publishing of a considerable quantity of inexpensive brochures written in simplified, didactic language" (p. 192).

Recall that popular psychological discourse measures family happiness to the degree that a family lives or assimilates toward the traditional nuclear family ideal (Parker, 2007). As such, the self-appointed task of psychologists to repair the family "when things go wrong" (Parker, 2007, p. 66) implies that families must maintain, or more closely align/assimilate to the ideal tracing in order to be happy.

CLIMATE PRIMED FOR FAMILY FAILURE

As a postmodernist thinker, I question not only the notion of the family ideal, but also the belief that family happiness requires alignment with the nuclear family tracing. From this critical frame of mind, I ask the reader to join me in questioning the way popular psychological literature promotes the maintenance/assimilation to this hegemonic family structure. Moreover, to join me in considering whether or not these unrealistic messages about family happiness contribute to a climate primed for family failure, lack, and inadequacy?

DR. INDOCTRINATION: FIXING THE FAMILY ONE PRESCRIPTIVE REMEDY AT A TIME

It is important to address popular psychological literature, because as noted in both Parker (2007) and Donzelot (1979), it plays a crucial role in constructing family happiness around the nuclear family ideal. For evidence that popular psychological literature effectively turns individuals and their families "into self-monitoring, self-regulating subjects" (Parker, 1997, p. 123), look no further than to the seepage of psychological "technical terms" or "therapy-speak" into the everyday lives of families (Parker et al., 1995, p. 68). The work of two widely syndicated Western psychological proponents, Dr. Laura Schlessinger and Dr. Phil McGraw, highlight how popular culture continues to promote family happiness and normality around the nuclear family structure.

DR. LAURA SCHLESSINGER: PARENTHOOD BY PROXY.

Bestselling author and syndicated radio show host, Dr. Laura Schlessinger, has a background in family counselling. On her website (http://drlaura.com), she includes in her education background, a Post-Doctoral Certification in Marriage, Family and Child Counseling from the University of Southern California, in Los Angeles, California. In addition, she was a Licensed Marriage, Family and Child Counselor (MFCC) who practiced privately for twelve years. Schlessinger (2008) addresses a wide range of "personal, work, and familial problems," and "preaches, teaches, and nags about morals, values and ethics" (Schlessinger, 2008). As a shameless promoter of the traditional family as ideal, Dr. Schlessinger (2000) has stated that,

> [d]ivorces, full-time working mothers, stepfamilies, shacking up, out-of-wedlock children, promiscuous reproduction, geographical fragmentation of the family, joint custody, and visitation are, to varying degrees, depending on the circumstances and the child—a disaster to the lives and emotional well-being of children. (p. 7)

In her book called *Parenthood by Proxy*, Shlessinger (2000) argues that with the exception of those who have suffered a "death of a spouse, severe illness, or abandonment," others who have chosen the above family forms are selfish, wrong, and non-normal (p. 7). Callers to her radio program, she states, "inevitably whine, 'But what about me? What about my happiness? When am I entitled to what makes me happy? When am I going to get what I want?'" (Schlessinger, 2000, p. 10). To this end, she states that,

> [s]omewhere along the way the focus of American thinking shifted from respecting obligation and character (sexual fidelity, commitment to sacred vows, sacrifice for family) to seeking self-fulfillment and selfishness (sexual freedom, entitlement to perpetual bliss, nix the kids, spouse as oppressive constraint). (Schlessinger, 2000, p. 10)

Overall, her arguments are based on the contention that society ignores "self-evident truths about children, families, child rearing, commitment, and responsibilities" and willingly sacrifices all that is "noble and right" in the name of "tolerance and the celebration of diversity" (Schlessinger, 2000, pp. 8–9). In the end, Schlessinger (2000) blames societal tolerance of non-nuclear family diversity for a tripling in teen suicide, the increased prevalence in juvenile crime, and more diagnoses of children with mental illness and learning disorders (Schlessinger, 2000). It is important to note that Schlessinger (2000) provides no references for any of her claims.

According to Schlessinger (2000), the following list of sources are to blame for the breakdown of the traditional nuclear family: homosexuals (male or female who want legal rights to get married, adopt, or use biotechnology), feminists (who want to have fatherless children and "be married without personal obligation to home and children" [Schlessinger, 2000, pp. 44–45]), the daycare industry (a money making enterprise), baby boomer types (and their kids who "treat the world as a candy store and see responsibility to children and family as an impediment to gratification" [Schlessinger, 2000, pp. 44–45]), sexually liberated (who feel that anything goes including "incest and pedophilia" [Schlessinger, 2000, pp. 44–45]), and liberated men (who "seek self-gratification like teenagers, frivolously divorce, and demand their ex-wives put the children in daycare and get back to work, so they don't have to pay much alimony and child support") (pp. 44–45).

Clearly, Dr. Laura Schlessinger aims to promote the maintenance and alignment to the nuclear family tracing, and she does so very explicitly, without any hesitation or double-speak. In contrast, Dr. Phil McGraw is less explicit, opting instead to bury his implications about nuclear family idealism within his "matter-of-fact," lay-person language.

PHIL MCGRAW: FAMILY FIRST.

In the introduction to his book, *Family First,* McGraw (2004) declares "I'm going to tell you what I believe is the truth about what you can and must do to create a phenomenal family, *even if* yours is a divorced family or a blended one" (p. 15). I highlighted the words "*even if*" to demonstrate to the reader how deep-seated beliefs about what an ideal or phenomenal family structure is, can be buried within the choice of language of so-called psychological experts. What I deduce from this statement is that divorced or blended families cannot be phenomenal families, without Dr. Phil McGraw's brand of truth and psychological expertise. But does this mean he favours the nuclear family ideal over all other structures?

Certainly, McGraw (2004) makes distinctions between the traditional nuclear family ideal and those families that are considered non-traditional. However, indications that McGraw (2004) promotes an alignment to the traditional nuclear ideal are not only less explicit than Schlessinger's, but are also far less extreme. For instance, McGraw does not suggest extreme conformist measures, as Schlessinger does (e.g., suggesting that a woman marry the man who got her pregnant to avoid explaining to a child that she is a slut who selfishly decided her child did not deserve having married parents [Schlessinger, 2008], all in the name of remaining a traditional nuclear family ideal. McGraw focuses more on encouraging acceptance that your family is non-ideal because it does not fit that traditional nuclear family ideal. He moves on to provide step-by-step suggestions as to what such families can do to become phenomenal… even if.

HELP OR ALIENATION

As a child, I hadn't sat down and read a self-help book about how to help my family, such as Schlessinger's or McGraw's. Although images of the perfect family were abundant in the children's books and movies I watched, I do not recall explicit instances where popular psychologists inundated me with their message about how shitty my family was.

My mother, on the other hand, did read self-help books. There is no question in my mind that she struggled to know what was best for my brother and me. I have no doubt that she read these books with the very good intention on bettering our family situation. Of the books that she read, her particular favourite author was Dr. James Dobson, who wrote a book called *Love Must be Tough* (1983).

In this book, she sought advice for her/our situation, but I argue that his denigration of divorce and religious sentiment for the traditional family, only served to alienate her further. In an indirect way, this literature served to alienate my brother and me as well. Her perspective on our broken family sometimes communicated tremendous shame and guilt.

For example, in situations of family distress after my mother married my stepfather, she would not hesitate to remind my brother and me that my stepfather would/could never love us unconditionally. That is to say, my stepfather would never love us the way my "real" father did.

This was a particularly cutting statement to me. When I had asked her where she had heard such a thing, I found it originated from that Dr. Dobson book.

By blaming non-nuclear families for all that is ill in the world, Schlessinger promotes a climate of failure for the majority of families. Her implication that non-nuclear families are selfishly chosen and abnormal, in turn, implies a need to make selfless sacrifices to maintain or assimilate as closely to the nuclear family structure as possible. Although Schlessinger (2000) does not have a step-by-step guide to the family ideal, it is safe to assume that she mentions every prescriptive guideline that rigidly aligns with traditional nuclear family ideals.

Within the context of her book, for example, she describes numerous non-ideal life circumstances, and follows them up with guidelines as to how to be less selfish by assimilating to the nuclear family ideal. Schlessinger (2000) recommends that it is "dumb" to argue that "You don't want to marry him 'just because you're pregnant'"; instead, she suggests that a woman should marry the man who got her pregnant because it would be selfish to "explain to a child that he just wasn't an important enough reason to get married, [while her] lust was important enough to risk unprotected sex"

(p. 131). This recommendation encourages the idealistic prescription that in order to be a happy and healthy ideal family, a woman must be married to the very same partner who impregnated her. Furthermore, Schlessinger (2000) suggests that to stray from the nuclear family ideal is to choose an alternative that can only lead to any number of negative outcomes, such as single motherhood, an outcome that *she* suggests (without providing supporting evidence) is related to higher incidences of mental illness (Schlessinger, 2000).

Whereas Schlessinger (2000) provides prescriptive remedies repeatedly throughout her book, Dr. Phil McGraw uses a step-by-step outline to provide the means to achieve a phenomenal family. Having appeared as a regular psychological expert on *Oprah*, Dr. Phil McGraw now has his own widely syndicated television show and has written numerous bestselling step-by-step books on topics ranging from weight-loss to the family.

Dr. Phil McGraw (2004) believes that "family matters because it is the single most outcome-determinative factor shaping one's outlook and achievement" (p. 7) and that is why, he continues, "among all [the] words in the English language, none means more to human beings than 'family'" (p. 7). As such, it is the duty of all heads of household to wake up each day and ask themselves, "What can I do to make my family better?" (p. 14). In fact, McGraw (2004) tells his readers, "you can begin to make choices and take day-to-day actions that will create nothing short of a phenomenal family" (p. 30). But what is a phenomenal family?

McGraw (2004) defines a phenomenal family as a healthy family that has bonded and interconnected family members who are "*painted with one another's brush*" and "leave no one behind" (p. 31). According to McGraw (2004), the phenomenal family is "no fantasy" but can be easily achieved by implementing and being willing to let the Five Factors for a Phenomenal Family become the foundation for your life (p. 31). You must decide, devote, reach, believe, and claim (*and other such action oriented words*) the mindset that you too can have a phenomenal family. But what are the Five Factors for a Phenomenal Family?

In his book, *Family First* (2004), McGraw outlines these five factors, but in order to demonstrate how popular psychological advice is constructed as universally applicable and realistic to implement, I provide only the pertinent points.

The first factor for a phenomenal family is the creation of a nurturing and accepting family system. According to McGraw (2004), phenomenal families require significant sacrifice in order to ensure that each member has a sense that their authentic selves are nurtured and accepted. Among other things, sacrifice may mean dedicating an hour each day just to the family or, perhaps, deeming it "family policy to give one another at least one supportive remark a day" (McGraw, 2004, p. 39). Overall, "the need for acceptance is more powerful in your family than anywhere else" (p. 39) and if this is not achieved a whole host of negative outcomes are possible (e.g., that children will turn to gangs) (McGraw, 2004, p. 32).

Second in the list of factors is the notion that phenomenal families have rhythm in their lives. Essentially, McGraw (2004) argues that a family should have a rhythm that communicates "this is where we're from, this is what we stand for and this is what we do together" (p. 43). For instance, he continues, "The McGraws don't lie, steal, cheat, call people names, make racist comments or be mean to other people", nor do they "make fun of people who are physically challenged", or "talk about or be disrespectful to neighbours or elderly people" (p. 44). By having a shared identity that is based on identical values and standards of conduct values, families can become phenomenal!

In terms of the third factor, McGraw (2004) states that phenomenal families establish rituals and traditions that are meaningful to each member. Repetition of such meaningful events will serve as "psychological and behavioural anchors for your values and beliefs, provide your family with a sense of stability and identity, reinforce your family's heritage, give your family meaning and continue to create rhythm in your family's life" (McGraw, 2004, p. 48). McGraw (2004) continues, "social scientists tell us that without [rituals], a family may be lacking in crucial ways" (p. 50).

Fourth in the list of factors is the need for being active in communication. Vital to every phenomenal family is active communication which entails that each member “listen with the goal of understanding, respond in a nonjudgmental way, share information openly and honestly and do so in a way that keeps your family relationships on solid, loving ground” (McGraw, 2004, p. 53). In his own clinical research, McGraw (2004) found that “the amount of trouble kids get into is inversely proportional to the number of words spoken in the home” (p. 53).

The fifth, and final, factor for a phenomenal family pertains to learning how to manage family crisis. In essence, this means that when you encounter a crisis (e.g., “your child is identifying with some counterculture like Goth” [McGraw, 2004, p. 55]), the key is not to panic nor turn against one another (McGraw, 2004, p. 55). Phenomenal families “should have a crisis management plan—bullet-point lines stating exactly what your family will do when things get out of control, every time something goes wrong in the family, written down so that you do not even have to think. The time to do this is now” (McGraw, 2004, p. 57).

Overall, McGraw (2004) states that his five factors for a phenomenal family are “tried-and-proven suggestions” that, when implemented with commitment, will produce “amazing progress in the quality of…home life” (p. 62). In cases when the five factors are not working for a family, McGraw (2004) suggests that the reason may lie in “you, or some other family member, [who] may be experiencing more than just a lack of knowledge about how to create healthy family behavior” (p. 63). For example, McGraw (2004) continues, “you may be suffering from deeply entrenched, serious conflicts or pain from your life that are blocking your ability to implement these five factors” (p. 63).

WHAT WOULD BE DIFFERENT?

To say that I disagree, or deem harmful, all popular psychological advice would be a misconception. Recall from my auto-ethnography purpose section, my aim is not to reject the possibility of an “ideal” or some "thing" that one holds in one's mind's eye as flawless and pure—the epitome of perfection. In fact, the notion of an ideal could be helpful, because I believe that the world does not lack: all to which one has ever aspired, wanted, or "needed" is hidden in plain sight.

On the other hand, I am critical of the notion that any ideal may be universally authenticated and/or ontologically "True." I am deeply suspicious of such rigid, binary, and idealized thought processes that produce prescriptive universalized definitions of the family as ideal or non-ideal.

As such, in regards to the aforementioned popular psychological literature for public consumption, I am leery and critical of its modernist undertones: (1) that each family should fit/maintain the hegemonic traditional nuclear family ideal; (2) that all non-traditional expressions of family need to be fixed/treated/assimilated; (3) that family therapy programs (self-implemented or not) can be universalized to apply across all lived expressions of the family; and (4) that these plans are the one "True" answer to a happy and phenomenal family.

Key to this list is the third notion, that help for families can be universalized to have standard prescriptive steps that apply to all lived expressions of the family. I suggest this mode of thought extends from the desire of psychology to align with the medical model. Doctors of medicine have standardized guidelines for treatment that they must follow, because their use is based on objective scientific research. Psychologists, too, subscribe to their own particular "brand" of standardized guidelines for therapy, in accordance to their chosen mode of treatment in the psychological field. Behavioural psychologists, for instance, adhere to the principles and practices of behavioural therapy that are widely accepted (for example, by insurance companies) as evidence based methods for treatment.

Thus, to remain within their modes of thought is a beneficial venture for psychologists, because it provides them with the same security mechanisms as those in the medical field, that is, evidence-based, ready-made, and easy to implement standardized treatments plans. Not unlike medical doctors, psychologists benefit from the ability to make diagnostic conclusions that are followed by a standardized course of treatment. Standardization of diagnosis and treatment also provides the opportunity for psychologist/researchers to share patient/client outcomes with the pre-existing academic research community which can potentially further their career.

As previously noted, alignment to the medical model allows psychology to gain status as a natural science and psychologists to attain authority as experts of human behaviour. The availability of prescriptive and standard definitions, categories, guidelines, treatments, allows medical doctors and psychologists to acquire a dominance that implies unquestionable expertise.

When a client does not respond to a standard mode of treatment, the blame is not placed on the doctor or the psychologist, nor is it placed on the treatment methods empirically validated research. No—the blame is typically aimed on some internal aspect of the patient(s)/client(s), and their (in) ability to follow the treatment plan exactly as prescribed or directed.

Hence, another beneficial aspect of adhering to standardized evidence based treatments for medical doctors and psychologists is that it shields them from being held directly accountable for treatment failure. Overall, by claiming faultlessness in treatment failure, professionals can further identify the problem as inherent in the patient(s)/client(s). For medical doctors and psychologists to stray outside of their chosen constrictive realms of thought, therefore, is for them to risk career suicide.

I must step back for a moment, however, and acknowledge the glaring difference between what is produced about the family in popular culture, and what actually transpires in the private therapy practice. Obviously, popular public therapists (e.g., Dr. Phil McGraw) and adherents to the traditional family (e.g., Dr. Laura Schlessinger) do not have the same level of interaction with the family as those practicing therapy in the privacy of the therapy room.

Given that public and private therapists differ in terms of their level of direct intimate contact with the family, the level of discourse also shifts. First, the family is psychologized by the popular psychological discourse of public therapists, which necessitates and normalizes the need for therapeutic intervention in the family. Second, the family is psychologized in the intimacy of the therapy room by the private therapist, and the particular "brand" of psychological discourse to which they subscribe. Ultimately, however, it is the first psychologization that often leads the family to the therapy room—that is, in so far as it was popular psychological discourse that successfully convinced the family of its existence as non-ideal, and therefore in need of therapeutic intervention.

The critical difference between the first psychologization of the family and the secondary experience in the private therapy room is level of intimacy between the family and the therapist. In the private practice, there is an added element of conversation between the family and therapist. What transpires in this intimate interaction varies greatly in direct accordance to the epistemological position of the therapist. That is, the therapist may or may not subscribe to the notion that the nuclear family is the ideal structure. In other words, the therapist may or may not identify the achievement of family happiness with the attainment/maintenance/assimilation to the traditional family form. Finally, the therapist may or may not take into account the messiness of the everyday lived experience of the family, that is, the contextual details that are not conducive to standardized methods of modern family therapy.

In Chapter Five, I explore the risk of stepping outside of the standardized, evidence-based, and prescriptive step-by-step programs for universal consumption, and consider possible alternatives for working with a variety of lived expressions of families.

CHAPTER 5

PUTTING THE FAMILY BACK ON THE MAP

CRISIS MEANS TO THERAPEUTIC EFFECTS: PART II

In the beginning, I called my auto-ethnography a parallel recursive analysis. As such, I set out to analyze the nuclear family recursively as the ideal, in a parallel exploration of my own, and others' points of view. In doing so, I have harped on (and on) about the harm of the nuclear family as ideal.

I have compared it to the Deleuzo-Guattarian (1987) concept of the tracing, implying the way the family is reduced to a pre-traced or ready-made concept, in particular, the nuclear family as the *ideal* tracing of the family; a tracing that covers over, the map of infinite lived realities of the family, where there is no pre-traced or ready-made family, but rather, infinite performative capacities of the family that exist free from dominant ideals or professional restriction (Deleuze & Guattari, 1987). I have provided the Canadian census family definition that is not only constructed by dominant national, but also international forces for the coordination of standardized research purposes (e.g., the United Nations Statistical Division [2007a] is facilitating the 2010 World Population and Housing Census Programme which requires "working systematically towards agreements about common concepts, classifications, standards and methods" [UNSD, 2007b]). I have noted the acts of discrimination, through overt (the negative attitudes and biases" that directly "affect an individual's access to services, employment and housing" [OHRC, 2007, p. 17]) and covert means, against those not fitting the hegemonic defined ideal. I have noted the nuclear family's internalization as the natural and normative family ideal. I have recognized mystification, the act of collusion that family members use (unconsciously), in an effort to maintain the (shared) family ideal. I have explored how the nuclear family became the normalized ideal within the social science disciplines and practices of psy-complex professionals. I have highlighted how psy-experts psychologize the family in such a way that they become self-surveyors of their own normalization, as evidenced by their own family's referral to child-care parenting clinics. I have recognized the role of popular therapists in the psychologization of the family, evidenced in the way therapeutic-speak is taken up into the everyday language of the family, and in continuing the normalization of a need for therapy.

But very recently, I have begun to ask myself: What am I *really* doing? Am I really "questioning" the hegemony of the nuclear family form as my internalized ideal family tracing, or am I just re-establishing it? In other words, am I just picking it up, looking at it, but ultimately placing it carefully back into its position as the dominant family form?

These questions have prompted me to reconsider Tyler's (1986) suggestions about (auto-ethnographic) writing as temporary retraction from the common-sense world, that it places the author/reader into a space of therapeutic crisis and in order to gain a therapeutic effect one must return to the common-sense world with a renewed point of view. At this point, I have one issue of contention for his suggestions.

I agree with his suggestion that writing an auto-ethnography can place the author/reader into a space of therapeutic crisis, but on the other hand, I do not agree that this space is immediately therapeutic. Personally, I have experienced a great deal of crisis, but until very recently, I have not felt the process of writing auto-ethnography as therapeutic. Why?

I do not know exactly why the space of crisis was therapeutically delayed. But I do know that I started to experience the writing process as therapeutic when I recently located my writing/auto-ethnography/self (all one-and-the-same, because my "self" is in the process/writing that produces the product/auto-ethnography) as stuck in a circular loop of thought.

* * *

CIRCULAR LOOPS OF THOUGHT

Picture this: The nuclear family form is a boomerang that I am holding in my hands. I look at it, grip its structure, pass it from one hand to the other, back again, and then I toss it out in a few different directions in order to see it cast in a variety of lights (i.e., historical, psychological). But all the while, its image/tracing remains in my mind.

How do I know? I see it evidenced in how I always return to it, and conversely, it always returns to me.

Hence, I recognize a circular loop of thought that is created by the tossing out of the boomerang, and our subsequent (mutual) return to each other.

A counter argument could be that the looping process was not only unavoidable, but integral to the process of writing. Another may argue that throughout the writing process I have been in a therapeutic space of crisis, but was just unaware of it.

While these arguments/suggestions may be very valid, I personally can only *now* consider myself, even in the position, for a space of therapeutic crisis. I think that it is because it is only now that I realize the harm I have put myself into by engaging in circularity of thought. I realize that I have ignored the freedom of thought/motion that could be found *through* the very statements I have explored; for example, both those of Deleuze and Guattari (1987), who point out that the brain is naturally "much more a grass than a tree," further adding that they are "tired of trees. We should stop believing in trees, roots, and radicles. They've made us suffer too much. All of arborescent culture is founded on them" (p.15), and Basaglia (1987), who warns that "the reality of today will differ from the reality of tomorrow, and in trying to freeze it, it either becomes distorted or irrelevant (p. 4).

I feel like a hypocrite, because I made reference to and praised their statements, while simultaneously going against them, remaining within a closed circular loop of thought. I feel as if I have reproduced the tracing. I worry that I have replanted the tree and fostered its roots. I contemplate whether I have frozen (my) reality of today which will differ from (my) reality of tomorrow. I ultimately feel as if I have produced a distorted version of my reality, one of utmost irrelevance.

It was by coming to these realizations, that I can now feel, that yes, I have arrived into the therapeutic space (which is different from the therapeutic *effect* of writing an auto-ethnography, which throws the author/reader into the *space* of abstraction/crisis to which Tyler (1986) refers). But then, I recalled his suggestion that in order for writing to have a therapeutic effect, there must be a return to the common-sense world with a renewd perspective, which will then produce the therapeutic effect.

* * *

BUT WHY RETURN TO THE COMMONSENSE WORLD AT ALL? PART II

In Chapter One, I shared my initial apprehension to Tyler's (1986) suggestion. I asked: "Why return to a common-sense world at all?" Over the course of writing, I revisited my initial reaction and thought: "Well now, Korinne, that was a rather defensive and knee-jerk reaction! Maybe a return to the common-sense world would not be so bad."

In light of my recent discovery, however, I think that my initial reaction was the closest I had gotten to freedom, that is, freedom from the loop of circular thought. But, at that time, I did not recognize it.

But what is a common-sense world? Frankly, I have no idea! In order for me to, as Tyler (1986) suggests, return to a common-sense world, you would think I should have a clue as to what a common sense world is. Does this mean that I thrive off a life of non-sense and chaos? I am not sure.

Just as I had commented in the beginning, "There must be a happy medium!"

* * *

WHEN YOUR BRAIN GROWS A TREE, IT'S ALL YOU CAN SEE!

My situation is not unique. Circular loops of thought are a common experience. In essence, our rhizome/map becomes territorialized or stratified by grounding structures that have circled around and taken root. They have proliferated into dominant trees in our brains. And when your brain grows a tree, it's all you can see!

In this case, the tree that has grown out of a mass of circular (non-free) thought is the nuclear family ideal, which is precluding other family expressions on the rhizome/map. Perhaps, now, by identifying my circular thought loop, I can (re)gain a freedom of thought.

Wouldn't freedom from the circular loop of thought create a therapeutic effect? Is it necessary for me to return to what Tyler (1986) calls the common-sense world? Won't a return to the common-sense world only serve to keep me within the circular loop of thought? Is it possible that there is a happy medium between the common-sense world and a life of chaos? Can I "acquire a consistency [of thought] without losing the infinite into which thought plunges"? (Deleuze & Guattari, 1994, p. 42). It seems so. By acknowledging the *possibility* of acquiring a level of consistency, without losing the capacity for infinite thought, Deleuze and Guattari (1994) confirm that "chaos has as much a *mental* as a *physical* existence" (p. 42). So, is acquiring a precarious balance between consistency and infinity (chaos) the alternative to the return to a common sense world?

I ask on behalf of not only myself, but also for anyone else who finds him/herself stuck in a loop of circular thought, whatever it may be. Lately, I've asked myself when I look in the mirror: Don't you get tired? What I am really asking myself is: Don't you get tired of all those thoughts that keep you all tied up in knots? Those thoughts that reify and reconstitute your being in its current state of mind and body, through the scrupulous execution of organized and methodical behavior?

Perhaps freedom from the loop (for myself, you, and all lived expressions of the family) may be found in the construction of what Mølbak suggests as a Deleuzian therapy.

DELEUZIAN (THERAPY?): A CONTEXTUAL INTRODUCTION

At the time of writing the article, "On Constructing a Deleuzian Psychotherapy," Rune Mølbak (2007) was still in training to be a clinician. He was completely frustrated by the focus training schools have on either the cognitive behavioural or humanist perspectives of therapy. In the article, he points out the lack of "philosophical reflection that informs current understandings of what therapy is and what it should seek to accomplish" (Mølbak, 2007, p. 474). In particular, Mølbak (2007) finds the lack of reference to Deleuze's work within psychology very strange because he feels that Deleuze has thought "through many problems of utmost relevance to the field" (p. 473).

Having said that, Mølbak (2007) suggests that "the time might be ripe for a Deleuzian therapy", and therefore, sets out to offer "some initial suggestions as to how Deleuzian thought can be made relevant to the construction of a new therapeutic ethics and practice" (p. 473). Prior to discussing his key points regarding the construction of a Deleuzian therapy, it is crucial to address Deleuze's perspectives on the logic of sense. Of particular and pertinent importance in understanding Deleuze's perspective on the logic of sense, however, is an understanding of his notions of sense and meaning, and the difference between the two.

(THE PROBLEM/QUESTION OF) SENSE.

Mølbak (2007) situates Deleuze's philosophy of the logic of sense as a continuation from Kant, who had originally raised "the question of sense after discovering that Descartes 'indubitable' truth 'I think therefore I am' is a logical tautology constructed in terms of a set of meanings that already presuppose their condition (existence of an 'I') to begin with" (pp. 474–475). Therefore, in order to explain, in the most simplest of terms, how Deleuze conceptualizes sense and meaning, I begin with the philosopher Kant who, according to Mølbak (2007) was the first to raise the "question of sense." Kant recognized that in order for us to gather *meaning* from this statement, we must presuppose, or *sense,* "the existence of an 'I'." As such, it was Kant who brought interest to the human propensity to presuppose, or accept as an *a priori* truth, the *sense* of a statement that cannot be verified empirically (i.e., the existence of an 'I') (Mølbak, 2007). Subsequently, Deleuze picked up the "problem of sense" proposed by Kant, but reformulated it as the problem "of where statements come from, what their production is related to" (Deleuze as quoted by Mølbak, 2007, p. 474). Essentially, Deleuze regards the question of sense as a problem of endless propositions that can never be recuperated, that is,

> I can never state the sense of what I am saying, [but can only] take the sense of what I say as the object of another proposition whose sense, in turn, I cannot state. (Deleuze as cited by Mølbak, 2007, pp. 475–476)

In other words, Deleuze did not believe that the sense of a statement can be determined by some original ground of truth as other philosophers did. Mølbak (2007) suggests that Kant and Heidegger both infer that sense can be recuperated from our pre-ontological or existential understandings, that is, some ground of intelligence that materializes as concrete. Therefore, Deleuze felt that the sense of any statement is always based on a presupposition of another sense, and so on (Mølbak, 2007). With our present reality being based on endless unverifiable sensed pre-suppositions, sense is a slippery construct.

Sense.

Sense has a strange and complex paradoxical nature, because it is "simultaneously presupposed by and lacking from the statement", or, in other words, it exists "*through* the statement, but not *in* it" (Mølbak, 2007, p. 476). In other words, there is a disjunction between the sense and meaning of statements. This disjunction pertains directly to a point of divergence between what Deleuze calls "an *actual* world represented, expressed or signified in thought and a *virtual* world of the unthought in thought which can never become present" (Mølbak, 2007, p. 476).

The actual world.

In order to explain what the *virtual* world is, it is first necessary to delineate the world of the *actual*. Basically, the actual world is what is represented and shown to us in the present. This actual world becomes the present as it "always presupposes something non-present as the basis of itself" (Mølbak, 2007, p. 476). In other words, our present is presupposed from the sense we gather from somewhere non-present. Yet, to admit that our unthought sense comes *before* what we experience as present, is to admit "of a temporality outside the present by means of which the present first *becomes* present" (Mølbak, 2007, p. 476). But how can a temporality outside of the present exist? Deleuze suggests thinking beyond the three dimensions of chronological time (past, present, and future) and proposes a fourth dimension called *the virtual,* of which he defines as "a time that is real but not *actual*" (Mølbak, 2007, p. 476).

The virtual world.

The *virtual* world, therefore, exists "outside the chronological series of presents," and basically "conditions the passage of this [present/actual] time" (Mølbak, 2007, p. 476). Because it is "presupposed outside of experienced time," it is considered to be the time of sense, the time of the moment, the time that is pure, and the time without content (Mølbak, 2007). It is in this way that the *virtual* world "has always already appropriated us to itself and always already refused itself to our direct apprehension" (Mølbak, 2007, p. 477). This is why Deleuze states that we generally "live" in the "temporality of the *actual*," or *the actual* world, because it is there that we feel in the present, and where we "identify and recognize ourselves" (cited by Mølbak, 2007, p. 478). Essentially, we feel secure in *the actual* world, because it is there where "an action can be considered complete…repeatable…and predictable", and "determinable actions…can be assigned…coordinates in chronological time and space" (Mølbak, 2007, p. 478).

BUT WHY RETURN TO THE COMMONSENSE WORLD AT ALL? PART III

Upon reading that the actual world is where the passage of time is conditioned by the presuppositions of the virtual world, it clicked that the actual world is the very same common-sense world that I am apprehensive about returning to! Therefore, the actual world is the very same common-sense world that Tyler (1986) argues I can return to with a new point of view and a therapeutic effect.

But I ask: Will I not just get (re)appropriated and stuck in circular loops of thought in this actual world that is so grounded in common-sense and predictable in chronological time and space?

If so, I do not think that even a "renewed point of view" will be sufficient enough to retain a freedom of thought! I fail to see where a therapeutic effect fits in with (re)appropriation to the actual/common-sense world.

At this point, therefore, I have not found a good enough reason to return to the actual/common-sense world!

The "space" between (the virtual and the actual world).

What exists *between* the virtual and actual worlds is a place of difference, not in a divisionary sense, but rather, a space of difference-in-itself. Deleuze describes the difference-in-itself as intensive, because it is comprised of tension points, that is, "pure unmediated distances, structures without content, positions without objects" (Mølbak, 2007, p. 477). Just like the virtual/actual worlds, we never become aware of the difference-in-itself or intensity, rather, we only come to know its intensities as developed extensities represented by all the phenomena that appear to us in our lived experience (Mølbak, 2007). In fact, and very importantly, it is in this "actualization of sense [in the actual world] and the cancelling out of intensity in extensity [in the difference]", that Deleuze acknowledges as the "defining characteristic of human life" (Mølbak, 2007, p. 479).

Before I get too far ahead, however, allow me to take a moment to pull forward concepts from the first two chapters and (inter)relate/parallel them to the current discussion's terminology.

EXTENSITIES COVER INTENSITIES = STAGNATION OF THOUGHT.

In *A Thousand Plateaus*, both Deleuze and Guattari (1987) recognize that the defining characteristic of human life is to allow extensities to cover intensities. In the context of their co-written book, they describe extensities using the arborescent schema of the tree (overgrown organizations and stratifications) that obscures the proliferation of the rhizome. However, although the rhizome gets obscured by overgrown trees, it will never allow itself to be over-coded but will continue to proliferate, and will always rebound through rupture of lines of flight. Intensities are related to rhizomatic multiplicity, described as the proliferation of grass. In short, to allow extensities/trees to proliferate, is to allow the infinities/grass to be covered over.

This is not to say that Deleuze and Guattari (1987) feel that trees or tracings should be done away with. Ultimately, it is not their intention to create dualisms of good and bad when they contrast the tree to grass or tracings to maps. In fact, they recognize their mutual reproduction of each other and ask:

> Is it not of the essence of the map to be traceable? Is it not of the essence of the rhizome to intersect roots and sometimes merge with them? Does not a map contain phenomena of redundancy that are already like tracings of its own? (Deleuze & Guattari, 1987, p. 15)

As such, they recognize the mutual reproduction of tracings to maps or trees to grass, but at the same time, they express discomfort in their capacity to propagate powerful redundancies. That is, tracings become dangerous when they reproduce the map/rhizome under the false impression that it is "reproducing something else," when it is "in fact only reproducing itself" (Deleuze & Guattari, 1987, p. 13). In regards to the family, the general state of affairs in the actual/common-sense world seems to be, "You must conform, or else live with your choice(?) to dissent". That is, if the individual "chooses" the external lived *with* family, as opposed to the internalized lived *by* ideal family, he/she must be prepared to accept the covert and overt family form discriminations to which dissenters from the nuclear family are exposed. When I use the term "choice here, I am mimicking the commonly held traditionalist perception of non-traditional families"; that is, that they have made the choice to be "other than" the "chosen family." Shlessinger (2000) illustrates the traditionalist opinion of family when she argues that with the exception of those who have suffered a "death of a spouse, severe illness, or abandonment," others who have chosen the non-traditional family forms are selfish, wrong, and non-normal (p. 7). Thus, the ideal tracing of the family in dominant culture is a redundancy that becomes dangerous as it continually reproduces itself, obscures free thought, and discourages the possibility of any alternatives for the family. It is the tree obscuring the growth of grass in our minds.

In the very same way, when we continually cancel out intensities for extensities, we surrender ourselves to the actualization of sense and "become enslaved by the meanings of the actual and incapable of opening to the sense of the virtual" (Mølbak, 2007, p. 479). In other words, Deleuze warns that by allowing our "intensive difference" to gain meaning as an "extensive identity," we are "slowing down the thought process" and bring the possible infinitive to an end (Mølbak, 2007, p. 478). Our view of the family in the actual/common-sense world, where infinite possibilities of the family exist as the majority, is, therefore, is obstructed by the dominant nuclear family because it is the representative extensity covering our intensive capacity for thought. Moreover, it is due to its ability to cover rhizomorphous/free thought that makes it difficult to think outside of its ideal construction.

Essentially, both Deleuze and Guattari (1987) are weary of the stagnation of thought created by the redundancy of overgrown trees and blanketing extensities, because they betray our capacity to think or act differently or outside the box of dominant culture. "We're tired of trees. We should stop believing in trees, roots, and radicles. They've made us suffer too much. All of arborescent culture is founded on them" (p.15).

To this end, it is not so much a problem of doing away with tracings or trees completely, but rather a "question of method" of how to put the tracings "back on the map" in an effort to reverse dangerous redundancies (Deleuze & Guattari, 1987, p. 13). As they say, "it is so important to try the other, reverse but non-symmetrical, operation" of plugging the "tracings back into the map, connect the roots or trees back up with a rhizome" (p. 14). As we re-situate our tracings and connect trees back to the rhizome we open them up to possible lines of flight.

But I still remain puzzled by our (unquestioned) affiliation for the nuclear family ideal tracing despite the fact that it is outnumbered by other family forms. For example, the Statistics Canada 2006 Census found that "[m]arried people are in the minority in Canada for the first time" with "51.5 per cent of people over age 15 [remaining] unmarried" (CBC, 2007). Further pertinent details from the report indicate that "the number of common-law families surged 18.9 per cent since 2001, to nearly 1.4 million families" and "26 per cent of families with children are headed by a single parent" (CBC, 2007). It seems to me, that to strive for an idealized standard that is attained by such a relative few, seems so counter-intuitive to our well-being. Deleuze and Guattari (1987) shed some well needed light on this confusing issue by addressing the complex notions of majority and minority.

MAJORITY AND MINORITY.

According to Deleuze and Guattari (1987), simple quantitative measures will not adequately explain the opposition between majority and minority. Why? It is because the majority will always imply a constant expression or content and serve as a standard measure for which to contrast and compare, despite being outnumbered by the minority (Deleuze & Guattari, 1987). Hence, my puzzlement regarding the strange affiliation for the nuclear family ideal, despite a less numerous quantitative expression, can be extracted and questioned from a theoretical perspective.

Deleuze and Guattari (1987) illustrate how a strange affiliation to the majority defies quantitative logic by highlighting how one version of "man" (the "average adult-white-heterosexual-European-male-speaking a standard language") is considered the majority despite being outnumbered by "mosquitoes, children, women, blacks, peasants, homosexuals, etc." (p. 105). The question then becomes: Why and how does this particular version of "man" acquire the status as the "obvious" majority, despite being less numerous relative to other determinations? In other terms, how does it come to pass that "a determination different from that of the constant will therefore be considered minoritarian, by nature and regardless of number" (p. 105)?

In the words of Deleuze and Guattari (1987), it is because this "version" of "man" (that is, "average adult-white-heterosexual-European-male-speaking a standard language" [Deleuze & Guattari, 1987, p. 105]) "appears twice, once in the constant and again in the variable from which the constant is extracted" (p. 105). Additional explanations they offer point to how the majority *assumes* both: (1) "a state of power and domination"; (2) the status of "the standard measure," "not the other way around" (p. 105). That is, the majoritarian "versions" of "man" or "the family" attain their dominance and standardization by *assuming* themselves as such. In this way, the majoritarian version of "man" (the "average adult-white-heterosexual-European-male-speaking a standard language") is not unlike the majoritarian version the "the family" (the nuclear family ideal), thus, the same (counter-intuitive) "logic" applies. We are strangely drawn to conform to what is considered the majority, despite its less numerous representation, due to its (hegemonic) power to *persuade* us of its dominance. Yet, we are *persuaded* in such a way, that we believe we have the freedom to choose otherwise.

THE (ILLUSION OF) FREEDOM TO CHOOSE OTHERWISE.

Deleuze and Guattari (1987) make the observation that we are often under the *illusion* that we have freedom of choice. To illustrate, they point to the electoral process wherein we believe we have the freedom to choose, but in actuality, we are *given* (privileged with) a choice "on the condition that [our] choice conform to the limits of the constant ('you mustn't choose to change society…')" (p. 105). Hence, we are free to choose to conform to the majority, and this assimilation process is no different for the family. As members of "the family," we each are drawn in by the need to conform to the majoritarian ideal; that is, the nuclear family ideal; the internalized synthesis of the family (Laing, 1969); or the ideal tracing of the family also known as the dominant tree of the family (Deleuze & Guattari, 1987). As such, each family member engages in any number of normalizing activities in order to attain, maintain, and assimilate to(ward) the majoritarian ideal object of family in dominant culture.

I have addressed some of these conforming/normalizing activities on two levels. On the societal level, I noted the way the psy-complex disciplines normalized interventions *into* the family by taking the main stage as judiciary and state powers remained in backstage. As Parker (1997) observes, psy-complex professionals, ranging from "psychology, psychiatry, psychoanalysis, social work, governmental agencies" (p. 7), govern "what abnormal emotional and correct mental functioning looks and feels like, and how child-care and family processes should be described and relayed to mothers and fathers" (pp. 3–4). On the family level, I highlighted Laing's (1969) notion of the transpersonal acts of mystification that family members use in order to maintain the internalized tracing of the shared family synthesis. Indeed, Laing (1969) states that each family member feels secure in the family to the degree they imagine the other family members to share their same internalized family.

Even with the knowledge that the majority is actually outnumbered by what is thought to be the minority, we still engage in acts of conformity. But the odds are stacked against us from the start, and we are set up for failure. More often than not, the family will fail to meet the external expectations projected from the psy-complex or the pressures of the dominant culture. In turn, family members will engage in the transpersonal defense processes of mystification until, eventually, more often than not, they strain or shatter the shared family synthesis. Overall, the danger lies in how the family and its members come to feel that: (1) they are failures to themselves; (2) they have failed each other; and/or (3) that they have failed to meet the expectations of the dominant culture.

CLIMATE PRIMED FOR FAMILY FAILURE: PART II

It is the feelings of failure and lack that concern me the most, whether they are transpersonal acts between and among family members, or projected upon the family by dominant culture. What I have found is that these feelings of failure and lack in the family can be related directly to Deleuze's original problem of sense.

Deleuze states that our meanings arise from endless unthought pre-suppositions. Therefore, in order for a family to feel failure, there must be a pre-supposed condition that imposes a feeling of lack in the first place!

Allow me to illustrate further what I mean:

> In order for a non-nuclear family to feel/gain their extensive identity as a non-ideal family, they must presuppose the condition existence of the nuclear family ideal.
>
> The opposite is also true…
>
> In order for a nuclear family to feel/gain their extensive identity as an ideal family, they must presuppose the existence of their own ideal status as the majority, and they must also presuppose the notion of the non-ideal family.

And so, the presupposition of a traditional/ideal/functional family incites the non-traditional/non-ideal/dysfunctional family to feel lack; a feeling of lack that emanates out of the part(s) that are missing from the traditional biological whole. For the family who lacks the status of the ideal family object of the actual world, there is a desire to acquire what is missing. In turn, the ideal traditional family object depends on the family's "essence of lack" in order to continually produce its "very nature as a real entity," thus, desire is what fuels this continual process.

* * *

WORLD – PERCEPTIONS = NOTHING: PART II.

Allow me to flesh out further the parallel to Deleuze's problem of sense by revisiting the introductory discussion of this auto-ethnography and its formulaic equation related to the blank art canvas. If you recall, I mentioned that I attended a symposium wherein the speaker suggested that an art canvas represents nothing until it acquires meaning though the perceptions of an observer.

Now, I (re)cognize that the art canvas is not unlike anything else appearing as an extensive object in this actual/common-sense world, in fact, I can (re)apply the previous formulaic equation:

World – Perceptions = Nothing

I extend this equation to the notion that the family construct means nothing until it acquires meaning from the perceptions of the observer.

World – Perceptions of the Family = Nothing

Furthermore, in Deleuzian language pertaining to the problem of sense, I reformulate this equation to I suggest that perceptions are synonymous with presuppositions.

World – Presuppositions of the Family = Nothing

My reformulation leads me to wonder: If post-modern thinking suggests that what remains in the nothing are taken-for-granted truths, then:

Is it even possible to gain freedom from the dominating extensive lived by nuclear family ideal?

Can we unthink what is already unthought?

Can we rethink the majority by becoming (re)cognizant of the minority?

Does this require the (impossible?) challenge of (re)cognizing what is the (unthought) pseudo-majority?

MINORITARIAN: THE BECOMING OF THE FAMILY.

What do I mean by unthinking the unthought? What does rethinking the majority by discovering the position of the minority mean? What I am asking is: How does the nuclear family form attain the position of majoritarian ideal in dominant culture, despite the fact that it is outnumbered by innumerable minoritarian forms of the family? Deleuze and Guattari (1987) confirm humanity's tendency to inflate wildly the prevalence of the majoritarian relative to the minoritarian. The majoritarian standard, they observe, is already at the representative threshold, in other words, it is without question the "Fact of Nobody" (Deleuze & Guattari, 1987, p. 106). In essence, the nuclear family as the majoritarian ideal is considered the (pseudo) majority, the unquestioned fact of nobody, regardless of its sparse representation in relation to the extensive expressions of minoritarian forms of the family.

Knowing that we tend to misconstrue how prevalent the nuclear family is: Can we rethink/unthink its position as the (pseudo) majority ideal version of the family? Deleuze and Guattari (1987) believe that we can, if we start to recognize the minoritarian expressions of the family "as a potential, creative and created, becoming" (p. 106). By recognizing the minoritarian families as infinite potential, creation, and becoming, perhaps it *is* possible to reconsider the notions of failure and lack associated with the minoritarian position. I suggest that we can reconsider the notions of family failure and lack by promoting a state of becoming.

Becoming.

Becoming is the state in which we allow ourselves to exist, neither in the virtual past nor the actual present, but, in the contemplations of "difference between the two, by releasing the movement of the infinitive" (Mølbak, 2007, p. 484). In this space of becoming, there is no beginning and there is no end, therefore we do not lack because we are in a place of excess (Deleuze & Guattari, 1987). A line of becoming negates any point(s) of origin because it "has neither beginning nor end, departure nor arrival, origin nor destination," instead, it has "only a middle" of infinite speeds of movement (Deleuze & Guattari, 1987, p. 293). Without a feeling of lack, the feeling of failure also becomes non-existent for the fact that they presupposed each other in the first place.

In this way, the minoritarian expressions of the family are less thought of as non-ideal, and more thought of as "the becoming of everybody, and that becoming is creation" (Deleuze & Guattari, 1987, p. 106). How can I suggest that minoritarian families are the becoming of everybody? Because the minoritarian (infinite) expressions of the family represent the epitome of continuous variation, as such they constitute "the becoming-minoritarian of everybody" (Deleuze & Guattari, 1987, p. 106). As Deleuze and Guattari (1987) point out, becoming-minoritarian is in opposition to the "majoritarian Fact of Nobody"; in fact, "there is no becoming-majoritarian; majority is never becoming" (p. 106). This leads Deleuze and Guattari (1987) to state that "[a]ll becoming is minoritarian" (p. 106).

The minoritarian families are the amplitude/intensity that "continually oversteps the representative threshold of the majoritarian standard, by excess or default" (Deleuze & Guattari, 1987, p. 106). Thus, minoritarian families are always in a state of infinitive becoming, as opposed to the nuclear family ideal that is arborfied as an extensive object in the actual world. As Deleuze and Guattari (1987) observe:

> [A]rborescence is the submission of the line [of becoming] to the point [while] [b]ecoming is the movement by which the line frees itself from the point, and renders points indiscernible. (p. 294)

As such, the minoritarian families should never ever strive to attain or acquire the majoritarian standard (nuclear family ideal)! Because, in doing so, minoritarian families are submitting themselves as a point into arborescence and are no longer in a state of becoming.

Deleuze and Guattari (1987) suggest that we can bring forth "the powers of becoming" by erecting the "universal figure of minoritarian" which represents pure autonomous and revolutionary becoming (p. 106). Deleuze and Guattari (1987) further state that the powers of becoming "belong to a different realm from that of Power and Domination" (p. 106). Therefore, by celebrating the universal figure of minoritarian (infinite expressions of the family on the map) as continuous variation, we are in essence celebrating the freedom of thought through the deterritorialization of the lines of segmentarity, and the rupturing lines of flight back into the of the rhizome/map.

Thus, as Mølbak (2007) points out: "Deleuze wants us to rupture, not to strengthen" the tracings/trees/territorialisation of the rhizome/map, because they will only lead "us to miss the essential: the genesis of the act of thought" (Deleuze as cited by Mølbak, 2007, p. 480). But the question then becomes: How does Deleuze suggest we rupture? That is: How do we weaken the strength or rupture the tracings/trees on our rhizome/map? How does one (re)gain a freedom of thought from a (pseudo) majority of the family ideal? These questions, of course, become the basis of what might be a construction of a Deleuzian therapy.

DELEUZIAN APPROACHES TO THERAPY

Mølbak (2007) presents very preliminary suggestions as to what a Deleuzian approach to psychotherapy might involve. The premise of the article, therefore, is not aimed at any one specific psychological issue or particular mode of clientele (i.e., individual or group). Nor does the article implicate specific practices or techniques because that is antithetical to everything Deleuze has thought out in the context of his own writings, and the literature he has co-written with Guattari. What can be extracted from the Mølbak (2007) article, however, is that a Deleuzian approach to therapy requires a re-thinking of what therapy is.

Such an approach would require a great deal of reconsidering pre-suppositions for what they actually are; that is, pre-supposed meanings based on continuously more and more pre-suppositions. In this way, a Deleuzian approach to therapy would be aimed at extricating people, or detangling the family, from their "current enslavement to the principles of lack" by recognizing the way that their identity has been pre-destined/chosen and grounded by the dominant culture of the extensive and actual world (Mølbak, 2007, p. 484). With this in mind, the ultimate goal of a Deleuzian approach to therapy would be "to make sense circulate freely again outside" of the constraining notions of the (pseudo) majority (Mølbak, 2007, p. 485).

WE ALL HAVE TWO FAMILIES: PART II

Once again, I return to the statement written by Gillis (1996):

"We all have two families, the one that we live *with* and the other that we live *by*" (p. xv).

Although I have stated that the lived *with* family is external and the lived *by* family is internal, I argue that they are both grounded in what Deleuze calls the actual world. After all, it is in the actual world where the lived with family presents to us as reality. Moreover, as an extensive object of the actual world, the lived by nuclear family imposes its position as the ideal upon/over our lived with family realities.

On the other hand, I suggest the differential/multiplicious/ minoritarian capacity of our lived with family, brings it closer, not in distance but in its in(tensity), to the virtual world.

Recall that between the actual and virtual world is the difference-in-itself, a place where thought flows in response to the tension produced by the varying speeds of the virtual and the actual world. This means that:

As lines flow closer to the actual world, they slow down, get more extensive.

As lines flow closer to the virtual world, they speed up, get more intensive.

Because of the capacity of the lived *with* family to be more differential, I argue that it flows closer to the virtual world than the lived by family, but is prevented from a state of becoming as a virtual intensity because it is grounded as an extensive object in the actual world.

What would a family-becoming, or becoming-family look like? Allow me to speculate.

BECOMING-FAMILY.

In the space of difference-in-itself, the moment of the happening, or in the state of becoming, I suggest that we could no longer say that the family *used to be healthy* (ideal), but *is now dysfunctional* (non-ideal), or vice versa. For in order for them to become one or the other to begin with, we must continually affirm their previous state (ideal/non-ideal) and current state (ideal/non-ideal) status simultaneously. In the state of becoming, the family, any form of family, can "transcend the present" by overturning its priority, and if they keep overturning it they can "postpone the moment of [their] actualization as a particular identifiable subject" (Mølbak, 2007, p. 478) (i.e., as functional/ideal, or, dysfunctional/non-ideal).

WHY RETURN TO THE COMMONSENSE WORLD AT ALL? PART IV

At this point, as I have just explicated preliminary thoughts about what could be considered a family-becoming, one could ask: Is this a realistic approach to rethinking the family and constructing a therapy?

I would counter argue that these preliminary thoughts about a family-becoming, and a Deleuzian approach to therapy, are no more unrealistic than the very dominant ideals that enslave the family to the actual world's ideal version of the family, and the subsequent feelings of lack and failure that lead the family to therapy in the first place.

It all comes back to my ongoing question(s) about the common-sense/actual world: What is a common sense world? And why is it necessary to return to it for a therapeutic effect? But it seems to me that a return to whatever is the common-sense world, would negate the state of becoming. So where do I go?

Deleuze and Guattari (1987) state that to do away with the common-sense world is to release your being to the rapid speeds of the infinitive into a state of becoming. Moreover, a pure state of becoming entails living in a pure state of chaos. In their collaborative book, *What is Philosophy?*, Deleuze and Guattari (1994) state:

Chaos is defined not so much by its disorder as by the indefinite speed with which every form taking shape in it vanishes. It is a void that is not a nothingness but a *virtual*, containing all possible particles and drawing out all possible forms, which spring up only to disappear immediately, without consistency or reference, without consequence. Chaos is an infinite speed of birth and disappearance." (p. 118)

However, Deleuze and Guattari (1994), themselves, caution against maintaining this state of chaos indefinitely. They describe the experience of living in a state of chaos as follows:

> Nothing is more distressing that a thought that escapes itself, than ideas that fly off, that disappear hardly formed, already eroded by forgetfulness or precipitated into others that we no longer master. These are infinite variabilities, the appearing and disappearing of which coincide. They are the infinite speeds that blend into the immobility of the colorless and silent nothingness they traverse, without nature or thought. (p. 201)

They therefore conclude that "we require just a little order to protect us from the chaos" (Deleuze & Guattari, 1994, p. 201).

Once again, I am brought to the point that I ask: Is there a "happy medium" between chaos and the common-sense/actual world?

A LITTLE ORDER/CHAOS.

Within the context of his article, Mølbak (2007) takes into account that a little order, in the form of repression, is not all bad because "it is a way for us to slow down the infinite speeds of the virtual in the face of a differential life that threatens to overwhelm us" (p. 485). As such, "to construct a Deleuzian psychotherapy is neither to do away with repression nor to seek to reify it, but to allow just enough reaction so that we may become able to actualize the sense of the virtual without becoming enslaved or destroyed by it" (Mølbak, 2007, pp. 486–87). In this way, it would be a "therapy of dual or variable speeds, in which the question to be answered is: How slow or how fast a life do we want?" (p. 487).

A "HEALTHY" DOSE OF CHAOS/NON-SENSE?

Perhaps this is the "happy medium" I have been seeking? That is, to (re)produce and (re)connect to some of the structure (found in trees and tracings) while retaining just a little bit of chaos?

DAN GOODLEY: RHIZOME/PARENTS

Certainly, other authors have taken the same bold step as Mølbak (2007) to describe how Deleuze and Guattari's philosophical perspectives and how they can be applied specifically to therapeutic contexts. For example, Guattari, a psychoanalyst himself, wrote extensively on therapy in writings such as *Molecular Revolution: Psychiatry and Politics* (1984) and *The Three Ecologies* (2000). Furthermore, Skott-Myhre (2005) wrote specifically about a Deleuzian approach to therapeutic encounters in his article, "Towards a Minortarian Psychology of Immanence and a Psychotherapy of Flight: Political Meditations on the Society of Control". Briefly, Skott-Myhre (2005) suggests that a "psychotherapy of flight" is "radically and overtly revolutionary in nature" and would be concerned with "the 'healing' entailed in the alternative ontology of the minority" (p. 54). In this "minoritarian psychology of immanence or psychotherapy of flight," therapy is an "encounter of potential" that "points the way out, reveals nothing and in fleeing closes the entrances off behind itself" until, finally, "we become everyone "that is to say no-on; which is to say no-thing" (p. 57).

Skott-Myhre, Skott-Myhre, Skott Myhre, and Harris (2004) also co-wrote a chapter pertaining to a Deleuzian approach to therapy, called "Radical Youth Work: Creating and Becoming Everyone" in Tom Strong's book, *Furthering Talk: Advances in the discursive therapies*. However, I have specifically chose to discuss Dan Goodley's (2007) article, "Becoming Rhizomatic Parents: Deleuze, Guattari and Disabled Babies," because it relates closely to this auto-ethnography about the family construct. More specifically, it parallels my suggestion of a family-becoming as resistance to the dominant knowledge's idealization of the majoritarian nuclear family. In the context of his article, Goodley (2007) addresses what might be called the becoming of parents of children with disabilities for the resistance to "a whole host of disability knowledges" (p. 146).

Goodley (2007) uses Deleuzo-Guattarian concepts to explicate how parents of children with disabilities can manoeuvre themselves around the dominant knowledges of their lived existence by becoming rhizomes. He literally describes parents as a "global phenomena" that should be considered rhizomes due to their capacity for infinite multiplicity. This description of parents as rhizomes parallels my description of the infinite lived *with* expressions of the family as existing on the rhizome/map. He also recognizes the same persistent threat of arborescence or reterritorialization for parents, as I have for the family.

> Rhizomes face blocks: strata are unavoidable. Inevitably, parents encounter organizations that threaten to re-stratify everything, that reinstall the order of significance and propositions. (Goodley, 2007, p. 150)

Goodley (2007) continues to say that parents who remain rhizomes are able to steer away from the dangers of arborescence or reterritorializations that "threaten to bind their children and their lives to old oaks" (p. 150). Thus, there "are exciting possibilities for rhizomes/parents" of children with disabilities because no longer are they bound by the dominant knowledges instructing their lives. Goodley's (2007) description of how parents become rhizomes or becoming-parents, will provide insight into how the family can get into a state of becoming-family.

Firstly, he acknowledges that becoming-parent would entail embracing uncertainty of the present with "seemingly scant regard for past and future" which would, in turn, demonstrate resistance of the dominant knowledges threatening their reterritorialization (Goodley, 2007. p. 155). Secondly, Goodley (2007) concurs with Deleuze and Guattari (1994) that a smidgen of order is required to protect us from never-ending nomadism, or chaos. As such, Goodley (2007) adds, "a further aspect of becoming to consider in relation to parents is appropriation" (p. 155).

Appropriation, he suggests, allows parents to "self-fashion" their lives (p. 156), or in other wor(l)ds, to keep some aspects of the common-sense/actual world while retaining some of the infinite/chaotic/virtual world. In essence, parents do not totally escape the repression or "imprisonment of powerful totalizing discourses," but gain freedom from them in other ways that are meaningful to them (Goodley, 2007, p. 156). In such a self-fashioned life, "it becomes possible to say…that one is not free in prison, but can nevertheless achieve freedom there" (Buchanan as cited by Goodley, 2007, p. 156). Life for rhizome/parents, therefore, essentially becomes a life of experimentation. A continuous experiment, a constant creation, an endless question of self-fashioning of when "to be" in the actual world, and when transcend into the virtual. According to Goodley (2007), what this approach to life means for parents of children with disabilities is an augmentation of their family's humanity through "celebrating their ongoing becomings" (p. 156). This is not unlike Deleuze and Guattari's (1987) celebration of becoming (continuous multiplicity or variation) by erecting the universal figure of minoritarian who represents the autonomous and revolutionary becoming of everybody. Whether it is Deleuze and Guattari's (1987) state of becoming or Goodley's (2007) suggestion to self-fashion, I argue that both concepts not only permit, but encourage a life of continuous experimentation.

What do the concepts of becoming and self-fashioning mean for people/therapists who work with parents and the family? In the context of his article, Goodley (2007) suggests that therapists apply these Deleuzo-Guattarian concepts in order to help parents enhance resistance to dominant disability knowledges, and empower their ability to pick and choose aspects of the dominant culture (i.e., medical or psychological practices) that work for them. I argue that the same Deleuzo-Guattarian concepts can be applied to all family expressions in order to enhance their resistance to the dominant knowledge that falsely portray the family as a stable construct (that is, the extensive object of the idealized nuclear family). Finally, and most pertinently, Goodley (2007) sees the value in applying Deleuzo-Guattarian concepts when working with parents and the family, because they "promote an attitude that embraces uncertainty rather than dismissing it as naivety on the part of particular people or the lack of allegiance to a specific view of life" (p. 157).

DISMISSING (A LIFE OF) UNCERTAINTY AS NAÏVE AND IRRESPONSIBLE

It is beyond words that I encountered this particular quotation today. As I near the end of this chapter and the entire auto-ethnography, I am once again steadied by simultaneous blasts of knowledge that focus my gaze and I achieve a brief moment of clarity.

If you recall, I had previously realized that my externally lived *with* family evolved much faster than my internally lived *by* notion of the family—which basically meant that it took longer for my internal feelings about my lived *by* family to "catch up" with the rapidly changing circumstances of my lived *with* family.

For reasons inexplicable, the above quotation by Goodley (2007) sparked a new parallel to yet another earlier realization I experienced regarding the variable speeds of the lived *with* and lived *by* family. I suggested that my lived *with* family flows rapidly as its proximity is closer to the infinitive of the virtual world, while the lived *by* family ideal flows slower because it becomes stratified as an ideal object in the slowness of the actual world.

Now, a new realization has dawned that I can clearly see: I have already lived what Mølbak (2007) refers to as a life of variable speeds! My external lived *with* family evolved faster than my internal lived *by* notion of the family *because* it flows closer to the infinitive speed of the uncertainty of life. My feelings of lack and failure can, therefore, be traced to my attempt to slow the infinitive. To remain connected to the common-sense/actual world's idealized extensive object of the nuclear family ideal.

Finally, I speculate that the delay between my lived *with* and *by* family pertains directly to the naïve attitude Goodley (2007) speaks of in the previous quotation. That is, I may have taken on the attitude that it is irresponsible to live a life that embraces the uncertainty of the present and has little regard for the past or future. Perhaps my negative/hesitant attitude toward the uncertainty of life, resulted in my fight to slow down the infinite speed (uncertainty/ unpredictability) of my lived *with* family.

* * *

THE MOURNING PERIOD

Faced with having to let my lived *by* internal image/tracing go, I hesitated to accept the circumstances of my lived *with* family. I fought against releasing it to the infinitive speed of the virtual. I was not ready. Internally, I held onto the lived *by* family in an effort to slow down my lived *with* family circumstances. Part of this fight to slow down the infinitive of my lived *with* family was a mourning period. I mourned for the piece of my biological nuclear family that was missing, my "real" biological father.

Missing from the family ideal/tree, was the limb of my biological father. Yet he remain(s/ed) extensive as a phantom limb, connected to me by a root system that grew incrementally weaker over time due to a lack of nourishment. It is through this phantom limb, that my lived *by* family was able to remain extensive in my mind as the lost ideal. This lost lived *by* ideal dictated how I felt about my lived *with* family circumstances.

In the early days immediately following the divorce, the connection was still fresh and the feelings I felt about his tearing away were insurmountable. Not only did I experience feelings of inexplicable failure and lack because I was no longer part of a biological and ideal whole, I felt that it was taken away by the force of his choice.

* * *

I WANTED TO BELIEVE

I wanted to believe otherwise. I wanted to believe that he left for any other reason except by choice. Most importantly, I wanted to believe that he really felt guilt and remorse for leaving us. I wanted to believe that he felt just as badly as I did.

I cried only once in his presence after the divorce. It was the first night my brother and I slept over at his new bachelor apartment. He got furiously upset with me and said that there was no reason to be so sad because I am with my father. But it was not his words that stopped my tears. It was the look in his eyes. I saw deep sadness and profound guilt… at least, that is what I *wanted to believe…*

* * *

NAMEABLE DRAMA/CEMENTED LIFE

Years of holding back tears and the feelings of sadness from my father, meant that other aspects and relationships in my life suffered. I was angry and sad most of the time. There were times that I felt that my sadness/anger were justifiable. But most of the time, I felt like I was "Being a baby" and I should "Just get over it already." Oscillating between these two feelings was both confusing for me, and for those around me. I often felt sad, angry and insecure, but not being able to explain in words exactly why. Therefore, I thrived on drama, any drama, just so that I could have a "nameable" reason to be sad and angry. It didn't matter what it was, I just needed a drama that I could name.

Not only did my family members accept the brunt of this sadness and anger, but also my early intimate relationships. Whether it was my mother or my first love, I latched on to these people, and held onto them for what felt like dear life. I stifled and attempted to manipulate and control them so they would stay with me. I would get jealous and anxious if they had other close friends. I wanted them all to myself. Insatiably insecure, these acts created the drama that I needed in order to name and blame.

As I look back to those years, I can see that it was all in an effort to cement in place a life that was certain and predictable. I wanted to have a person, just one person that I could depend on to be there forever.

Eventually, I learned that no amount of manipulation can make forever happen. A whole series of "after-school television specials" could be produced based on the attempts I made to slow down and cement a life of certainty! One could be premised on my early tumultuous marriage to my first love, for instance, and all the subsequent unpredictable events that led to its demise. What a lesson to learn, and learn from!

Until now I dealt in fear
These years of cloak and dagger
Have left us disappeared

(Good, 2003)

Despite the fact that all my attempts to cement a life of certainty would inevitably end in my disappointment (because life is uncertain and people are unpredictable) I do not have any regrets. I believe that I did the very best that I could in each moment/phase of my life. I forgive myself for the "mistakes" I made. I can see now that all those acts and events were a reflection of the sadness and anger I felt. Although these events backfired, they were the evidence of a struggle. A struggle to slow down my life, to a more comfortable/manageable speed, a speed that flowed closer to my internalized lived by idea of what family life *should* be. Recall that Mølbak (2007) suggests that a "therapy of dual or variable speeds" would involve asking the question: How slow or how fast a life do we want?" (p. 487).

It took time, and what many may consider "bad choices," but I eventually started to accept that life is uncertain and unpredictable. I gradually learned that no amount of mystification could slow life down and make it predictable. I incrementally released myself to the infinitive. Not only did I gain freedom from the tracing/tree of my extensive lived *by* family, but also, I gained the ability to deal with the remaining haunt of the phantom limb of my biological father.

What role, if any, did therapy play in this gradual acceptance?

* * *

EARLY EXPERIENCES IN THERAPY

Intermittently throughout my childhood, adolescence, and early twenties I was a consumer of various forms of psychological therapy.

One particular visit to a therapist comes to mind that is representative of most of my therapeutic experiences as a child. Although the description is limited and subject to the fallibility of my memory and perceptions, I believe that it captures the essence of my childhood therapeutic experiences.

"He just didn't get me!" I recall of the psychologist that I visited as a young girl of eleven or twelve years.

Sitting in a stiff leather chair in his dark, stuffy office, he sat and looked at me from across the huge oak desk. He asked me question after question, all of which did not seem at all relevant, for instance: "Tell me Korinne, what is your favourite colour?"...only in the next breath to ask..."What is it that you dislike about your step-dad?"

I remember thinking... "When did I say I dislike my step-dad? I like him! He is not the problem, I am just sad. Why can't I just be left alone to be sad? This guy just doesn't seem to get me at all, nor did it seem like he was trying to!"

* * *

WHAT WOULD BE DIFFERENT? PART III

What would have been different if I, as a child, had been a consumer of therapy that involved Deleuzo-Guattarian concepts? Would I have been asked the same questions that seem to be based on the presuppositions and assumptions of the therapist? Would I still have felt so misunderstood and alone? In my late teens and early twenties, would I have still acted in ways that essentially tried to slow my life down?

Most importantly: I wonder if I would have accepted the infinite speed of my life, and lived *with* family circumstances sooner?

* * *

A SELF-FASHIONED LIFE

Recall Goodley's (2007) suggestion that appropriation allows one to "become active, [in order] to self-fashion" a life that keeps some aspects of the actual world while retaining some of the virtual world (p. 156). Deleuze and Guattari (1987) concur with Goodley (2007), stating that staying somewhat stratified (organized, signified, and subjected) "is not the worst that can happen" (p. 161). But there are no guidelines as to how to self-fashion your life. There are no instructions or standardized approach. Each and every self-fashioned life must make its own path.

Personally, I picture a self-fashioned life like a ship at sea. It sets sail in a general direction, but is always free to alter that route. It loads on/in selected cargo, but can unload or throw overboard if it starts to feel toxic, harmful, or unsatisfying. I picture this ship as engaged in a life that accepts that life's waters are uncertain and unpredictable. Most importantly, I imagine that this ship is aware that it does not lack and has the freedom to alter routes, throw overboard toxic cargo, and live a life of uncertainty without feeling irresponsible!

How can I apply this concept to the family and therapeutic contexts?

* * *

FAMILY THERAPY(?)

Although it has been my dream to work with families, there are two cnetral aspects about being a therapist with which I feel tremendously uncomfortable: first, I will be in a position of dominance where I can deem families as dysfunctional; and second, I will be considered an expert of human behavior.

In other words, I am afraid of becoming just like that therapist that I visited as a child. I do not want to work with families and children under the contention that they are dysfunctional and that I as an expert know exactly why. Most crucially, I do not want to make assumptions or ask questions that are based on my own presuppositions about their lives.

That being said, my perspective is not unlike that of radical psychiatrists and other prominent postmodern therapists who valiantly shared their discomfort with the hierarchical and power dynamics that develop inevitably between clients and the therapist. Thus, I turn to their perspectives to gain insight into how I can self-fashion an approach to family therapy that, as Goodley (2007) suggests, keeps some aspects of the actual world while retaining some of the virtual world (p. 156).

In this way, I can discuss ways to accommodate some aspects of dominant culture (for instance, employer expectations) while still retaining some aspects of the virtual world. Ultimately, I cannot predict how I will react in specific "real world" situations, but I feel that this final exploration will be helpful so that I can have some basic navigational tools for my future career.

SELF-FASHIONING AN APPROACH TO FAMILY THERAPY

As a future practitioner or therapist working with all expressions of the family, there are two key areas that I am most concerned: first, I will be in a position of dominance that I can deem families as dysfunctional; and second, I will be considered an expert of human behaviour.

DEALING WITH THE ABILITY TO DEEM A FAMILY DYSFUNCTIONAL.

If you recall, the ultimate goal of a Deleuzian approach to therapy is "to make sense circulate freely again outside" of the constraining notions of the (pseudo) majority (Mølbak, 2007, p. 485). As I self-fashion an approach to my work with families, I extract from this Deleuzian approach and make my ultimate goal to promote freedom of thought from the binary notions of an ideal/functional or non-ideal/dysfunctional family.

Although releasing the family from these constraining dualisms has been my aim all along, I am deeply concerned that my surrounding dominant culture (including my employer and the families themselves) will encourage me to engage in such divisionary acts. How can I prepare myself to deal with the pressure to determine a family as non-ideal/dysfunctional?

If we follow the logic of sense proposed by Deleuze, in order to suggest that there is a non-ideal or dysfunctional family at all, we must presuppose the existence of an ideal or functional family in the first place. Where do such dominating pre-suppositions arise? Narrative therapists Michael White and David Epston (1990) suggest that dominant culture ingrains in us presuppositions or truths in the form of grand narratives, for instance, the story that an ideal and perfect family exists and is represented by the nuclear family form. In order to prepare myself for the pressure to determine a family as non-ideal or dysfunctional, I need to accept that this grand narrative is not going anywhere (at least for now), and my role is to help families to re-author a story that more accurately reflects and empowers them.

Narrative therapy is a complementary and viable possibility to consider because it addresses head on dominant totalizing stories that are harmful and can disallow the space for another more preferred story. In fact, as Michael White and David Epston (1990) point out, families and individuals most often present themselves to therapy because they

> feel situated in stories that others have about [them] and [their] relationships, and that these stories are dominant to the extent

> that they allow insufficient space for the performance of the person's preferred stories. Or [they are] actively participating in the performance of stories that [they] find unhelpful, unsatisfying, and dead-ended, and that these stories do not sufficiently encapsulate the person's lived experience or are very significantly contradicted by important aspects of the person's lived experience. (p. 14)

My role, therefore, is not to keep families situated in stories that, for one reason or another, are not working for them. Instead, my role is to enable families to re-author and perform new meanings and possibilities that all members will "experience as more helpful, satisfying, and open-ended" (White & Epston, 1990, p. 15). White and Epston (1990) also offer other specific narrative therapy techniques that include finding unique outcomes, externalizing the problem, re-authoring, and recruiting external audiences. Already, I can foresee that conflicts will arise between what dominant society deems dysfunctional/ideal (including the perspective of employers) and what the family is re-authoring as more acceptable to them as a story for their lives. Certainly there will be specific problems that will require me to step into the realm of the modernist actual world. For instance, White and Epston (1990) acknowledge that problems such as "violence and sexual abuse" cannot be externalized and re-authored because this only leaves the clients open to further oppression (p. 49). In these, and other instances of oppression, they suggest that the therapist address the underlying "attitudes and beliefs that appear to compel the violence, and strategies that maintain persons in their subjugation, for example, secrecy and isolation" (White & Epston, 1990, p. 49).

The above scenario is a perfect example of where a self-fashioned approach to family therapy will help me to discern when to draw upon aspects of the actual world and my employer expectations, or when to remain on the side of the virtual. As such, regardless of what therapeutic setting I find myself in, I can incorporate (self-fashion) aspects of narrative therapy into my work with families. By personally operating from the general narrative theoretical perspective, wherein there is no one truth or totalizing story or view of the ideal family, my concern about categorizing families as dysfunctional is eased because the narrative perspective works against the dominant dysfunctional story through techniques such as re-authoring. Finally, no matter what venue in which I find myself working, I can incorporate White and Epston's (1990) perspectives on the role of the narrative therapist as the supporter of new and more satisfying possibilities.

Essentially, however, all of this becomes a question about how I will navigate the pressure to engage in a hierarchical dynamic with the family, wherein I am the expert and they are my subjects or clients that I am called upon to "fix."

DEALING WITH BEING CONSIDERED AN EXPERT.

Alan Parry and Robert Doan (1994) suggest that it was Freud who primed the entire psychotherapeutic field to see the therapist as an expert, or the interpreter of foundational truth and clientele experience:

> [W]henever there is an underlying foundational theory of truth, there must be an expert to interpret it. When the area of supposed expertise is another person's experiences, the expert is, ironically, taking that person's voice away from her/him. Thus, what Freud gave away with one hand he took back with the other, and virtually the entire succeeding field of psychotherapy followed him. (p. 8)

That being said, Parry and Doan (1994) suggest that a meaningful therapeutic experience will "help clients gain a sense of being their own experts" on their own lives "via enabling them to author stories based on their experiences, thoughts, and feelings" (p. 46). In their 1994 text, Parry and Doan (1994) provide a relatively detailed description of their approach to therapy. In general, however, they suggest that therapists should connect their clients to "meaningful narratives [that are] compatible with their preferences" which for a family means joining with others in "multiple authorship" (p. 43).

Heavily influenced by the postmodern perspective of Michael White, Parry and Doan (1994) describe their own version of narrative therapy for the family as

> a way of thinking rather than a particular type of treatment. Individuals compose families, families compose cultures and sociopolitical systems, and cultures and political systems compose countries. There are individual stories and story interactions at each of these levels, as we have previously pointed out. Individual stories are important in relation to shared or colliding stories, and shared or colliding stories are important to individual stories. We think in these terms, whether we are seeing an individual or a group of individuals (e.g., a family or a business). (pp. 47–48)

This "way of thinking" is helpful to my future work with the family because it reminds me that clients are not only experts on their own individual life stories, but also on their shared family stories. Parry and Doan (1994) further suggest that "narrative family therapists have a very important role to play in assisting families in finding ways of making their members feel connected meaningfully and pleasurably to one another" (p. 29). By and large, therefore, they suggest that narrative family therapists conduct themselves as facilitators, assistants, or catalysts that work *beside* family members in an effort to promote their status as experts of their own lives and family and to find meaningful interconnectedness (Parry & Doan, 1994).

From this viewpoint, I feel confident that I can self-fashion my position as a therapist to be a *facilitator* as opposed to *dominator.* As a facilitator, I will remain conscious that the client(s) are the experts of their own lives and my role is to provide a frame of reference where the multiple family members' stories can interconnect.

In a similar vein, White and Epston (1990) suggest that therapists support people by helping them to identify and perform new meanings *on their own.* They call this the "standing-behind posture" wherein the therapist "consistently endeavours to identify with the position at which the person was previously and maintains a cautious attitude, so as to not catch up too quickly with developments in the person's life" (p. 149). In general, what this stance counters is the "possibility of getting ahead of the person and thus contributing to a disempowering distinction," and most importantly, it privileges the client(s) as the only author(s) of the new story (p. 149). As a therapist, therefore, I can incorporate this "standing-behind posture" to avoid making assumptions or presuppositions about the lives of families and their members. By self-fashioning this stance in family therapy I can avoid asking pre-suppositious questions similar to those asked by my therapist as a child, such as "Why do you dislike your step-father?"

THE ANTI-CONCLUSION: A SELF-FASHIONED/BECOMING

This auto-ethnography mirrors my life as a state of becoming. No beginning, no end, only a middle. It is contemplation and difference, both of which are mine, but are available for you to discover if you so choose.

Opening up more questions/possibilities than answers, this auto-ethnography is evidence of an infinite struggle. What kind of struggle? The struggle to accept that life is ultimately uncertain and unpredictable. A life that can be all-at-once be exciting, alienating, and confusing. Indeed, Laing (1967) himself acknowledged that this approach to life and style of thinking "offers no security, no home for the homeless" (p. 47). On the other hand, Laing (1967) continues to state that "we must continue to struggle through our confusion in order to insist on being human" (p. 47).

How does this uncertainty fit in therapy? Laing (1967) contends that the most helpful moments in therapy "are unpredictable, unique, unforgettable, always unrepeatable, and often indescribable" (p. 47). Thus, uncertainty can fit just fine in therapeutic contexts if therapy can be (re)considered as a "re-search" that is "validated by the shared experience of experience regained in and through the therapeutic relationship in the here and now" (p. 47). Having said that, Laing further adds: "We all hope to share the experience of a relationship, but the only honest beginning, or even end, may be to share the experience of its absence" (p. 48). Essentially, what Laing (1967) is trying to convey is that our lived experience, including in the therapeutic context, is based on what we *want* to believe is true and certain, our pre-suppositions, our unquestioned truths.

To live purely in the common-sense world is to have unquestioned faith in what we believe to be true in the actual world presented before us. Many people prefer life in this box of dominant truths and unquestioned belief. They find the existence of clearly defined borders as exhilarating as life-giving breath. On the other hand, as Laing (1967) observes, "some people can stand a lack of oxygen better than others" (p. 47). I am one of them.

Needless to say, my auto-ethnography has provoked "a rupture with the commonsense world" and evoked "an aesthetic integration," but its therapeutic *effect* has not been "worked out in the restoration of the commonsense world" (Tyler, 1986, p. 135). Instead, realizing a life of becoming and self-fashioned experimentation (which can include aspects of both the actual/common-sense and virtual world) has been the therapeutic *effect* both in my personal life, and in therapeutic contexts of my future career. Embracing the uncertainty of life involves an ongoing struggle, because it is so easy to fall back into talking ourselves into believing that we lack, or that we are failures.

To illustrate further the therapeutic effect of my writing here, how it is evidence of a struggle, and how it will continue to deeply influence my personal life and career, I turn to a particularly meaningful piece from the book *A Separate Reality* by the author Carlos Castaneda (1971) who states, in the voice of Don Juan speaking to his pupil.

> You talk to yourself too much. You're not unique at that. Every one of us does that. We carry on an internal talk... We talk about our world. In fact, we maintain our world with our internal talk… Whenever we finish talking to ourselves the world is always as it should be. We renew it, we kindle it with life,

we uphold it with our internal talk. Not only that by we also choose paths as we talk to ourselves. Thus we repeat the same choices over and over until the day we die… A warrior is aware of this and strives to stop talking.

How can I stop talking to myself?

A warrior is aware that the world will change as soon as he stops talking to himself, and he must be prepared for that monumental jolt.

What do you mean Don Juan?

The world is such-and-such or so-and-so only because we tell ourselves that that is the way it is. If we stop telling ourselves that the world is so-and-so, the world will stop being so-and-so… Your problem is that you confuse the world with what people do… The things people do are the shields against the forces that surround us; what we do as people gives us comfort and makes us feel safe; what people do is rightfully very important, but only as a shield. We never learn that the things we do as people are only shields and we let them dominate and topple our lives.

What do you call the world?

The world is incomprehensible. We won't ever understand it; we won't ever unravel its secrets. Thus we must treat it as it is, a sheer mystery!

An average man doesn't do this…in his stupid confusion he believes that the world has no more mysteries for him. What a wretched price to pay for our shields!

A warrior is aware of this confusion and learns to treat things properly. The things that people do cannot under any conditions be more important than the world. And thus a warrior treats the world as an endless mystery and what people do as an endless folly. (p. 218–220)

Although this passage is literary in nature, I argue that its message encapsulates the message that many of the academic based authors I have referenced were trying to convey. That is, that life is uncertain and unpredictable, and by trying to deem it otherwise (as certain and predictable) we only slow ourselves down and shut ourselves out to endless possibilities of the infinitive world. It captures not only the overall feel of the struggle to embrace uncertainty within my auto-ethnography, but also how my life will proceed in a state of becoming. As proceeding from the middle in the contemplation of the difference, as a warrior that embraces the mystery in a state of becoming.

Part II
Learning My Mother's Magic

Kathleen S.G. Skott-Myhre

PREFACE

As a post-modern feminist whose ultimate goal is to appreciate and be a part of the growth of other human beings, I have found myself longing for a method of inquiry that would both satisfy my quest for erudite knowledge of the human mind as well as my innate desire to understand more deeply my heartfelt connections with other human beings. At the outset of my training I searched for the empirically based answers to the complex issues of the human spirit. The further I travelled along the well-worn roads of empiricism, the more skeptical I became that I would ever be satisfied with any "Truths" about humankind. That said, I was intrigued by the numbers and statistics surrounding various maladies encountered by the people with whom I worked. However, I always seem to find myself asking for the stories behind the numbers. It seemed that I needed to hear the voices behind the statistics.

This desire to discover the narrative behind the numbers led me to the qualitative methods of inquiry. Even here, I struggled with what I perceived to be the objectification of empirical qualitative methods. I tried a number of routes to understand better the richness of the stories behind the figures, but still found that, for me, the charting, coding, graphing, and analyzing of themes seemed to be leeching the life out of the evocative nature of a person's personal struggle.

As I listened to the stories of my clients, my students, my friends and my family I felt that something was being missed in the phenomenological and coded analysis of personal narrative. Then it struck me—what was missing was me. I realized that this obvious but incredibly important aspect of my work was missing. My engagement with the people I encounter as a therapist was only partially about being a change agent in their lives. There was another aspect just as important. It was that as I listened to their stories, I *felt* their stories and they changed me.

This realization forced me to re-evaluate the kind of research methodology I felt I could employ. When I set aside the numbers, facts, codes, and themes and reflected on what they said, I realized that I needed to understand how every story had an impact on *me*. I needed to explore the ways in which my reactions and heartfelt responses were transformative for both the storyteller as well as myself. The idea initially made me a little nervous. I considered that perhaps this is what is meant by counter transference and that I needed to examine my own feelings about the stories in order to be an objective listener and therapist, but the idea of disengaging at that level left me cold. How could I not be moved and changed by every encounter with another person? For the past five years I have thought about how to express to the academy the importance of this experience.

As an academic I consider understanding theory to be invaluable. I insist that my students think critically about what they read and what they hear. I urge them to challenge the information that they receive at multiple levels and to question most everything. However, I can't stop there. I ask that my students demonstrate through reflection how theory applies to life—be it teaching, learning, counseling, or just plain living. Given that, my teaching methods can sometimes step outside the traditional boundaries of imparting knowledge. I tell stories of my own life to demonstrate theory or methodology and engage in discussions that bring lived experience into the classroom.

Of course, as a therapist I was trained to keep the personal out of therapy. The therapist is to be a blank slate onto which the client can paint her story without being encumbered with the values, judgments, or critique of the therapist. I was educated in the tradition that it was my job to listen and offer feedback in a non-judging manner. I could, when necessary, confront the client gently with inconsistencies in her own narratives but never give any indication of what I might be experiencing in reaction to her story. This approach never really rang true for me. Instead, what became true for me, as a therapist was how valuable it is for my clients to see me as a human being with many of the same insecurities and vulnerabilities that she faces.

As a result, I share with my clients relevant stories of my own life when I have faced similar struggles and how they came to shape the person who I am becoming. However, I don't share everything or just anything. For example, I don't share stories about overcoming obstacles and persevering in the face of adversity (this would present me as possibly heroic or self-valorizing), rather I share stories that let my clients know that we are two people struggling together to make sense of a sometimes senseless situation. Together we work out how we might look at her story in a way that helps to shape a brighter future for her as well as many other people in her life—including me.

I am by nature a storyteller. I come by my stories honestly and through a long line of storytellers. My mother would advise me that it is the nature of being an Irish woman.

The articles that I have written (Skott-Myhre, 2008; Skott-Myhre & Skott-Myhre; 2007; Skott-Myhre, 2005) have always included stories of encounters with the various groups with whom I am working at the time. The stories that I write are not meant to explicate the intricacies of a particular diagnostic disorder nor are they meant to illustrate a particular therapeutic intervention. The stories that I have written have always come back to the ways in which I have been transformed, changed, and altered in some way by the person or people with whom I come in contact. For me, teaching, learning, counseling, and writing is not preparation for life. They are life. They are everyday lived experiences that deserve reflection.

CHAPTER 6

BACKGROUND: A PERSONAL JOURNEY

I am an Irish Catholic American woman. I am also someone committed to working with others toward producing a more just and equitable world. I have had the opportunity to work with many different people from many different geographies, cultures, ethnicities, genders, capacities, and sexualities. In this work, it has become obvious to me that without understanding what it means to be Irish Catholic American, I can't possibly hope to understand what it means to be anything else. How could I hope to work with the first generation Hmong young woman who is striving to be both Hmong and American? How could I hope to work with the African American woman who continues to battle racism? How could I work with the Native American youth who is determined to reclaim his heritage while his family is trying to deny theirs?

I grew up in a blue collar, Irish Catholic neighborhood. I went to school being taught by nuns. To me, my family was the richest in the neighborhood. My three sisters, two brothers and I all got brand new shoes and new clothes for school every year. Many of my friends from the neighborhood got the dreaded hand-me-downs. My mother made sure that we were "cultured" as we grew up. She took us to the theatre, read to us the classic American stories, made sure that we all dressed properly for church (making us late for mass every Sunday!), and made sure all of our teeth were straightened. She corrected our grammar and would not tolerate the "abuse" of the English language.

Where my mother left off, Gramma Hamilton, my paternal grandmother, took over. My sisters and I would each take turns going to Gramma's house for cookies and milk and Emily Post. We learned how to sit at the table while dining, how to place our napkins in our laps, which fork to use, and how to eat a cup of chicken noodle soup without slurping.

Gramma Gallagher, my maternal grandmother, on the other hand, taught us how to blow bubbles in our milk, how to speak with a Brooklyn accent, how to make ourselves small enough to fit into the tiniest of hiding places, and how to comb through the Johnny jump ups in the back yard looking for fairies—dirty knees be damned!

As I think about this many years later, I wonder whether my mother and Gramma Hamilton were not simply training us to be nice girls. Perhaps they were training us *not* to be Irish, *not* to show our blue-collar roots, and certainly *not* to let on that we were a family of modest means. On the other hand Gramma Gallagher made sure we never forgot who we really were. Of course this is just one possible story about what happened; perhaps it wasn't like that at all. I wonder though, because such an experience is not an unfamiliar story for immigrant groups who feel they must assimilate to a dominant culture and the Irish, as I will argue, certainly fit this profile.

The women in my family were not encouraged to become educated, although my mother did go to University and earned a degree in nursing. We were not encouraged to work outside the home, although my mother insisted that she return to her nursing career once my youngest brother began first grade. We were encouraged to do what was important first and play later, although my mother would give up a sink full of dirty dishes to help us blow bubbles in the back yard or show us the robin's nest complete with blue eggs that she had found in the garden.

In a sense I was raised between classes. While my Gramma Hamilton aspired to produce us as thoroughly middle class, there was an alternate set of family values that both accepted this on the surface but rebelled against it on the margins. We always thought of this as the "crazy" part of our family when it came to the whimsical and creative expressions of fun that my mother embodied, such as teaching her grandchildren to juggle plates of food at the dinner table or gargle milk until the bubbles ran down their chins. This alternate set of values was also was expressed in the large family gatherings of infinite quantities of food, drink, and displays of uninhibited behaviour complete with vulgar humour, loud singing, and the occasional complete family breakdown into a good fight. Of course, there was also the complicated role that alcohol played in the family. The heavy drinking by almost everyone led to a great source of joyful celebration but also to alcoholism and physical abuse for some of us.

In addition, being between classes also meant that we could never quite figure out the exact boundaries of our family. Strangers, friends, ex-boyfriends, ex-girlfriends, and relatives flowed into and out of our lives, sometimes living at my parent's house for years at a time. Indeed, boundaries in the conventional sense of the nuclear family of the United States in the 1950s and early 1960s were only known to us through television shows such as *Ozzie and Harriet* or *Father Knows Best*. Our family looked nothing like these fictionalized accounts of order and authority. That said, the face we presented to the outside world reflected a conventional middle class life in the suburbs of the American dream. Inside the house it was a different story. This alternative way of life that violated the bourgeois standards we were supposed to be aspiring towards was never spoken about. It was the secret of the family and the hidden legacy of my mother and her family that provoked serious contestation with my father's family and their aspirations toward middle class respectability.

When my sisters and I stepped outside the roles that were set out for us by decorum, my mother would not be overtly supportive. Indeed, she would even feign disapproval, but she would not push us to behave and somehow, we knew that our small rebellions were making her proud. This same sort of solidarity showed when we would visit my mother's mother. Unlike the rules and etiquette that surrounded a visit to my father's mother, visiting my mom's mom gave us full permission to be loud and get dirty. Visiting Gramma Gallagher meant fun and freedom. Visiting Gramma Hamilton meant cookies and quiet play. Gramma Gallagher, through unspoken affirmations, let my mom know that she was a wonderful mother. She and my mother would sit and talk for hours while we played, only pausing long enough to show us how to carve animals out of ivory soap or to perfect the water to dirt ratio in a mud pie. These differences and contrasts were integral to my learning about what it meant to be a woman. Indeed, the complexity of these contrary formulations produces ambivalence about social codes to this day. On the one hand I feel compelled to be polite, clean, and well behaved and on the other, to throw all of that out the window to break the rules, dirty my hands, and laugh too loud.

My sisters and I came to be educated much later than what would be considered the norm. We each had a failed attempt at higher education directly out of high school and then each followed an entirely different path out of the family home. Two of my sisters ventured off to Alaska to "live off the land," one went to the mountains of Colorado to ride horses, and I earned a cosmetologist license and got married. In my family, women were not supposed to be "smart" in the academic sense of the word. We were supposed to be caretakers and nurturers. However, there was always an inherent sense in each of us that someday we would return to learning. The timing simply had to be right. We had learned this from watching our mother who balanced her desire for education against the demands of her family. We watched as she patiently waited for the time she could return to school and finish her education several different times in her life. We all knew at some level we would finish some kind of schooling beyond high school but we also knew this had to be balanced against life circumstances in which other people's needs and demands came first.

BEING AN IRISH WOMAN

In the book *Erin's Daughters in America: Irish Immigrant Women in the Nineteenth Century*, Diner (1983) characterizes the stereotypical Irish Catholic woman in the American protestant imagination as "not very bright or dependable, she was a horrendous cook and fanatically bound to her priests...[she was] not someone of great consequence" (p. xiii). The reality, however, was somewhat different,

> Irish women differed from most other immigrant women in terms of numbers. They were the only significant group of foreign born women who outnumbered men...they accepted jobs that most other women turned down and their rate of economic and social progress...outdistanced that of the women of other ethnic groups...[they] viewed themselves as self-sufficient beings, with economic roles to play in their families and communities. (p. xiv)

Diner goes on to note that they made decisions for themselves, were involved with trade unions, held assertive roles in their families and had frequently boisterous public behaviour. They "asserted their economic prerogative in myriad ways and basically ruled their families, frequently leading them up the ladder into the middle class, but they never rose to challenge the public hegemony of men" (p. xiv). On the other hand, these women, "subscribed to a set of religious imperatives and conformed to a set of behavioural patterns enunciated by the Catholic church and by the traditional structures of Irish life which had no use for the 'feminist-women's rights' model of the 'new woman'" (xiv).

Diner notes that women's roles as workers and wage earners would seem to indicate a certain kind of independence and self-assertion but in actuality this was not so. She argues that their behaviour was rooted in family loyalty and the desire to support their families while remaining committed to traditional Irish Catholic values.

In spite of the fact that the world described by Diner is several generations removed from that of my mother and my family, a very similar set of contradictory imperatives, actions, and desires permeate the world of my family and upbringing. The stereotypes that Diner notes are almost word for word self-descriptions that might be given by mother who constantly demeaned her own cooking and intelligence. The women in my family have always been economically self-sufficient and in some cases have been the sole providers for their families but would never describe themselves as particularly powerful or publicly assertive. While these contradictions may appear confusing at first glance, my experience of them was not particularly disconcerting. It was just life as it had been presented to me.

In the book *A Thousand Plateaus*, Deleuze and Guattari (1987) discuss the ways in which language and description encode and order our world. They propose that language orders life into certain configurations that appear to us as natural or normal. We accept such descriptions as presented to us without much question. Our lives are filled with codes that often obscure our own lived experience. Such codes give order to lives like the Catholic Church gave order and behavioural prescription to the Irish immigrant women Diner discusses.

However, Delueze and Guatarri (1987) also propose that "language is not life, it gives life orders" (p. 76). That is to say, language can describe the world but only insofar as it turns it into code. The ways in which this coding process occurs shapes life into different configurations, fitting it into certain ways of knowledge and truth. Foucault (2002) calls this process the "will to truth." He says that this will to truth organizes knowledge constructions about the world that have tremendous force. As certain truths are organized, various groups lay claim to these truths and use them to exercise modes of dominance and control. Foucault calls these organized truths to which groups lay claim discourses. He maintains that even the most benign forms of social organization exert covert discipline and domination through these discourses. The human sciences of psychology, psychiatry, and sociology are all complicit in producing truths that are utilized to control and discipline groups of people.

However, Foucault (1977) also argues that for every exertion of control there is a moment of resistance. I am going to argue that some of these moments of resistance arise because life is more than just description—it is also experience. Deleuze and Guattari (1987) take this up when they suggest that language and discourse are not complete systems of control. Indeed, even within language itself, they suggest that there are what they call passwords below the truth claims that order our world into docility and obedience. They would say that there are ways of making meaning that elude the dominant codes in society. They call these alternate meanings passwords. These passwords are the hidden codes of resistance embedded in the alternate possible meanings of each word or phrase. Foucault (1980a) refers to this kind of knowledge as subjugated knowledge or those sets of truths cast aside or even actively suppressed by the existing regimes of dominant truth-values in any given society. These embedded meanings are what allow life to express itself outside the structures of dominance.

In my own life, as my sisters and I have grown older, these passwords have allowed us to resist and exceed the codes of dominance or disciplinary truths that have regulated the lives of our mothers and grandmothers. Of course, that is not to say that each generation doesn't have its own passwords and moments of resistance. Rather, there lies the possibility that each generation pushes against both new and old dominant truth claims in unique ways that both draw on past struggles and go beyond them.

Indeed, in what follows, I hope to explore the ways that these passwords of resistance, these hidden discourses of subversion allow a certain kind of power to be passed between generations of women. I want to explore, briefly, how dominant constructions of gender, race, and spirituality have disfigured and obscured indigenous feminine knowledge among women. I intend to explore the alternate codification of hidden knowledge and how such codes are passed on through body practices, sayings, gestures, stories, and turns of phrase. Finally I want to discuss the implications this has for working with young women in a counseling relationship.

Theory: Making Sense

To begin to make sense of my experience, I need to find a way of decoding and unpacking the descriptions of Irish, Catholic, American womanhood that were given to me so that I can find the passages hidden within those codes. To do this I will engage the language of postmodern philosophy. I do this because the philosophers of the postmodern, such as Foucault (1980a), specifically read between the codes of the dominant society to find what they refer to as hidden histories of struggle and resistance, subjugated knowledge, and forgotten histories; and new forms of knowing that can challenge the systems of social dominance. Put another way, I want to look at how certain constructions of knowledge inherent in language produce certain forms of power. However, to discuss postmodernity, I must first begin with modernity.

Modernity is an historical period that begins in the 1600s and enters a significant crisis in 1968 according to some scholars (Hardt & Negri, 2000) because at that point we begin the shift from industrial capitalism to global computer driven capitalism. The most distinctive characteristic of modernity is that it produces the concept of Truth with a capital "T". That is to say, "Truth" that is true across time, place and people; a universal kind of truth. For example, in psychology many of us subscribe to the idea that attachment occurs in all societies. There is healthy attachment and there is unhealthy attachment but there is always attachment. There may be cultural variables and differences, but attachment *per se* simply exists as "Truth" (Best & Kellner, 1997).

Modernists believe that the world is discoverable through observation, reason, and rationality (Best & Kellner, 1997); that is, empiricism, rationalism, and logocentrisim. If science can carefully observe something by filtering out the distortions of perception, then the scientist can discover the truth of what is being observed. Reason is one way to filter out distortion and is used to reduce the reliance on the body's perceptual mechanisms. According to modernist thought, the body's perceptual mechanisms can be easily distorted by emotion or faulty perception. Reason allows the scientist to distinguish accurately between one thing and another. Science argues that by using reason, one can set up experimental conditions that overcome the weakness of physical perception. Finally, rationality is the ability to separate the mind and the body so that one can think clearly without the interference of the passions. What all of this means is that for a modernist thinker, the most reasonable rational people who can observe most clearly are those people who are most separated from their bodies (Best & Kellner, 1997).

This idea that the closer one is to the body the less capacity one has for reason has had significant impacts for women in general and particularly women of color, working class women, and women from colonized areas of the world. Throughout the male dominant theories of modernity, women have been inextricably linked to their bodies through childbirth, menstruation, and through religious ideas that link them with the fall of man through sexuality. For non-white women, working class women, and, in particular for this project, young women, this association with the irrational body is doubled through the fact their daily labour is accomplished with the body. These associations have been used to justify the denial of political inclusion and access to education among other disenfranchisements. Interestingly, for us as therapists, we can see many of the same kinds of arguments being deployed with young women today (Stoler, 1995; Roediger, 1991).

The modernist line of thinking also believes that knowledge is teleological in nature and insists that time moves forward in a linear fashion (Best & Kellner, 1997). For example, many of us in the field of psychology assert in the concept of human development (see, for example Piaget [1968] and Kohlberg [1984]); that human beings evolve in predictable ways across the life span. Under this system of belief, adolescence is a stage of development that is a precursor to adulthood. This means that adolescents have certain developmental tasks determined by their stage in life that they must accomplish to move forward through time to becoming a mature adult. Knowledge increases in both quality and quantity over time and the older person has more and better information than the young person.

Modernist knowledge also produces the concepts of progress, productivity, and individuality (Pietrese & Prekh, 1995) that deeply influence the ways in which we, as psychologists, view the young women with whom we work. We see them first as separate individuals who have certain characteristics, traits, and difficulties. We tend to work with them as individuals, often only adding family and community as an afterthought. As individuals we believe that they should be progressing towards a model of the mature adult who is productive with her/his time and fits well into the dominant culture.

This way of thinking about young women is hierarchical and ordered and is strongly devoted to scientism. Again, this has had a strong influence on psychology in the ways we set up our practices or organizations and perceive adult roles as being about appropriately ordered discipline and authority. We worry about families and organizations in which the youth might be "in charge". Similarly, science with its "facts" about adolescent biology and psychiatric disease has had a ubiquitous effect on our therapies and interventions.

In French philosophy, postmodernity arises in the late 1960s to early 1970s primarily as a challenge to scientific theories of society and politics. Postmodernity challenges the modernist idea of discoverable "Truth" and would argue for a small "t" truth found in the local knowledges that each of us has about our own experiences. Although these local knowledges are not generalizable, they represent each person's own unique way of knowing the world and make each individual an expert in her/his own life. Modernist thinkers would argue that this kind of knowledge is overly influenced by personal, distorted passion, or subjective perception. Postmodernity suggests that this kind of knowledge is important because it enriches the field of ideas out of which new societies might be built (Best & Kellner, 1997).

Postmodernity further critiques the "grand narratives" of modernity such as the narratives of attachment, development, maturity, and psychiatric disease mentioned earlier, that make claims about being true for everyone. The postmodern critique is based on the idea that truth is always spoken in language and that language is neither stable nor predictable. This interest in language is sometimes talked about as what is called the linguistic turn. Derrida (2005) suggests a certain kind of relationship between the reader of a text, the writer of that text, and the text itself. What he proposes is that each reader brings to the text his or her own system of signification that translates every text into a different text every time it is read.

The process of reading is not directly related to any intentional meaning of the author, who even when she is writing, changes the meaning of the text with every reading. In other words, as I write this I stop every so often and read it. When I read it I find the text often holds different meanings than what I had originally intended. These different meanings influence both my editing and my thinking. Sometimes, the meaning of what I have written changes so much with my second or third reading that I can no longer recall what I had originally intended. Which is to say that the intention of the author, although it exists, loses any direct connection to the text itself.

Derrida suggests that because the text is independent of the author's original meaning and is available to an infinitude of interpretative possibilities, the text itself is infinite in possible meaning. That is to say, all knowledge has multiple interpretations. These interpretations, of course, have an immense influence over what we believe to be true about the world. As in the case of the meanings we produce about young women, there are struggles over what things mean. For example, is a young woman's defiance of authority a legitimate act of rebellion or a psychiatric problem called oppositional defiant disorder? Interpretations are always subject to power struggles over what things mean and these struggles have real world consequences. To relate this back to my own history, how am I to make sense of the contradictory meanings I have been given about my class, my gender, and my status? I propose that the meaning that I give these things will have a profound effect on who I think I am and what I am capable of and that the meaning I ascribe to myself is mutable and unstable but nonetheless powerful.

Foucault (1980a) in his essay called *Two Lectures* describes what he calls the "insurrection of subjugated knowledge" (p. 81). He says that each of us lives in a world of knowledge subject to power. Such a world, he suggests, is built out of two kinds of power. The first and most familiar of these is what he calls dominant power. This, he asserts is a monarchical power or the power of the sovereign. This power is centralized, operates from the above and is exercised directly on the body. This sort of power is used to repress and oppress.

Examples of this sort of power are abundant and can be found in any sort of structured environment. In the home it is corporal punishment, globally it is war, and it is torture, within the legal system it is imprisonment and the death sentence. In the early formulations of family therapy by Jay Haley (1978), this kind of power was central to untangling what he saw as the confused hierarchies of authority in the families he consulted. However, his mentor and colleague Gregory Bateson (1981) reflected later that he had become "bored and disgusted by ...my colleagues' obsession with power" (p. 187). He felt that therapists had become "power hungry" (p. 188) in their desire to centralize their truth constructions about others and cure them through coercive power.

Foucault (1977) argues that dominant top down hierarchical power is not a complete portrait of power. He proposes that for every instance in which power is used to dominate there is an immediate act of resistance and that act of resistance is a form of power as well. In fact, he says that it is the relationship of resistance to dominance that creates society. In this, Foucault defined power as relations of force; force meaning the creative drive of life itself. He described this force as a web moving in all directions at once and colliding with technologies, histories, biologies, language, law, and so forth. Power then can be simultaneously productive and destructive in those collisions.

This productive/destructive force can be thought about in much the same way as the productive/destructive force of a bolt of lightning. Lightning is produced by the collision of positively and negatively charged atoms. The lightning that is produced strikes a tree and causes a fire, the fire destroys a forest but in destroying the forest, causes certain sorts of seeds to open and produce more trees and plants. In this sense, every time something is destroyed, something is produced.

Power similarly is produced like lightning as a relation. For lightning it is the relation of positively and negatively charged particles. For power it is the relation of force between that which is coming into being and the infinitude of possible forms that becoming could take. In this relation, as with lightning, every time something comes into being, something else is destroyed. However, every time something is destroyed it both clears the space and provides the elements for the next production.

Another way to think about Foucault's power analytic is in much the same manner as one might think about electricity. Electricity is something that we cannot see, we cannot hear, we cannot smell, taste, or feel, yet we know that it exists and flows around us at all times. We can never observe electricity in its own right, but it becomes available to us at points of collision, such as turning on a light. When we experience electricity, we are only experiencing its effects. Just like electricity, power is everywhere all of the time. It cannot be perceived directly, it is constantly in motion, it is only visible at points of resistance, and we can only experience the effects of power.

The effects of power are both dominance and resistance. As noted previously in my discussion of discourses, Foucault suggests that dominant power always operates as a certain kind of dominant truth. This dominant truth is what we think of as expert knowledge or common sense. Foucault proposes that every time there is a dominant knowledge, it covers over alternate ways of knowing things. The kind of knowledge that is hidden from view by dominant knowledge he calls subjugated knowledge. Subjugated knowledge is uncommon knowledge. It is the knowledge of the delinquent, the subaltern, the insane, and the knowledge of women and youth (Foucault, 1980a).

Essentially it is the knowledge of all groups that do not hold dominant power within a society. For the purposes of this auto-ethnography, that would include the knowledge that the women in my family have about our own lives that the dominant culture does not share and dismisses. Subjugated knowledge is all of the knowledge or descriptions of the world not accounted for or that which is discounted by dominant knowledge through the practices of dismissal, forced silence through coercion imprisonment or death as well as the silence of assimilation of homogenization. Even so, Foucault says that dominant knowledge acts as though truth is neutral in terms of its power. It is simply "True". But Foucault also says that all truth is a power struggle and that subjugated knowledge contains the hidden history of struggle covered over by dominant description. Foucault suggests that there is the possibility that subjugated knowledge can revolt against dominant knowledge under certain conditions and this is what he calls the insurrection of subjugated knowledge (1980).

In *Two Lectures* (1980a), Foucault discusses two notions. The first one is the idea of parallel dominant knowledge, for example, in medicine. In the medical culture, there are both the local knowledges, such as that of people whom we call patients, who are seeking help and the dominant knowledge that the dominant discourse proscribes and that describes the role of the doctor, the role of the nurse, the role of the patient, and the role of the delinquent.

When local knowledge is held up to the scrutiny of the dominant discourse, or dominant knowledge, local knowledge is declared insufficient or inadequate. However, what is not said is that it is specifically in the local application or the local interaction between the patient and the doctor that all potentials for medicine to change and evolve occur.

It is in the insufficiency of the dominant discourse in that specific interaction at the very local level, between the patient and the doctor, between the doctor and the nurse, between the doctor and the institution of the hospital, that the insufficiencies of the dominant discourse become apparent. This parallel function wherein all advances in dominant knowledge are dependent upon interaction with local knowledge is reflected in the work of Marx (1978), when he points out that dominant systems of power such as capitalism produce nothing themselves. They simply appropriate what people in their daily lives produce. Foucault is making a similar point here when he identifies the dependence that the doctor has on the lived experience of the patient. It is within these interactions between dominant knowledge and local knowledge that new knowledges are generated that are then appropriated by the dominant discourse and claimed as its own.

This is what I was struggling with at the opening of this writing when I said that my work is not about being just a change agent for those with whom I work in my practice but also about how those interactions change me. Foucault elaborates this when he suggests that it is by the force of the opposition that the local knowledges are not able to extend themselves fully because they are held back. This was Bateson's (1981) intuition when he left his investigations into therapy and psychiatry in disgust because he felt the pull of dominant power as a seduction that actually covered over useful ways of knowing. He elaborates on this point when he claims behaviourism as a failure because it ceases to pay adequate attention to the lived world that exceeds the capacity of causality and statistical analysis.

For me, any therapeutic approach that closes off possible avenues to knowing cannot be fully useful to human beings. For the field of counseling to evolve, it calls for the lived experience, stories, and alternative knowledges about living which interactions with others supplies. When we think we know a truth about someone else without taking into serious account what they know about themselves, we lose the point of the encounter. We lose the value of subjugated knowledge.

In my family, the women could not fully express that knowledge. There is a great deal of knowledge that cannot even be spoken amongst us that must in fact be denied. There is a history or tradition amongst the women in my family to deny being smart or having any wisdom. Intelligence has to be refuted, debunked, renounced, and disclaimed and as a result of that, there is a potential of unexpended energy force, knowing, wisdom, and information that still somehow is passed from generation to generation. This passing on of hidden knowledge gives support, in a subversive way, to the insurrection of such knowledge.

This insurrection is the combination of subjugated knowledge with the unread academic histories of struggle available in the libraries that produces a new kind of knowledge that allows for new meanings.

This means combining the knowledge that the women in my family have about their own lives with the unread or untaught histories of struggle one can find in the library. It is in the insufficiency of the dominant discourse to describe life and events completely that the struggle for meaning can be mounted. No accounting of history, science, medicine, or philosophy can produce complete truth about the world. Foucault would argue that dominant truths can only be produced by ignoring inconvenient alternate experiences. Interestingly, these alternate experiences are often recorded and documented within the academic writings to be found in the back rooms of the library. Foucault (1980a) suggests that new knowledges can be generated out of these discrepancies when combined with the local knowledge of people's lives. The suppression of alternate ways of knowing by the force of dominant knowledge produces local knowledges that are not able to fully extend themselves.

In my family, what women know can seldom be expressed fully without being discounted in the same breath. The rules are that the women are to make sure that any uncomfortable truth is covered over or held at a safe distance. We are the great distracters using an appearance of being scatter-brained and unfocused to diffuse family tensions. It is up to us to create the stories that deny the actuality of any trauma or painful event. We are given the task of protecting the men from any accountability for their actions or self-reflective knowledge of their own behaviour. In this, we cannot allow anyone to know that we are doing these things. In addition, since this takes up a great deal of our time, we cannot talk about ourselves, what we know, who we really are, what our dreams might be, and certainly not our desires. In spite of all of this, we as women somehow know a great deal about these unspoken aspects of ourselves.

However, even though that history of struggle in my family cannot be spoken about, somehow with daughters, mothers, and sisters it is passed on. It is somehow passed on in a common sort of way in body practices, in language practices, in relational practices, and in the sense of potential that we each carry. Put in another way, the knowledge that we hold, while it cannot be spoken, can be lived in the rhythms of our daily lives. This subversive rhythm of voice tone and inflection, a certain toss of the head, a glance away, a forceful stride, a determined set of the lip, holds the information without the articulation of language. Over time those on the inside of a subaltern group learn the codes without ever being to articulate what they mean—in some cases even to themselves.

We carry this local knowledge, this "potential," in such a way that it is carried for our mother, our nieces, and daughters. On the other hand, as I have noted, we carry forward this force but can't articulate it. It becomes buried so deeply that we give in to the "I don't know" and the story about how working class women are not supposed to know things outside the tasks of their given class (Diner, 1983). Interestingly enough, this force, because it cannot be fully expressed, actually builds potential. It is the potential of unexpended unknown, the not yet, the knowledge of the minority (and here I use the term "the minority" as Deleuze and Guattari [1987] do when they refer to any identity that refuses the logic of the majoritarian system), the knowledge of that which is contrary to the majority knowledge (Deleuze & Guatari, 1987). It is the potential of what is unspeakable. To begin to render the unspeakable into terms that can be expressed, I will use what follows to look at two frameworks, feminism and critical race theory, that have influenced my ability to articulate my struggle. These frameworks have produced new ways of knowing myself that have influenced the work I do with young women.

FEMINISM/WOMANISM

In this section I would like to introduce what I call a double insurrection: the personal knowledge that I have of being female and Irish combined with the academic history and theories of feminism as well as the history of the Irish people in the United States. It's the interplay of Irishness and feminism that intersects with the subject positions or relations of being a mother and a daughter. As Irigaray (1993) points out there has been considerable effort on the part of the patriarchy to diminish both the force and knowledge of the mother and to present her as weak and trivial. Indeed, many women internalize this discourse and trivialize their own intelligence or accomplishments within the family context. My own mother would often disclaim her own intelligence by acting silly or making a joke that discounted a strong or incisive comment at family gatherings.

This places the daughter in a highly ambivalent position of revolt in which her own attempts to become powerful and independent must repudiate her own mother and model themselves on the strong and independent male subject. This flies in the face of what every woman knows intuitively, which is that all of her force as a woman must be grounded in the unique subjugated status of being female which can only be transmitted from the mother to the daughter. This places the daughter in the awkward and confusing position of only being able to sustain an affective loyalty to the mother if she wishes to exert her own force in the world. No truly female-based way of knowing holds any honor within this relationship. In my own family, there is a strong tradition of alternate spirituality that includes a range of pagan knowledge about supernatural phenomenon such as angels and fairies, alternate healing practices, and intuitive knowledge about future events. These ways of knowing are either discounted through silliness and humour or spoken together in secret.

In spite of all of this nullification and disqualification of the role of mother, I will argue that power is in fact passed from mother to daughter, generation to generation. This process of covert transmission is of particular interest to me as a therapist. I believe that it would be of considerable use to me in working with young women and their families to understand how power is passed covertly from Mother-Daughter within a patriarchal society and family structure.

This interest is based in my own personal knowledge of my mother and my family. I combine this personal knowledge with the history from the library that tells me that historically Irish women were powerful holders of spiritual knowledge and that prior to the invasion by Cromwell in 1649, Ireland was once a matriarchal society in which the women were the spiritual leaders and healers. The old religion was connected to earth and involved the stories of

magic, fairies, and ritual. This way of knowing was founded in knowledge of the senses rooted in the body. This connection to the wisdom of the body precedes the modernist split that separated sensate perception from reason.

Of course, the Catholic Church began to undermine the matriarchal structure of knowing in Ireland long before Oliver Cromwell led the brutal protestant invasion by the British that eventually colonized Ireland. Cromwell, however, went even further and did everything that he could to eliminate the old religion. He even went so far as to send women and children into slavery to the Caribbean in order to break the back of the matriarchal pagan religion. It is during this time period, which covers the advent of full modernity, the industrial revolution, and the birthing of early capitalism that the Irish family structure becomes overtly patriarchal while covertly matriarchal.

An historical example of this is in the tragic story of Bridget Cleary (Bourke, 1999). Bridget Cleary was a young married women living in Ireland in 1895. While the story takes place during the modern period with all its assertions of modernity, it also shows the continuing struggle as late as nearly 1900 between the old matriarchal religion and the emerging force of patriarchal power with its support by the Catholic Church.

Bridget Cleary was a woman with her own financial means, who was quite outspoken and encouraged other young women to be the same. She was both revered and reviled by the women in the community for her assertiveness and independent nature. Her husband was shamed by his inability to keep his wife "under control" and so claimed that she was mad/crazy. Eventually, with the help of the priests and doctors in the community, (a powerful conflation of modern and pre-modern patriarchal force) they drugged her and burned her to death under the guise of attempting to force the demons from her over an open flame.

As I started to recognize the oppression of women in Ireland, I began to contemplate the juxtaposition of strength and tenderness with which Irish women must have struggled on an ongoing basis.

I couldn't help but think about the relationships among women under such brutal conditions. I wondered about that primary female relationship, mother to daughter. Imagining this relationship within this context, I began to think differently about complexities of the mother-daughter relationship. I wondered how women under conditions of patriarchal force might interact in ways that call for new relational structures that defy the patriarchal structures of hierarchy and discipline.

Investigating this led me to the feminist theorist Luce Irigaray (1993), who said the following about mother daughter relations:

> ***In a sense...[we] need to establish a woman to woman relationship with our mothers, in which we might possibly also feel them to be our daughters. In a word, liberate ourselves along with our mothers. That is an indispensable precondition for our emancipation from the authority of fathers (p. 50).***

Irigaray (1993) is suggesting that the relationship that women have with their mothers holds within it the possibility of liberation and new ways of forming society and family relations. I found this intriguing as I thought about how to work with young women and their families. On the basis of this, Irigaray (1993) also suggests that, "In our societies, the mother-daughter, daughter-mother relationship constitutes a highly explosive nucleus. Thinking it and changing it, is equivalent to shaking the foundations of the patriarchal order" (p 50).

Here, she is suggesting that among women there is a possibility for building relationships in which both daughters and mothers can learn from each other and give birth to a whole new world.

While working at a University counseling center I had the opportunity to work with a graduate student who had been wrestling with disordered eating since she had been about nine years old. She had in common with both her mother and her grandmother a long history of struggling with negative body issues and eating disorders. During one of our sessions we were having a conversation about reconnecting with spirituality and through a series of questions, we came to the conclusion that she might benefit from talking with her grandmother.

The following week, she came back and described a transformative conversation in which she and her grandmother connected in a way that she never thought possible. She said that she heard from her grandmother stories of a different sort of spiritual journey that were unlike her traditional religious upbringing. It was a story of her grandmother's own resistance to the patriarchal version of religion and how her mother had given her the wisdom to make it her own. She said that as they talked, an image formed in her mind of a long line of the women in her family standing behind her in support. She formulated a different image which altered the weak and submissive women that she believed her mother and grandmother to be into women who had, in their own ways through their own unique spirituality, resisted the patriarchal oppression which could have ended them.

I felt that my own family experience was that the women in my family had a certain kind of spirituality that the dominant discourses of society didn't describe very well. Yes, we were Irish Catholic with all of the piousness, obedience, and guilt that went along with it, but I sensed a different sort of connection to it that my mother, my sisters and I were both attracted to and repelled by. There was a sense of secrecy, an unspoken understanding of the mysticism that was hiding beneath the ritual and formality of the church.

Like my Irish foremothers, to call myself a feminist initially felt awkward and ill fitting. There was something about the term "feminist" that didn't feel right to me. When I thought about feminism the picture that would come to my mind was that of thousands of white women on the march standing up for all women and denouncing the normative standard of the highly educated white male by which we all are judged. I hadn't given much thought to the idea that women of color, lesbians, or women from a lower socioeconomic status might view feminism any differently. After all, aren't we all being judged by the same standard?

What I came to understand, however, is that the feminist movement was initially formed by women of bourgeois status. It was actually an elitist group leaving out or marginalizing women of color, lesbians, and women from lower socioeconomic structure. This was highly problematic for me in my desire to identify with other women in their struggle for liberation. I certainly did not identify with upper class white women; my background was far too blue collar for that. However, my knowledge of other struggles was limited, and I found myself wanting to know about how the identity politics of race, gender, class, and sexuality both divided women and formed new possibilities for alliance.

There are many levels to the oppression that woman of color and women of different classes experience. One might call this group collectively women of difference. We are not all the white middle class suffragettes. After all, these women achieved the vote in 1920 while black women had to wait until 1964. For me as an Irish-American woman living between my bourgeois training and blue-collar experience, the white upper middle class composition of the feminism of the late 1960s didn't fit.

Indeed, it was a peculiar aspect of the feminist aspiration for liberation that it became a dominant discourse in its own right that required an insurrection of subjugated knowledge by women of color to make it available to me. The alternative to traditional feminism that worked for me in beginning to understand my own social positioning as a woman has been called womanism (Moradi, 2005).

Womanism brings a racialized and often class-located experience to the gendered experience suggested by feminism. Womanists perceive feminists as being protected by white privilege without the multiple oppressions with which other subaltern groups to contend. White women simply have not suffered as much as Black women. A womanist is someone who is seen as rooted in her community and committed to the development of herself and the entire community. Womanism offers a way for Black women to address gender oppression without attacking Black men and thereby allows them to maintain connections with the entirety of the Black community (Moradi, 2005).

Black Feminism, on the other hand, disrupts racial solidarity. It breaks the rule that black women will support Black men no matter what. Black feminism comes into conflict with codes of silence surrounding problems between men and women in the Black community including such issues as domestic abuse. The feminist emphasis on individualism, individual subjectivity, and personal advocacy takes away from whatever strength there is in the Black culture's collectivity.

The summer that my mother turned sixty-five and retired from a twenty-eight year nursing career, my husband and I gave her the gift of a literature course at the University of Minnesota. She was immediately hooked. My father was, at first, amused and supportive of my mother's new interest. But, the more work and effort my mother put into her schoolwork, the less amused and supportive my father became. In fact, one might consider my father threatened by my mother's participation in higher education. Yet, I rallied around my father, trying to keep him occupied and included while my mother did her homework in near secrecy so as not to take too much time away from him.

Why would I, a self-proclaimed feminist, choose to support my father when his behaviour toward my mother is so appallingly juvenile? I can only conclude that like the womanist who complicates the relation between race and gender, I also find class and gender to be a complex field. My father is a white male, however he is not of the highly educated elite. Despite the fact that my father may have some of the privilege that comes with his race and gender, he is not fully privileged because of his class. While this relation of different levels of privilege even among white men does not excuse oppressive behaviour, it makes it more complex. White men of blue-collar status certainly benefit from and take advantage of their association with the dominant ruling class. However, their privilege is always unstable, particularly in the economic sphere and psychologically they have a sense of ongoing second-class status.

This, of course, often makes their assertion of their privilege even more brutal (Roediger, 1991). However, for those of us who live with them and love them, the relation is complex at best. I have compassion for my father in his confusion and sense of inadequacy while fully repudiating his sometimes brutal and oppressive behaviours.

When I first began to examine race relations, I had initially amassed all "White" people into one category, that of the privileged. What I came to understand through personal experience is that white women are not as homogeneous as I had once thought us to be. Within the white culture there are various points at which some people are deemed more privileged than others, one of those being the difference of class. The working class woman is more inclined to think in terms of the collective rather than the individual. Therefore, as a working class woman I am more prone to being womanist than would be the elite or the bourgeois. It is the elite and the bourgeois that have been at the vanguard of the feminist movement with the result that many working class women have actively resisted the movement.

That said, like the white working class male, working class white women have held an ambivalent, sometimes hostile relation to women of color as well as women of alternate sexuality. In their desire to capitalize on their racial association with the dominant class, they have often overlooked the commonalities of the subordinate status they share. It's a peculiar kind of denial that we also see in the emerging black middle class in the United States. The repudiation of our own in hopes of affiliation with those in charge is an old story. In the case of white blue-collar women of Irish descent, it goes back to our common ancestry in the United States as slaves and the proclamation of the Irish as white. I will have more to say about this later.

The blue-collar dynamic of repudiating the politics of feminism had a deep influence on my own struggle with the idea of feminism. To me, feminism was attached to the man-hating, political radicals of the seventies. Many of these women were standing up to the men who had the power. I had difficulty aligning myself with that idea when I was working shoulder to shoulder with men, like my father, who were simply trying to scrape out a living. To me it made more sense to work with these men rather than against them. What I couldn't define at the time was that I, unlike the elite feminist, was working *with* the collective and, like the elite feminist, was also *against* those in power.

Moradi (2005) suggests that what she calls the "womanist identity model" has the potential of moving in different kind of way on race/gender to "capture the diversity and complexity of women's self-concepts as shaped by multiple personal and group identities (e.g., race/ethnicity, class, sexual orientation)" (p. 226) She notes that in doing this the multiple and complex identities held by women could be better articulated and lead to a richer source of self-understanding.

The fact that traditional feminism was the province of upper middle class women made it inaccessible to my mother and grandmother both in their status as working class women but also in their ambivalent status as Irish-American. As I will explore in the next section, the racial identity of Irish immigrants to the United States was never truly white. As colonized people, they were considered people of color until the revolution of 1776. This shift from being a subaltern group to being nominally "White" produced a complicated and ambivalent identity for Irish-American women when attempting to challenge their own subordinate position (Roediger, 1991).

For me, being able to find the academic literature that offers the possibilities inherent in womanism in combination with my own local experience of the women in my family, offers precisely the insurrection of subjugated knowledges proposed by Foucault. It provides an alternative and more local way of knowing that might allow me the possibility of making sense of my own local experience as the ground from which to challenge power. The fact that womanism arises in the African-American community but holds such force in my own life-world is not entirely accidental. The history of

African and Irish communities in the United States has a long and complicated story of struggle, betrayal, and possibility. It is this possibility, through the transformative process of "undoing" Whiteness, which I will elaborate in the next section.

CRITICAL RACE THEORY

As I have inferred, the identity of Irish-American women is both complicated and troubling. So much of the history of Irish-American women is obscured from view by the complexities and brutalities of the British colonization and the marginalization of the immigration experience. The anxieties provoked by the struggle to achieve acceptance within the dominant culture have produced a certain degree of collective historical amnesia. For many of us, we don't want to remember or admit our histories of struggle. However, to ignore our complicated historical position as immigrants to the United States fleeing a brutally repressive regime of occupation creates us a people who no longer can explain to our children who we are or who we might become.

For me, it was crucial to my understanding of myself that I unpack my own lineage of struggle. I found that to do this I not only needed to examine my status in terms of class and gender but also my dubious status as White. In fact, I would argue that it is Whiteness itself that frames and gives force to both class and gender.

Critical Race Theory (Degado & Stefancic, 1997; Roediger, 1991; Stoler, 1995; Said, 1979) suggests that whiteness is not simply a delineation of people by skin color but a set of beliefs and practices. These beliefs and practices are produced by the intersection of the concepts of modernity I have outlined previously (rationality, reason, productivity, and progress) with the project of European colonialism. While the complexities and full implication of this intersection are beyond the scope of this project, what is notable is that colonial modernity produced a binary relationship between the colonized and colonizers that rigidly defined and prescribed who they were and what they were able to do.

Put simply, those designated as White were ascribed the desirable attributes of the modern project. Such people were considered to have the capacities of reason and rationality. On the basis of this, they were supposed to be more productive and their achievements marked the heights of evolutionary progress. Non-white peoples were irrational and unreasonable. They were considered to be behind Whites on the evolutionary scale and considerably less productive. This, of course, meant that to be White was to have access to privilege and power and to be non-White was to become available for exploitation, marginalization and, in the worst cases, genocide.

Although the Irish are now generally considered White, this is actually a fairly recent development (Ignatiev, 1995; Roediger, 1991). Roediger (1991), in tracing the ways in which the Irish were not White, notes that until the late 1700s the Irish who came into the United States were sold into indentured servitude on the same slave blocks and transported in chains across the countryside with African slaves. In fact, the first American Revolution, often referred to as Shay's rebellion, was instigated and carried out by a combination of Irish and Africans living together in slave quarters. This revolt so badly frightened the merchant class that when they decided to revolt successfully in 1776, they constitutionally split up the Africans and Irish by declaring the Irish White and free while leaving the Africans as slaves. The Irish were then given jobs as overseers of their previous comrades in arms. However, the legal production of the Irish as White was highly ambivalent and there are political tracts in both Britain and the United States questioning the white status of the Irish well into the 1860s.

This troubling history held its costs for Irish-Americans. These included an ongoing racial anxiety that manifests as virulent anti-black racism among significant sectors of the Irish-American community, as well as what I have described in my own family as an ongoing ambivalence about adopting the bourgeois standards of becoming white. As I have suggested previously, this has had a

profound impact on the relation between blue-collar Irish women as womanists and their sisters of color.

In talking with my mother and my sisters, it became very clear that our own history and knowledge as Irish women was clearly influenced by a need to appear "white". For example, there was a total denial of the fact that my grandmother on my father's side was not only Irish but of African descent as well. Interestingly and perhaps predictably given the history I have traced here, it was she who most adamantly insisted that we all behave in an extremely restrained and middle class fashion. This has been at considerable cost to the women in my family whose inherent nature is to be rather wild and free.

The idea that the dominant discourse is one of dominance over nature and over people associated with nature led me to investigate the role of colonialism in the identity of myself as a woman and the nature of colonial identities such as whiteness for young women. To investigate this, I looked to critical race theory. I came to understand that in order to uncover my own lineage of struggle, I had to undo my understanding of myself as "white". Critical race theory (Roediger, 1991; Stoler, 1995; Said, 1979) suggests that whiteness is not a skin color but a set of beliefs and practices. These have been identified as rationality, reason, productivity, and progress, which are also the characteristics of modernity as well.

Roediger (1991) traces the ways in which the Irish were not White until fairly recently. In the United States, the Irish were sold into indentured servitude along with African slaves until the American Revolution when they were declared "white" and released from slavery. Roediger further traces the costs culturally and politically to the Irish in becoming white.

Whereas Irish men eventually won their white status, becoming major players in finance and politics (even becoming president), women, and therefore Irish women, have never become fully White, as they are not considered to have the modernist qualities or the patriarchal practices that define the term (reason, rationality, and mind/body duality).

Women, of course, have always been linked to their bodies and sexuality in western mythology from Adam and Eve forward. They are considered to be hormonal, irrational, hypersexual, and responsible for the sexual downfall of men. They are further connected to their bodies in ways that men are not, as they have menstrual cycles, PMS, give birth, and have obvious and external secondary sex characteristics. In short, they are inescapably physical in western thought. This has been the justification for such things as denying them the vote, and questioning their ability to succeed in the "hard" sciences.

Indeed, Marx (1978), writing at the height of industrial capitalism and modernist thought, claimed that the model for all oppressive systems is rooted in the role of women within the patriarchal family. If so, then perhaps male/female relations constitute what Foucault (1977) calls a social diagram or a model of social control designed for a specific historical purpose that expands across the social in unpredictable ways. I would argue that this binary model of reason and rationality initially applied to women and then colonized and racialized others has gained a new currency with what Foucault (1988) calls the silencing of unreason in our diagnosis of mental illness. Science has found a new province for the binary constructions of reason and biology in the ability to construct the neuro-pathological subject. This is, of course, of huge importance for those of us in the counseling profession. If, in fact, this evolving construction of the body as a site of unreason premised in biology has its roots in Whiteness and gender, then we should be extremely cautious in its application to our practice.

The idea of aspiring to Whiteness covers over the histories of struggle and resistance in which women engage daily. For example, in private conversation, women will often speak of ways of knowing things about their children or their lives that are non-rational. Take, for example, the notion of intuition. Such ways of knowing are demeaned and dismissed as trivial sources of knowledge in our society. However, as I have been pointing out, there is always that element of resistance predicted by Foucault

(1977) to every instance of domination. In this case, we might note the rise in feminist research of the auto-ethnography or the research project, such as this one, that highlights such subjective knowledge as an attempt to overcome this kind of whiteness.

As a therapist, I have found that in order to be fully able to hear what young women are telling me, I have needed to challenge my whiteness. This is partially because as an Irish-American woman, my own training as white and the surrounding anxieties of that position create barriers to hearing non-white descriptions of the world from marginalized and oppressed young people. In addition, however, there is an increasing use of the non-white discourse to describe all young women as irrational, unproductive, hyper-sexual, and dangerous. To the degree that I don't understand and challenge my own induction into whiteness, I can be seduced into believing these descriptions and that can severely interfere in my ability to hear the stories I am being told.

WRITING FROM THE INSIDE

In the preceding sections, I have traced my own evolution as a therapist and researcher. I have argued for a reflective form of writing that takes into account my own life and context as a way of understanding the power relations and identity formations that I bring to the counseling encounter. In this, I have argued that counseling is a mutually transformative experience for both the counselor and the person seeking counseling. The mutuality of the relationship requires the counselor to account for the constitutive aspects of that relationship. In other words, how does this relationship impact both parties in terms of how to come know themselves?

I have suggested that this process of mutual influence is not neutral but laden with power dynamics that go beyond the common sense notions of who we think we are. Following Deleuze and Guattari, as well as Foucault, I have argued that the language of counseling is riddled with the beliefs and practices of the dominant society in which we live. I have traced the impact of modernity with its grand narratives regarding gender, race, and class and have shown how these discourses have influenced me as a woman in the context of my family. I have specifically pointed out how the discourses of whiteness with their assumptions and practices of reason, rationality, and scientism have had a muting effect on women in their relations with each other. In particular, I have illustrated how these sets of knowledges subjugate certain kinds of knowledge held by particular cultures and individuals silencing certain voices and driving them underground. Using Foucault, I have made the argument that there is inherent within this subjugation an equal response of resistance that I trace in his concept of the insurrection of subjugated knowledge.

In all of this theory, I have used my own experience as a reflective tool to illustrate how these effects have played out in my own life and family. In this reflective process I have come to wonder about how women pass subjugated knowledge between generations so that wisdom that cannot be overtly articulated is still sustained as potential knowledge. I have noted that the specific relation of the mother and daughter within the patriarchal family structure holds promise for this investigation.

In the next chapter, I will show how certain counseling practices allow for this potential knowledge to be accessed by women talking together. I will provide a case example that will demonstrate how this can occur. Finally, I will make a proposal for rethinking the form and structure of family genealogy. I will argue for a genogram of flight that can accommodate post-modern thinking about family relations so that we, as counselors, can find new ways to work in a liberative fashion with those who come to consult with us.

CHAPTER 7

THE JOURNEY CONTINUED—TOWARD A JUST AND EQUITABLE PRACTICE

When I first began to imagine who I might be as a therapist, I thought about with what sort of population I would want to work and with what population I would not want to work. At the time that I was about to go out on my first practicum experience, my son was entering "adolescence." As a single mother, I worried that, without adequate back-up, I would not be able to handle the stage of storm and stress that I had been studying (Hall, 1904). My son was relatively easy to deal with at that point, but the friends that used to come home with him were another matter. Somehow, my son found the most marginalized young folk with whom to socialize. There was one young girl in particular who troubled me. She had taken to sitting at the kitchen table and talking with me while the rest of the "crew" were downstairs doing whatever it was that young teens were doing at that moment. Somehow she had bonded with me and decided that I was a safe adult with whom to share her sordid history. She told me about the numerous times she had run away from home, about the various types and quantities of chemicals with which she had been experimenting, the sexual assault she had experienced, and the promiscuous lifestyle that she was leading. I felt for this young girl, yet at the same time concluded that this was most definitely a population of young people with whom I did not want to have anything to do. As fate would have it, my practicum placement was at a shelter for runaway youth.

On my first day at the shelter I arrived with my proverbial bags packed with all of the psychological theory on adolescent development and family systems approaches. I approached my first day "on the floor" with my flimsy liberal beliefs that one only needs to treat all peoples alike and justice would be served. Of course, some youth were the exception to that philosophy, as some of them needed adult help and guidance to assist them in the navigation of the stormy sea of adolescence. One of the first young persons with whom I had the opportunity to work was an African American girl who, on the surface, personified the hard, tough, and vulgar black female stereotype.

One of the steps in the intake process with young people coming to the shelter for assistance is to search them and their belongings for any sort of "dangerous" paraphernalia. This is usually done toward the end of the intake. Admittedly, I was so intimidated by this 16-year-old girl, that I used this process at the beginning of the intake to feel as though I had some authority over her. She made me nervous. As the interview proceeded, I came to find a very different girl beneath a very tough exterior. She was tough, but not in the way that made her dangerous or difficult. She was tough out of survival. She had a tremendous love and devotion toward her mother and her siblings but was having an incredibly difficult time with her father and some of the social situations surrounding her family. Her way of negotiating her life and circumstances created unexpected and often hidden assets and strengths. This experience made me question some of the theories and assumptions I had about young people who are raced, classed, and socially constructed, and led me into a new way of thinking about therapy and counseling.

THE TRADITIONAL LENS

The very process of studying theories of adolescent development had prepared me to view young people through a lens that created them as going through a period of chaos and rebellion (Hall, 1904; Johnson, Roberts and Worell, 1999; Levy-Warren, 1996). Following this traditional modernist line of thinking, I was taught that it would be my job to help the young woman described above to understand how to comply and follow the rules for her own personal well-being. Conceptual frameworks such as stage theories (Kohlberg, 1984; Piaget, 1968), psychoanalytic theories (Freud, 1938; Erikson, 1963; 1968), and socialization theories (Bandura, 1977; Maccobi, 2007) might well lead me to focus on the negative and view this young woman as narcissistic and pleasure seeking (Hall, 1904; Johnson et al., 1999; Wolfe & Mash, 2005) with no regard for her family or future consequences (Kochanska & Aksan, 2006). I have to note, however, that had I been fully indoctrinated into this line of thinking, I might well have missed hearing her concern for her mother and her sisters, her dedication to her grandmother and learning her families' traditions, and her apprehension and aspirations for her own future.

It was my experience that using adolescent theory based on Piaget (1968), Kohlberg (1984), Freud (1938), Erikson (1968), Bandura (1977), and most recently Maccobi (2007), as a framework for working with young people can become a way of marginalizing yet another group within the population. By positioning young people within the confines of so called "adolescence" we treat persons within this age group (the parameters of which are growing ever wider) in a particular way that may have a huge impact on how they see themselves and how that view of themselves is acted out in our culture (Burman, 2008; Males, 1996; Raby, 2002; Skott-Myhre, 2008).

In this regard, we might note that youth spend most of their day in developmentally isolated confines separated from the rest of our society, ostensibly so that they can be educated. Yet, as Foucault (1977) has pointed out, a good deal of what we call education in our society is actually designed to shape and control young people. This is, of course, a certain kind of education, but it is a kind of pedagogy that has powerful effects. Some of these effects include a degree of alienation, as young people find themselves not only isolated from the rest of the community but under constant surveillance from metal detectors, police in the hallways, barbed wire on school yard fences, and security cameras on school buses and in hallways (Giroux, 2005; Kozol, 2005; Raby, 2005).

In addition, when they leave the school confines, young people continue to be under surveillance in stores and malls. In fact, many stores now have signs limiting the number of youth who can congregate within the store at any time. The media contribute to this sense of isolation and alienation through constant horror stories about youth and the use of drugs, alcohol, and uncontrolled sexuality (Males, 1996; Raby, 2005; Skott-Myhre, 2008). These stories utilize the developmental discourse of adolescence to explain and amplify the perception that youth are biologically incapable of reasonable decision-making. (See Blakemore [2006] for developmental psychological claims regarding brain development and adolescent judgment.) I find these conceptions of youth both troubling and unconvincing.

While developmental psychology has much to offer in terms of understanding young people in their growth and development, I would propose that the field might overreach itself in its negative portrayal of adolescence. This seems particularly cogent for me when comparing social statistics of pathological behaviour between young people and adults. Statistically it is not youth who have the highest rates of depression, suicide, drug addiction, drug overdose, mass shootings, or other types of violent behaviour (Males, 1996). It is, in fact, adults. If adults are actually engaging in high-risk behaviours at statistically higher rates than young people, why are we given the impression that the obverse is the case? One possible explanation is that our own children have become scapegoats for irresponsible adult mismanagement of society (Males, 1996; Giroux, 2005). Of course, to create a group of people as a scapegoat, one must produce a social discourse that marginalizes them as either dangerous or inferior. This was discussed in Chapter One when I looked at the process of producing whiteness. Indeed, Giroux (1996) argues that young people have been socially constructed in western society since the 1970s as non-white, regardless of skin color. Supporting this contention, Males (1996) and Skott-Myhre (2008) point out that the developmental adjectives we use to describe youth are the very same adjectives we have used to describe other disenfranchised and marginalized groups that we have historically categorized as developmentally inferior by race, gender, or class.

When one works with young women, this social dynamic is amplified by the discourses of gender as well as race. As discussed in the section on whiteness, women in our culture are seen as emotionally incompetent, volatile, and hyper-sexual (Burman, 1998; Stoler, 1995). Certain psychological and psycho-dynamic theories see them as overly dependent on their peers and pathologize what is described as a particular importance on maintaining their relationships with their "best friends" (Aapola, Gonick and Harris, 2005). According to Lawrence Kohlberg's stages of moral development (Kohlberg, 1984), which continues to pervade the current literature, women lag behind men in their ability to reason logically. According to this archaic, yet ever present, description, women are stuck in the middle stages of adolescence, as suggested in critiques of Kohlberg's theory offered by Erica Burman (1998), Carol Gilligan (1993), and Ian Parker (2007). The end result of this particular stage of development is to pass successfully through the process of individuation and separation with the ultimate goal of being able to operate morally within the realm of universal principles. As Carol Gilligan (1982) points out in her critique of Kohlberg, women tend to think in terms of relationships, not universal principles such as justice. Kohlberg, in his research, found women unable to reach stages five and six of his moral reasoning hierarchy. Gilligan asserts that this is because women found their ethics in material human relations, not ideal principles. Erica Burman (2008) following Gilligan suggests that this focus on relationships leads to a lowered importance for individuation and autonomy. Many cultures would refute autonomy as being the objective of adolescence and entry into adulthood (McGoldrick, 1998). The Western/capitalist notion of youth and many of the theories of adolescent development are not easily generalized and, I would argue, they are culturally bound (Parker, 2007).

As I continued my work at the runaway shelter, these cultural discourses on what adolescence means and who young people are began to break down through my actual interactions with young people. As I began to do more work with their families, these discourses eroded even more. I came to find that young people and their families are complex and multifaceted. My encounters with them, at some of the worst moments in their lives, led me to see them as quite different from the stereotypes we hold about gender, race, sexuality, or age.

It was in relation to my evolving understanding of these complexities as a family therapist that I really came to understand how much I had to learn from the people who came to see me. Working with families in an inner city multi-cultural context showed me how inadequate my psychological training was in preparing me to work with the wide range of families and family culture that came to see me. Family systems theory (specifically the theories of Gregory Bateson, Murray Bowen, John Bradshaw, Jay Haley, and Salvador Minuchin) did not capture the complexity and diversity of the families with whom I was working. As I began to work with African American families, Hmong families, Native American families, and Latino families, I realized that all family structures were not alike. The extended kinship networks that I encountered in some families reached well beyond what I had been studying about the traditional nuclear family system. How do I include mom's best friend whom the young person with whom I'm working calls Auntie? What about dad's fourth cousin who replaced him as the father figure when dad disappeared?

CASE STUDY: ANA AND HER MOTHER

The complexities of this kind of multi-cultural work became very clear to me when at the runaway shelter, I had the opportunity to work with a young Latina girl, to whom I will refer to as Ana. Ana and her family are a combination of many of the families with whom I have worked and all names are pseudonyms. Ana had come in with her mother, Julie, to discuss how they might be able to come in together to talk about Ana's drug and alcohol use and her tendency to stay away from home some nights. Both Ana and her mother seemed open to discussing the struggles they were having and I sensed a good but strained relationship between them.

After the initial interview, it was decided that we would figure out a time that would work with all of our schedules and they would call me when they felt ready to begin. That next weekend the Ana showed up in the shelter. That was the first in a series of stays at the shelter during which time I worked with Ana around the circumstances that prompted her to drink and use drugs.

TOWARD A MULTI-CULTURAL THERAPY.

The first step toward working with Ana for me was beginning to acknowledge that I needed to pay attention to the role of culture in her life. In exploring Ana's sense of her own culture, I found that she was actually not just Latina but Norwegian on her mother's side. Through talking with Ana it emerged that she was torn between her loyalty to her white mother and her desire to reclaim her Latina culture. Talking about this together, and through much trial and error, we found that it was helpful for Ana to connect with her paternal grandmother and learn what it means to be a Latina woman. Her mother in the meantime, started to reconnect with her own mother for support and in the process she began to revisit those things that were a part of her Norwegian culture. As time went on, Ana learned from both her mother and her paternal grandmother how to blend and honor both aspects of her history and culture and how she might begin to define herself as a young woman growing up in a diverse and blended culture.

REFLECTING ON ANA.

I found that for me to begin to see Ana in the kinds of terms that allowed me to explore her culture, I had to set aside much of what I had been taught about working with adolescents. I wanted to begin to see Ana, not in terms of her behaviours but in terms of her lived experience. This was challenging because, like most of the clients that I saw, it was Ana's behaviour that worried everyone around her. For example, her mother, Julie wanted to meet with a therapist from the shelter for a couple of reasons. First, because she was obviously concerned with the things that her daughter was doing (staying out all night, drinking, partying) and second, because she wanted to provide Ana with a safe alternative should she decide to run away from home. Ana was also experiencing angry outbursts at home and at school, which Julie found to be quite puzzling from a daughter who had always been quiet, polite, and a superb student. Ana also described experiencing anxiety and panic attacks. I discovered in an individual session with Ana that she had been gang raped and was experiencing significant repercussions from the incident.

To begin to work with Ana and her mother, Julie, in a way that fit my developing cultural awareness and was not problem-focused and rooted in empirically based research, such as the approaches used by cognitive behavioural therapists (e.g., Beck, 1999; Ellis & Dryden, 1997; Foa & Rothbaum, 1998), seemed very risky to me in spite of my determination to work in a culturally competent manner. I had just begun to experiment with the postmodern methods of working with people (e.g., deShazer, 1985; Berg, 1994; White & Epston, 1990) and had a sense that this might have some potential, but I had barely read through and internalized the methods one might employ to do such therapy. I seriously thought about abandoning the prospect of using any of the aspects or philosophies of this new approach and returning to what I felt was the safety of having a stepwise process in place.

In retrospect, however, I believe that had I gone the route of my traditional training, which was cognitive behavioural therapy (CBT, particularly that suggested by Foa and Rothmans [1998] specifically for the symptoms of post-traumatic stress disorder), things would have gone very differently. Using CBT, I very likely would have employed the protocol outlined as follows. I would have elicited from Ana her inaccurate thoughts that were associated with the feelings that caused her both to drink and party all night long. We would have worked on restructuring those "damaging" thoughts that were getting in the way of the former happy, well-behaved Ana. We would have broken down all those tasks that in her current state she found to be so overwhelming that she simply would give up and drink instead.

I believe that CBT feels safe for a new therapist for a number of reasons. It diminishes the necessity of getting into any sort of discussion regarding a client's history. Digging into the past can lead to some very difficult stories that a newbie may feel ill equipped to handle. For a new therapist, CBT offers a clear step-by-step process that can be ticked off throughout the session as the client and therapist move forward. This in itself can be rewarding for both client and therapist as both can feel that there is a tangible process underway and a resolution is not far behind. The therapist is in charge and the expert in this sort of treatment modality and that can be a powerful thing for a new therapist to experience. The "giving over" of power can feel like a relief for the person experiencing distressing symptoms. Both may have a momentary feeling of accomplishment in such a relationship.

Finally, the documenting of such a process (both for the client's file as well as for reporting back to a supervisor and professor) is a fairly simple paint by number procedure. One can then check back and make sure that all the proper steps were followed and should success be slow, one would pump up the volume. Instead, I resisted the pull toward the familiar and opened up the postmodern box and began.

PROBLEMATICS OF DOMINATION.

I would argue that the first difficulty in using a CBT based approach in a complex multi-cultural situation is that in focusing on symptom reduction. I might well have lost the rich cultural resource of Ana's mother, grandmothers, and cousins. Using CBT, I most probably would not have paid attention to the issues of culture that played out so richly in the work I have briefly outlined. Ana's mother, Julie, is a Norwegian woman raised Lutheran in the suburbs of a large Minnesota city. Julie is very close to her mother, which has often been a source of contention between Luis (Ana's father) and Julie. This conflict in cultures between Ana's father and mother amplify the effect of Julie's status as female in a patriarchal, racialized, class based, and gender biased culture. Surely, for a young woman, issues of gender and culture that are important factors in shaping her mother's life will have an impact on her own sense of self as a becoming woman.

Julie had been divorced from Ana's father for several years. She had been raising her three children on her own and had only recently begun to have difficulties with Ana, her middle child. She described herself as a typical "Minnesota girl" growing up in the suburbs of St. Paul. Her family was not particularly "religious," although they did attend services on the important religious holidays. Julie was raised to be in an environment in which mannerisms and emotional affect were kept to a minimum. The role of the wife within her family was essentially that of the communication center. Girls within the family are expected to take on adult roles earlier than boys and begin to help their mothers with gender appropriate tasks at about the age of eight; boys do not begin to help their fathers until age eleven or twelve (McGoldrick, 2005). In Julie's family, hard work is highly valued and if a woman was able to have a job outside the home and keep up her duties at home, she was considered to be industrious and useful. Julie earned an undergraduate degree at the local university but did not go on to educate herself further as planned after meeting her future husband.

Many of the early Norwegian settlers who left their homeland and settled in Minnesota were farmers in Norway and the rich farmlands of Minnesota were most appealing to them. Around the time that many people left Norway for the United States, people lived under a rigid class system. People of the lower classes were expected to show their respect to those of a higher status. For example, when in the presence of a person of higher status, the person of lower status was required to remove her/his hat and be silent unless the person of higher standing addressed him/her. This of course was a very humbling experience for those in the lower class and traces of this formality can be seen within the Norwegian population of Minnesota today (Gjerde, 2002; Zempel, 1991).

Luis (Ana's father) was raised in a fairly strict catholic household and expected that he would raise his family in the same tradition.

Luis had strong affiliations with his family and had a particular affection for/attachment to/honouring of his mother. It was her father's strength and his devotion to his mother that Ana admired about her father. In the Latino culture, particularly that of the Mexican-American Latino culture, there are rather specific roles for each member of the family (Garcia-Preto, 1998; Ginorio, Gutierrez, Cauce, & Acosta, 1995; McGoldrick, 2005).

Similar to what western culture has come to describe as a traditional family structure, the father is the head of the household. He is expected to be the provider and protector of his family, while the wife is to take the role of the homemaker and caretaker. Within the Mexican-American family the bifurcated role of male as dominant and female as submissive is still the predominant public norm.

The children are important aspects of the family and take on hierarchical roles as well. The first-born son is given the most authority and is often given the task of exerting that authority over his younger siblings. During adolescence, the children are segregated by sex and girls are given the household chores for the boys, who in turn, chaperone and protect the girls. Girls within the family are expected to remain pure and "virginal" until they begin to court and even then are to maintain their virtue until married. In a Latino home there is the expectation of loyalty at all levels of the family formation. The children are to be especially loyal, and respectful to their mother. Within the family, hierarchies are clearly defined and parents would not expect nor want to be friends with their children (McGoldrick, 2005).

THE IMPACT OF PATRIARCHY ON THE MOTHER/DAUGHTER RELATIONSHIP.

Ana found herself in the position of being both Norwegian and Mexican-American. She faced the struggle between being a strong, emotionally repressed, industrious woman that her mother represented and being a virginal, submissive, dutiful Latina daughter. This is further complicated by the hierarchical relations between mothers and daughters as prescribed by both of the cultures within which she is embedded. In the Norwegian community, children are not to be overly praised as to avoid the sin of pride and are expected to develop into productive, considerate, and obedient adults based on the idea that given the proper atmosphere for development, their unique, inborn potential will naturally evolve. That individuality must not be expressed too openly as inflated self-regard is unacceptable for a respectable adult (McGoldrick, 2005).

In the Mexican-American family the status of the child remains quite low compared to that of any adult within the family. The children are expected to be loyal and dependent upon the mother while the mother is to be submissive to her husband's rule. Older children are in charge of the younger children and the boys in the family hold power over the girls. Each of these cultures supports a hierarchical and patriarchal family model that covers over alternative sets of relations that might be available to women within these structures (Garcia-Preto, 1998; Ginorio, Gutierrez, Cauce, & Acosta, 1995; McGoldrick, 2005).

THE ISSUE OF HYBRIDITY IN MULTI-CULTURAL COUNSELING

One of the problems with defining a family by culture in a reductionist or simplistic fashion is that culture is not a static thing. Different groups of people within any given culture are going to experience the same phenomenon differently depending upon their status within that culture. Therefore, women are going to experience and use the elements of their culture differently than men based on the way that patriarchy manifests itself within the culture.

Homi K. Bhabha (1994) is associated with the use of the word "hybridity" and may well be helpful in delineating the problem as stated above. His analysis of the colonizer/colonized relationship can be used to discuss the struggles that might present themselves to a family brought together under multiple ethnicities. Obviously, these categories have multiple implications for Ana and Julie both in terms of culture and gender. The way that the previously subaltern immigrant group that constitutes the Norwegian culture (they were thought to be intellectually inferior and barbaric in North America—

called square heads) attained its current mainstream status is often obscured in pioneer histories of Minnesota. In addition, the fact that Norway was colonized by both Sweden and Nazi Germany is also rarely discussed.

The history of Latino culture is even more complex as those of Spanish heritage were involved in the brutal colonization of the Americas and those of indigenous heritage suffered its effects. The fact that most people of Latino heritage carry both histories makes this very complicated, especially when we add in the savage annexation of Mexican lands to the United States and the current controversy over Latino immigration. Of course, each and every one of us carries these histories with us, whether we know them or not. The dynamics of these historical struggles play out in our social relations and habits often outside of our conscious awareness (Sangari, 1987). These struggles also help shape our identity, those subjugated voices that become an essential part of who we are.

In his analysis, Bhabha (1994) stresses the interdependence and mutual construction of subjectivities between the colonizer and the colonized. Under colonialism, indigenous cultural forms were either forced underground or took on colonial meaning. This forced set of colonial meanings takes two forms. The first of these is assimilation, in which indigenous practices and ways of knowing are absorbed into dominant structures of the colonial system. This is how the history of Norwegian struggles against occupation in Europe and subjection to discrimination in North America are obscured. People of Norwegian descent think of themselves as just another group of white people. The second response to colonialism is resistance, where indigenous practices and symbols come to stand for resistance to colonial domination. This can be seen in the proliferation of Latino murals and flags throughout the communities in St Paul and Minneapolis.

However, it is not only the colonized who are influenced by the colonial process. The influence of the colonial process was engaged to some degree in Said's (1979) work on orientalism where he notes the mutual identity production between colonizer and colonized.

Both subjects produce each other. In this context, it becomes very important to recognize that both the culture of the colonized and the colonizer are changed by the interaction. Neither culture can sustain itself in an essential or foundational form. The colonizer influences the indigenous peoples and the indigenous peoples influence the colonizer.

Bhabha (1994) refutes the old claim that there is a fixed, pure culture in which the leaders (elders, parents, and priests) know what that culture is. He states that culture is an evolving system influenced by outside forces as well as contradictions within the culture itself. Differences in status, ecological events, shifts in geography, and shifts in the economy all produce fractures and ruptures that consequently affect the ways in which a culture is played out. He contends that all cultural statements and systems are constructed in a space that he calls the "third space of enunciation." It is the space between. It is not an either/or; it is a third space from which one could speak. He argues that cultural identity always emerges in the contradictory and ambivalent space of cultural collision. This makes the claim to a hierarchical purity of cultures untenable. According to Bhabha (1994), the recognition of this ambivalent space of cultural identity may help us to overcome the exoticism of cultural diversity. He suggests that this could allow us to recognize an empowering hybridity within which cultural difference may operate.

I would argue that for clients such as Ana, positioned between two cultures, this is a very important idea. The idea that there is a radical separation between cultures and one must choose one over the other and betray one aspect of one's lineage is a highly charged emotional field for a young person. The possibility that one may be able to shape the confluence of cultures within one's own lived experience can be quite empowering.

Another view of hybridity is offered in the work of Deleuze and Guattari (1987). They conceptualize hybridization as a rhizomatic formation. A rhizome is a fluid, anti-hierarchical structure that "ceaselessly establishes connections between chains of meaning, organizations of power, and circumstances relative to the arts, sciences, and social struggles" (p. 7). They imply that culture is not structured like a tree that grows up in binary forms originating in a single a root. Instead, culture is made up of infinite connections of everything that is changing, fluid, and unpredictable.

Another possibility for describing culture is found in their concept of the map versus the tracing when they say that

> [W]hat distinguishes the map from the tracing is that it is entirely orientated toward an experimentation in contact with the real...it fosters connections between fields...The map is open and connectable in all of its dimensions; it is detachable, reversible, susceptible to constant modification. (p. 12)

The tracing tries to give an exact copy of culture, which is impossible according to Deluze and Guattari (1987), as well as Bhabha (1994). One cannot get an absolute replica of culture. Anything one says about culture is a map and maps are experimental. Any map is a certain moment in time and selects only certain elements from that particular moment.

For example, one of the critical relations formed within colonial structures is the role of gender and sexuality (Stoler, 1995). The replications of the hierarchical structures of dominance play out in the micro-politics of the family in very powerful ways. Indeed, Marx (1978) states that it is from the family that all other forms of oppression and domination spring. These relations are fundamental to any essentialist reading of culture. Gender roles are powerful structures that each family member is supposed to trace upon their own lives.

Ana and her mother broke the "rules" of both the Norwegian and Mexican families and developed a close relationship with each other as women, separated from their culturally defined roles as mother and daughter. Although unspoken, there was encouragement given to Ana by her mother via furtive glances and hand holding during our family sessions instead of the appropriate disciplinary distance. It was as though Ana and her mother had a pact between them that Ana would break the barriers of the patriarchal regulations put into place by both of her cultures and move on to a stronger, more assertive life. Julie seemed to be waiting for her daughter to lead the way to her own emancipation.

The traditional mother/daughter relationship in both of these cultures is formulated through a history of patriarchal power and matriarchal submission (Garcia-Preto, 1998; Ginorio, Gutierrez, Cauce, & Acosta, 1995; McGoldrick, 2005). Yet within each of these cultures, women hold their own subversive forms of power. Within the Norwegian families, women were raised under similar expectations to their male siblings to be productive and industrious, but the end result was to show themselves to be good wives. The role of the wife in the traditional Norwegian family is to be the communicator and social net worker. Through this, women learn tactical, yet veiled, negotiation skills and pass them on from mother to daughter.

Julie had been the ideal daughter, going to school, working in gender appropriate part time jobs while she completed her degree, and married shortly after graduating from university. Rather than becoming the stay-at-home mom as was the expectation from her family, as well as the expectations of her husband and his family, Julie chose to pursue a career and stayed home with her children only as long as her maternity leave allowed after the birth of each of her three children. Julie engaged the negotiating tactics learned from her mother to subvert the gendered role prescribed to her by her culture.

Of course, this becomes much more complicated when there are multiple cultures involved. A daughter of multiple heritages faces double oppression in that there are at least two forms of patriarchal practices to which she is responsive. She also faces two kinds of practices of resistance manifested overtly through her mother's culture and more obliquely through women in the extended family network of the father's culture.

Julie has taken the industrious nature of the Norwegian culture and adopted some of the progress of the feminist movement by declining to follow the patriarchal role of mother as seen in the Latino culture. This resistance to both her husband and her mother-in-law's directions as to how be a good wife and mother was amongst the issues that ultimately led to her decision to divorce her husband.

Unlike the traditional distanced mother/daughter relationship in the Norwegian culture, Ana and her mother had formed a close intimate bond during Ana's younger years which Ana felt she was betraying as she sought out her Latina roots. During her visitation with her father, Ana was spending more time with her paternal grandmother and her paternal cousins. She experienced a more traditional Mexican culture during those visits and became drawn to that aspect of her heritage. She struggled with the ideas of being the submissive, virginal Latina girl that her father and grandmother painted for her, and found an alternative when with her cousins.

Some of her cousins belonged to and introduced her to the Mexican gang culture that was a prominent element of the neighborhood in which they lived. Ana was intrigued by the strength and presence of the Chola[1] within the gang. She began spending more and more time with her cousins and their gang, and ultimately fell into a pattern of drug and alcohol use as a means of demonstrating her independence and brave nature. It was during one of the many parties that she attended with her new found "family" that she was raped as part of an "initiation" process into the gang culture. It was soon after the rape that Ana began to experience panic attacks and self-medicating them via alcohol and drugs.

COGNITIVE BEHAVIOURAL THERAPY FOR POST-TRAUMATIC STRESS DISORDER

For many psychologists, this sexual assault would become the center point of the therapy. The complexity of the culture and relationships that surround this event would be overshadowed by the trauma and deficit based models that would predict a diagnosis of post-traumatic stress disorder (PTSD).

Using CBT to reduce the symptoms of PTSD as applied by Foa and Rothboum (1998) would begin with the process of relaxation training with the client. This would counteract the effects of the panic attacks by reducing the amount of oxygen flowing into the blood stream alleviating the light-headedness, rapid heartbeat, and shortness of breath that often accompany such an attack. Once this process has been repeated and seems to be mastered by the client, the next step would be to pair relaxation with the traumatic memory. The therapist would talk the client through the traumatic incident and essentially help the client to "relive" the event over and over again for periods of up to 60 minutes at a time to reduce the visceral reaction to the memory of the incident. The client would use her newly found skill of relaxation to calm herself after reliving the event. Once success with this step has been achieved, the client would be instructed to imagine herself approaching situations that remind her, directly or indirectly, of the event, allow herself to become agitated and then calm herself down using her relaxation exercises.

The next phase of the process can take some time, as the client will begin to expose herself to the various situations that cause her to experience her anxiety and panic. With the therapist's help, a hierarchy of avoided or panic-inducing situations is made along with homework assignments to accompany each situation. The client is to expose herself to each of the anxiety provoking (but realistically safe) situations and remain in each situation for 30 to 45 minutes until her anxiety is reduced by at least half. The client is then to continue exposing herself to the situations further and further up the list until she succeeds in exposing herself to the highest anxiety-provoking incident and successfully calming herself in said situation. The entire process should take approximately 10 to 12 weeks to complete with a few additional sessions available at the discretion of the therapist. If the client does not show significant improvement after a reasonable number of sessions, the therapist should consider another course of action.

While this approach has obvious humanitarian effects in reducing the traumatic effects of the assault, it does little to empower the client as political agent. For women within a patriarchally driven system, sexual assault is more than an emotional or physical event. It is also a political act of domination by men. As I have argued previously, this kind of domination extends beyond any particular traumatic event and is woven into the very fabric of patriarchally defined/derived culture. In this sense, while it is very important to triage the immediate psychological trauma, it is not sufficient. Although it can be useful to deploy traditional techniques that may assist clients as an initial approach, I would argue that psychologists need to address the broader socio-cultural contexts that continue to allow these events to occur with disturbing frequency. In this sense psychotherapy/counseling becomes a site of potential revolutionary politics (Parker, 2007) and it is to this end that the present project is dedicated. That is, that psychology should be a site for revolutionary politics, not just limited to the issues surrounding sexual assault but to a political analysis that encompasses issues of trauma, power, and domination. Clearly, CBT as the only treatment is unable to address this aspect of counseling psychology.

LIMITATIONS OF A MODERNIST APPROACH

Certainly one of the most problematic aspects, for me, in using a more modernist approach such as CBT, is that I would be placing myself in a position of privilege and a position of knowing. It would be my responsibility to lead the way through the process of decreasing the symptoms and increasing quality of life. Using such a process creates a significant power differential between the therapist and the client. This relation of power and knowledge as an arena of privileged truth is central to my concerns in forming a just and equitable practice. In this regard, to position myself as holding my own contingent knowledge as an element of co-construction with the client's knowledge moves us into postmodernity as a realm of uncertain and constructed knowledge. This is a very different position than the more technical positioning of the modernist clinician.

Another concern that I have about using a modernist approach in this situation is the mandate to observe families from a disconnected vantage point and bring in what the experts have to say about single mothers and their teen daughters. If we look at Ana's family from the perspective of the mandate described above, we might well focus on the fact that Julie is divorced from Ana's father. We have a single mother attempting to work, maintain a home, and raise three teenage children on her own. Red flags are flying all over the place: father absence, children feeling abandoned, neglected, overworked mother with possible resentment toward her daughter for having her youth and her freedom to do what she will with no real life responsibilities. Ana is 15 years old and is at the perfect age to be placed into the storm and stress description of adolescence. She is just starting high school and is being noticed by boys. Perhaps this is simply a "phase" and that she will grow out of it. An argument might even be made that with the proper discipline and consequences for her behaviours, the difficulties that Ana is having will work themselves out.

FROM MODERNITY TO POSTMODERNITY

As I delineated in Chapter Six, the primary difference between modernism and postmodernism lies in what each posits about "truth" (Foucault, 1980b; Kogan & Gale, 1997). Modernism, which is rooted in the ideas of the Enlightenment, proposes that there are fundamental truths, which can be discovered through objective observation and the application of rationality and reason. These truths are true across time and circumstances and comprise what post-modernists have described as the "Grand Narratives" of western civilization (Lyotard, 1984). A classic example of this is the application of psychological concepts such as Oedipality (Freud, 1938), developmental theory (Piaget, 1968; Kohlberg, 1984) or cognition across cultural contexts (Malinowski, 1964), which may hold ways of knowing quite different than those of psychology.

Postmodernism has been quite critical of the modernist "Grand Narratives" and emphasizes an anti-objectivist epistemology (Kogan & Gale,1997). The postmodernist approach is concerned with the ways in which "...modern sciences control and discipline their populations by sanctioning the knowledge claims and practices of the human sciences: medicine, psychiatry, psychology, criminology and so on" (Philp, 1985, p. 67). Psychology's assertion that it can know the essential qualities of mind and behaviour is challenged by postmodern thought on the grounds that such knowledge is premised in linguistic constructions of the world not the material reality of that world.

But this construction has implications. From the postmodern view, the creation of the "Grand Narratives" of modernism obtained their "truth value" at the expense of other ways of knowing. The postmodern approach aims to unseat these grand narratives in favor of what Foucault (1980b) has termed "local memory". Instead of large systems of thought capable of broad and sweeping knowledge, postmodernism is interested in "local and specific knowledge" situated within each of us (Philp, 1985, p. 68). In terms of therapy, postmodernism assists us in avoiding any search for absolute truth. Instead, we investigate the ways in which the idiosyncratic truths of our clients play out in their lives. In this sense, truth is never stable; it is always being produced anew through the relation of power and knowledge.

My experience at the runaway shelter where I met Ana and her family brought the differences between modernist and postmodernist approaches into a progressively clearer focus for me. It was at this site that I was met full force with the dehumanizing effect of the dominant discourse of the medical model of psychology. In my experience there, I worked with youths who had been treated like machines on an assembly line. The parents of these youths described to me conforming behaviour, which they viewed as progress, when their child was on medication. However, the youths' "local and specific knowledge" had them viewing themselves as flawed or malfunctioning because the medication was necessary in order to keep them to functioning in accordance with the rules of the adult world. Here, I want to make it clear that I agree with the statement made in Freeman and Combs (1996) when they say:

> We are not against medication. Nor are we against clinical research or the naming of problems. What we do object to is using medication, research, findings, or diagnostic terminology in mechanized, routine, and/or dehumanizing ways. (p. 21)

Or put another way, I believe that medication should be an option that is used with the full consent and participation of the client. Moreover, I believe such use should not be predicated on an inflexible diagnosis of illness, but rather as one method for managing the effects of living in today's society.

In *Narrative Therapy*, Freedman and Combs (1996) also discuss the "objectivity" of the modernist worldview, with its emphasis on the scientific aspects of observation, reason, and rationality to inform their conclusions about people and how using such a scientific methodology causes one to lose sight of the individual person and the localized meanings embedded in their lives. They go on to argue that "when people are treated with this kind of 'objectivity,' they tend to be regarded as objects, thus seducing them into a relationship in which they are the passive, powerless recipients of the knowledge of the doctor who is in turn the sovereign, direct questioner, the observing eye, the touching finger" (p. 21). It is in response to this idea that I attempt to do away with the hierarchical character of the therapist as the holder of "Truth". Addressing this, Kenneth Gergen (1992, p. 57) writes, "the postmodern argument is not against the various schools of therapy, only against their posture of authoritative truth."

Using a modernist approach in family therapy, the therapist would turn to the scientific processes of observation, reason, and rationality in order to compare the family against preexisting, normative models of the family. The therapist would then offer her/his expertise via enlightenment, guidance, or premeditated intercessions as a means to bring the family into alignment with a more normative family model (Freedman & Combs, 1996).

Kathy Weingarten (1998) proposed two dilemmas in moving forward with this approach. First, a modernist therapist supports belief in her/his role as the expert by identifying her/himself as separate and apart from those who seek her/his help. This separateness allows her/him to perform her/his task of observation in order to diagnose, assess, and formulate a treatment plan while exempting her/himself from the same analysis as the family s/he is treating. Furthermore, the locality of understanding the complexity of the issues presented by the family is presumed to lie within the therapist's vast knowledge of the human condition. From a postmodern perspective, however, the rich understanding and knowledges lie within the client and it is the function of the therapist to shed light on and acknowledge the significance of those knowledges (de Shazer, 1985; White & Epston, 1990). In this sense, the client is the sole keeper of knowledge about her/his lived experience. That said, this knowledge is always contingent and incomplete and requires interaction with others to extend, clarify, or amplify the capacities for growth and creativity contained within that experience. What the therapist brings to this encounter is not the ability to know the client's world, but her/his skill in using the encounter as a space for creative co-constructions of new possibilities.

The second dilemma noted by Weingarten (1998) concerns the dimension of power. A modernist therapist assumes that everyone who is present in the therapy room has the equal opportunity to have a say to the therapeutic process. S/he may even delude her/himself into believing that by giving each a turn to contribute and respond to the discussion in the room that s/he is leveling the playing field and giving each person an opportunity to be heard. Often, this is not the case. The same power relations that exist outside of the therapy room bias each person's participation in the process. It would be quite easy to overlook this aspect of the family/social dynamic, but doing so unintentionally upholds the existing relations of power and thereby silences certain voices (Hare-Mustin, 1978; Pare, 1996; Weingarten, 1998).

This is particularly true in the case of Ana and Julie given the traditional relation of hierarchy between mothers and daughters that can obscure their common struggles as women within a patriarchal social structure. This was further exemplified when the family joined with both father and older brother performing their traditional familial and cultural roles of power within the therapeutic setting.

These dilemmas as outlined above do wane. However, it would be unrealistic to say that they disappear completely, when working from a postmodern narrative position. The postmodern therapist can acknowledge that s/he alone is not the holder of the truth about this family's life. S/he alone is not the one to prescribe a treatment for the problems that have been holding this family captive. S/he sets her/himself up within the family and commits her/himself to working side-by-side with the client/family in order to investigate and honour the various strengths and solutions that often have been buried under the dominate discourse of normality. It is through the course of illuminating the buried voices, strengths, compassions, and understandings, and through the resurrection of subjugated knowledges (Foucault, 1977) that the unique outcomes and alternatives to the problem-saturated story will surface.

Because a postmodern narrative therapist does not ascribe her/himself to fixed truths or master narratives that cover the situations of our lives, s/he has very little interest in a conversation that tries to discover the aetiology of a problem (Freedman & Combs, 1996; Parry & Doan, 1994; Weingarten, 1998). What s/he is interested in are the conversations that uncover the many alternative possibilities that will offer ways in which to move forward once a problem has become a strain on the person's or family's life. The postmodern narrative therapist will work with a family to co-construct a preferred description that is more aligned with the family's or individual's lived experience "…regardless of whether they fit anyone else's idea about 'persons like that' or 'couples like that' or 'families like that'"(Weingarten, 1998, p. 4)

In Ana's case, positing her situation against the normative family structures of the dominant culture would have led to potentially serious misunderstandings of an extremely complicated cultural mix. For example, to understand the impact of the sexual assault outside the cultural factors involved would lead to a treatment based in the statistical norm of the dominant culture. However, this would leave aside the fact that the rape was an initiatory event gone wrong; that it was a complex mélange of machismo and subjugation by the patriarchal culture bound up with the subjugated status of men within that culture. Women from within such a culture have a very complicated relationship to their subordinate status as was discussed earlier in the description of womanism. This is then heavily linked with the expectation of "virginal" submission and cultural shame that is then complicated by the passive injunction from her Norwegian mother to assert herself; a mother who is not inducted into the same cultural set of beliefs and practices that led to the assault. I would argue that there is no template of norms and dominant values can adequately address such issues.

As Weingarten (1998) so eloquently pointed out, in order to accomplish the task of co-constructing a preferred narrative that takes into account the surfeit of knowledge contained by the client or the family, the therapist must be present in way that is very different than that of a modernist therapist. The therapist must shift her/his attention from what s/he thinks about her/his client's stories to trying to understand what her/his clients think about their stories. S/he goes on to describe the process of this shift as a feeling of free falling. I had much the same sort of dizzying experience when shifting to this way of hearing my clients' stories. It reminded me of the scene from Jim Henson's *Labyrinth*, in which the character of Sarah falls down a passageway leading to an oubliette. As she is falling, she is caught, slowed down, and eventually stopped by disembodied hands that ask her if she would prefer to go back to where she came from or if she would like to continue into the unknown.

Like Sarah, I chose to let go of the systemic belief system along with its possible solutions in order to experience that which I may not know but which offers new opportunities for a different kind of knowing. Much like Weingarten (1998), as I become more comfortable with this new way of knowing, I have found a level of congruency between my work and the politics, ideas, and beliefs through which I interpret and interact with my world. My education and experience in working with people have allowed me particular knowledges and I can concede that "I do have certain knowledges and expertise and I [can] share what I know when these seem relevant. I am not the expert. I don't know the 'truths' of peoples' lives and I don't know what they should do. It is a great relief no longer to believe that I must know" (Weingarten, 1998, p. 2). In the case of Ana and Julie, my own personal knowledge as a woman from a similar community to Julie's, as a single mother, as a daughter, and as a woman struggling against the same patriarchal discourses of normativity, I am able to hear their stories not simply from an objectivist stance, but from a position of knowing from the inside.

TOWARD NARRATIVE THERAPY

White and Epston (1990), following Foucault, writes that we easily fall into the trap laid by hegemony and will internalize the "dominant narratives" of our culture, believing the commonsense idioms that seem to speak the truth of our identities. We become the "docile bodies" under "the gaze" of those who control the discourses of power in our culture. These dominant narratives, in turn, can bury the possibilities that other more hopeful narratives might have to offer us.

White and Epston (1990) argues that people come to therapy either when dominant narratives are keeping them from living out their preferred narratives or when

> [T]he person is actively participating in the performance of stories that she finds unhelpful, unsatisfying, and dead-ended, and that these stories do not sufficiently encapsulate the person's lived experience or are very significantly contradicted by important aspects of the person's lived experience...persons experience problems, for which they frequently seek therapy, when the narratives in which they are "storying" their experience, and/or in which they are having their experience "storied" by others, do not sufficiently represent their lived experience, and that, in these circumstances, there will be significant aspects of their lived experience that contradict these dominant narratives. (p. 14)

Problems develop when people internalize conversations that restrain them to a narrow description of self. These stories are experienced as oppressive because they limit the perception of available choices.

According to Foucault (as cited in White & Epston, 1990), in recent history, western society has increasingly relied on the practices of the "objectification" of persons and their bodies to "improve and extend social control" (p. 66). He refers to the "power of the state" that produces an increasingly totalizing web of control that is intertwined with and dependent upon its ability to produce and increasing specification of individuality. In order to understand the operation of power in its modern form it will help to understand the wider context of person's experiences of subjugation.

GOALS OF COUNSELING.

> The central goal of a narrative therapy must be the facilitation of a sense of personal authorship or agency concerning the events of one's life. Once a person is able to realize that her life is less a matter of things happening to her and more a matter of her authoring the things that happen, the closer she is to becoming an artist of her own life. (Parry and Doan, 1994 p. 9)

Another goal of narrative therapy as outlined by Allen and Allen (1995) is to help a client to liberate potential stories that have been concealed, bringing up interpretations and possibilities missed or forgotten. The client can then choose the one with which s/he prefers to identify. The therapist can then encourage the client to give him or herself permission to continue to reshape her or his story in a richer fashion.

To use narrative therapy in family therapy, White and Epston (1990) suggests that language be used carefully to uncover previously hidden stories and exceptions to the problem-saturated story. By emphasizing the exceptions through carefully crafted questions, he begins the process of discovering other stories of exception and the times when the client or family has ignored, defeated, or defied the problem. Solution-focused therapies (Berg, 1994; de Shazar, 1985) are similar in this regard. The client is asked to imagine her/his life with the problem already resolved. Each of these techniques seeks to ferret out a narrative that has been covered over and suppressed by the families' current circumstances and a running account of the problem's significance in their lives. White and Epston (1990) see their task as liberating the subjugated knowledges and life stories. Narrative therapy is a hopeful approach that is premised in a collaborative effort between client and therapist. By externalizing the problem and redirecting the problem-saturated story towards uncovering hidden strengths, the therapist is able to help her/his clients deconstruct the oppressive narrative that has compelled them to seek help. The therapist guides the client to re-read the oppressive text and then invites them to author a new narrative, one that is more satisfying, empowering and promising (Freedman & Combs, 1996; Weingarten, 1998; White & Epston, 1990; 1996).

A desirable outcome of therapy is the development of alternative stories that integrate critical and previously ignored aspects of lived experiences, insofar as these stories incorporate alternative knowledges. These alternative stories are often generated through conversations with both the therapist and members of the client's family and community. Including outside resources such as family and community is referred to as building a *community of concern* or *outside witness group* ((Freedman & Combs, 1996, Parry & Doan, 1994, White & Epston, 1990). Indeed, it can be argued that the naming of and providing the space for the performance of these knowledges is a central focus of the therapeutic task. In the case of Ana and Julie, I would bring forward the stories of women of strength from their own histories' commonalities as women and the ways in which they share struggle against patriarchy. In essence, narrative approaches are designed to free individuals and families from their difficulties by helping them verbally construct new mental frameworks that diminish the powerful hold that problems have had in their lives and/or opens new possibilities.

PROCESS AND TECHNIQUES.

Narrative therapy first requires a different sort of listening to the stories that clients bring into the therapy room. This sort of listening involves turning off the expert ear that necessitates listening for diagnostic information. Instead, I listen and try to put myself into the client's shoes. Rather than attempting to sort their stories into the neat categories of pathology, I listen for what I don't know (White & Epston, 1990). Of course, to listen for what you don't know takes both skill and experience. We are trained within the dominant culture to listen only to what is said. It may well be a very particular social role that the therapist fills in being a technician of listening for what is not there or for that which has not yet been said. In this the therapist holds a very different kind of power. In Foucault's terms, this is power as creative force rather than domination or control.

This sort of listening gives the client the opportunity to define the problem that then provides me, as a therapist, with the opportunity to conceptualize the problem as an external entity. By separating the person from the problem, we are given the capability to view the problem from many different angles in order to discover both the strengths and weaknesses of the problem itself. By giving the client the chance to see her/himself apart from the problem we have opened up an alternative viewing of the problem. We are able to determine the many different relationships involved with the problem as well as the differing effects the problem has on persons within the family.

Family members are then given the opportunity to understand their own relationship to the problem and how they might be encouraging the problem in their own lives. Most people, when coming to therapy begin their work by giving a *problem saturated description* (White and Epston, 1990) of the family. They tend to point out the one person in the family they believe to have the problem. By externalizing the problem and separating the problem from the members of the family, the family gains the opportunity to describe themselves, each other, and their relationships from a problem free perspective. This allows an alternative story of the family and family members' relationships to each other to shine through. From this perspective, the family is then able to tease out the essentials of their lives and how the problem has come to interfere and blind them to their preferred reality. By setting aside the problem in this way, families are given the opportunity to describe exceptions to the problem-saturated story that has brought them to me. White and Epston (1990) refer to these exceptions as *sparkling moments* or "unique outcomes" (p.17). As these exceptions are acknowledged, each person is encouraged to "engage in performances of new meaning in relation to them" .

By deconstructing the problem in such a manner, each person involved in the therapeutic process is given the opportunity to examine her/his own relationship with the problem and how it involves her/him. It allows the family to understand that the problem does not belong only to the "identified client," but that each of them has a relationship with the problem and each of them has contributed to sustaining the life of the problem. This in turn gives the entire family the opportunity to come together to take back the control from the oppressive symptom.

Taking back control via the process of externalization and mapping the influence of the problem on the lives of each of the persons involved sounds almost too good to be true. White and Epston (1990) warn therapists not to fall too quickly into universal descriptions of a given situation; rather they should keep in mind the specifics of each circumstance and consider the possible outcomes of particular courses of action. They go on to argue for a level of consciousness on behalf of the therapist. They suggest that:

> Lest the therapist inadvertently contribute to persons' experiences of oppression, this consciousness requires an appreciation of local politics—that is, politics at the level of relationships. This consciousness discourages therapists from inviting the externalizing of problems such as violence and sexual abuse. When these problems are identified, the therapist would be inclined to encourage the externalizing of the attitudes and beliefs that appear to compel the violence, and those strategies that maintain persons in their subjugation, for example, the enforcement of secrecy and isolation. (p. 49)

Once the problem has been situated in such a way that allows for the understanding of the influence of the problem on the lives and relationships of each of the persons involved, it paves the way for the family to begin to explore contradictions to the problem-saturated description of family life and give each member the opportunity to examine her/his own capability and resourcefulness in the face of hardship. In the cultural and gendered context of the familial structure, it can be helpful also to access possible historical accounts of persons contradicting adversity. Examining the influence of the problem across the various intersections of time, location, technology, and culture can provide even more occasions for the family to search for alternative stories to facilitate performance of new meaning.

However, this familial aspect of narrative work has received much less elaboration than other aspects of the work. I believe that in working in a multi-cultural context this aspect is crucial. In the last section of this chapter, I would like to examine a rather traditional approach to the role of multi-generational family relations and then propose a new possibility. In the following section I will explore a very traditional modernist approach to diagramming the family. I am going to do this in order to set the stage for an alternative approach based in more postmodern concepts immediately following this next section.

BOWEN'S THEORY: BACK TO MODERNITY

Family systems theory (Minuchin, 1974) conceptualized the family as an emotional unit that is comprised of a network of interlocking relationships. The family is best understood when analyzed within a multigenerational framework. This theory suggests that individuals cannot be understood in isolation from one another, but rather must be seen as interconnected and interdependent individuals, none of whom can be understood separate from the system. The theory goes further to state that it is not simply the present system that must be understood in order to alleviate distress within the family, the investigation of the distress must include the systems upon which the present family is built (Goldenberg & Goldenberg, 1996; Nichols & Schwartz, 1995). This was very radical thinking at the time of its development in the late 1950s and early 1960s when psychodynamic individual therapy was the predominant model of theory and therapy. The originators of this approach such as Murray Bowen (1990), Richard Fisch, Lynn Segal, and John Weakland (1982), Jay Haley (1978), Salvadour Minuchin (1974), Virginia Satir (1972), and Paul Watzlawick (1974), drew upon the most progressive and radical thinking in science and philosophy. They were deeply influenced by cybernetics, existentialism, and phenomenology, as well as the theories of Ludwig Wittgenstein and Whitehead (see Weakland & Ray, 1995). Nonetheless, in spite of these influences, they were still very modernist in their conceptions of the family as a machine-like system of cause and effect.

Murray Bowen was a pioneer in family systems theory (Goldenberg & Goldenberg, 1996; Nichols & Swartz, 1995). His contribution to seeing the family in the context of many generations was groundbreaking. He centered his analysis on eight (six developed in 1963, two more added in 1975) interlocking concepts. These concepts were tied together by the still quite psychoanalytic premise that chronic anxiety is a universal phenomenon of the human condition. He argued that human beings are living in this state of chronic anxiety, which will manifest itself differently at different times, under different circumstances, under different family situations, and differing cultural considerations.

Bowen centered his theory on two counterbalancing forces: togetherness and individuality (Goldenberg & Goldenberg, 1996; Nichols & Swartz, 1995). Ideally, each of these forces will be in balance with one another and the individual will experience the ability to distinguish between the intellectual process and the feeling process s/he is experiencing. In other words, the individual has a healthy balance between her/his emotional and cognitive processes which is the goal of attaining differentiation of self. We might note that this split between the emotional and cognitive is an extremely modernist concept developed by Rene Decartes (1990) and commonly referred to as the Cartesian split of mind and body. For the purpose of this auto-ethnography, I will focus upon differentiation as the first out of the eight forces that Bowen developed in order to explicate the shaping of family functioning.

Bowen's theory is further guided by the assumption that rooted within each individual is the instinctual drive to become an emotionally separate person able to think, feel, and act as an individual (Goldenberg & Goldenberg, 1996; Nichols & Swartz, 1995). This, of course mirrors the teleological modernist psychoanalytic thinking of Erik Erikson (1980), who proposed individuation as a key element of healthy development. According to Bowen, while individuation is important, at the same time, there is a corresponding instinctual life force to maintain an emotional connection to the family. As a result of these counterbalancing forces, no one ever fully achieves full emotional separation from her/his family of origin. There are however, more or less healthy ways of becoming a well-integrated adult. This is due to the different parental relationships established between children and the degree to which a person is either fused within or differentiated from the family.

Harkening back to systems theory, Bowen argued that families and their systems develop typical ways of being which are reliable and predictable. Drawing on cybernetic theory, he suggested that family roles and family rules are some of the ways in which families maintain their equilibrium, or what in cybernetics was called homeostasis (Fisch et al., 1983; Watzlawick et. al., 1974). Whether these roles and rules are adaptive or not, the chronic anxiety of the family situation begs the system not to change, but rather to remain the same and function as it always has in homeostatic equilibrium. However, when one part of the system moves (does something outside the rules or roles) the rest of the system becomes unbalanced and anxiety is heightened as the system attempts to right itself again. Noteworthy here is the way in which the living complexities of family relations are diagnosed in the same manner that a malfunctioning machine might be analyzed. Of course, these kinds of metaphors harken back to Freud's description of human consciousness in mechanistic terms of force, drives, and so on.

Bowen went on to suggest that during periods of low anxiety and calm external conditions, families will experience greater or lesser degrees of comfortable back and forth exchanges usually between dyads. When an increasing degree of anxiety is experienced, a dyad will pull in a third person by either channeling their emotional energy into the third party or the third person may be emotionally programmed to initiate involvement. Either way, the addition of the third party serves to defuse the anxiety felt by the dyad. Once the anxiety within this triangular relationship resolves, the emotional configuration returns to that of the peaceful dyad. However, should the anxiety within the triangle become too much, one of the persons within that triangle may reach out to an additional person creating yet another triangle and so on until any number of people both within and outside of the family may become involved. The higher degree of fusion within a particular family system, the more persistent and powerful the formation of triangles becomes. Deleuze and Guattari (1987) have critiqued this model of triangulation as being rooted in the fundamental Oedipal triangle proposed by Freud (1991). They argue that this model is far too reductionistic to be applied to complex living systems.

Bowen would argue that the triangle is the smallest stable relationship system; therefore, a two-person system is always unstable. The triangle is meant to offset and equalize the anxieties experienced by the two-person dyad. When anxiety becomes too much for the triangle to contain, more and more persons are pulled into the system and the system may become a series of interlocking triangles and leaving multiple triangulations to be resolved.

Bowen would assert that all generations are a part of the person's acquired ability to differentiate and shape the individual "self". The process of transmission occurs at many levels within the family including the active shaping of an offspring via the conscious teaching of information as well as the unconscious programming of emotional responses. Bowen goes on to say that each child within the family will likely formulate either a greater or lesser degree of differentiation than their parents and that each of them in turn will seek out a life partner with a similar level of differentiation. This pattern will continue to repeat itself through the subsequent generations producing families with more or less functioning than the generation before. Those with poorer differentiation are increasingly vulnerable to anxiety and fusion. As this vulnerability is transmitted through the generations, ultimately a level of impairment is reached that is consistent with dysfunction. However, this mapping of progressive degeneration did not offer me the kind of information that I wanted to use in this auto-ethnography to explore patterns of multigenerational power among women.

Bowen's modernist model that covertly expands psychoanalytic diagrams firmly rooted in modernist concepts of teleology, progressm and cause/effect, is particularly problematic if we wish to engage a culturally competent model of psychotherapy. Like Malinowski's failed anthropological project to prove that the Oedipal triangle is a cross-cultural phenomenon (Spiro, 1993), Bowen's expansion of the triangle to the social world of the family as an ever-expanding array of triangles is also rooted in peculiarly Euro-centric notions of the universality of structure. I will argue in the next section that there may be another mode of analysis that allows both more cultural flexibility and that steps outside the scientific approach of modern Euro-centric thought.

FEMINIST NARRATIVE THERAPY AND COMMUNITY

One of the fundamental techniques of narrative therapy is the mapping of the influence of others (White & Epston, 1990). This mapping helps to illustrate how important others can be in the ways we know things. This is knowledge held in common in the relationships and roles biologically ascribed in Western families, such as mother, sister, parent, cousin, and aunt as well as the knowledge held by multiple people who hold these roles through non-biological social history. Transmission of power, knowledge and creative force between generations of women is not necessarily only between two people or even between two people related by blood; although, very probably, certain rhythms and biological sensibilities are only available through these channels. Nonetheless, the binary structure of the traditional genogram proposed by Bowen is exploded in lived relational experiences into a multiplicity of women all educating each other through the stories they tell and the experiences they share. Like Lynn Hoffman's (2000) metaphor of the braided challah to describe the interweaving of therapeutic traditions in her work, I use the symbol of the Celtic knot to signify the pattern of knowing that women weave across generations and which sustains their infinite creative force. We reach back and bring forward knowledge and creativity and combine it with new knowleges and technologies to create a fluid, endlessly intertwining construction of creative force. This is not only meaningful to us in our current time, but also to our daughters, nieces, grandchildren, cousins, and sisters as well as our mothers, grandmothers and ancestors.

As feminist therapists we must always place ourselves first in relation to the women we see as both mothers and daughters. We have to recognize, as Luce Irigaray (1993) pointed out, the mutual interdependence of feminine knowledge. We must give way to the shape-shifting ability to become mothers to our mothers and daughters to our daughters. Unlike patriarchal knowledge, women's ways of knowing do not flow from mother to daughter in a top down fashion, but are mutually created in the collision between generational worlds. Of course the barrier to these conversations lies in the "dominant discourses that produce and sustain the status of those who have power against the competing discourses of those on the margins of society, like women, ethnic minorities, old people, and poor people" (Hare-Mustin, 1994, p. 2).

When we see family situations within the Bowenian framework, we impose a dominant discourse of binary hierarchy and western notions of individuality. These dominant discourses hold a "presumption of essential gender characteristics [that] mask the relations of power" (p. 3). Hare-Mustin cites Waldegrave as suggesting that "therapy enshrines patriarchal meaning, supporting rather than challenging hierarchies of gender" (p. 8). If we wish genuinely to explore the relationship of power between mother and daughter, we must step aside from the traditional models of familial flow. We must look to a more female centered way of knowing that is focused on mother/daughter relations, and that violates both the teleological and special restrictions of patriarchal genealogical models.

As Janet Lee (1997, p. 10) points out, "[m]uch feminist psychology has been a movement toward understanding, getting in touch with, and/or revaluing a feminine subjectivity that has often been defined in somewhat static and universalizing ways." This means that to be a subject who is gendered as woman is to be produced socially as more than simply a reaction to patriarchal practice. If we are to conceptualize the transmission of power between women then we must find a way to see the relationship between female subjects as radically distinct. We must "...pay attention to gendered meta-narratives and specifically analyze the social construction and interpersonal co-constructions of meaning engaged in by women as marginalized persons" (Lee, 1997, p.11). To do this, we, as feminist therapists, as mothers to our own daughters, as daughters to our own mothers, rather than therapist to client "must pay attention to [our] own self-narratives and [be] in touch with [our] own meaning constructions...feminist narrative therapists must be aware of their own stories as well as the way they co-create therapeutic stories over the course of treatment" (p. 12). This means resisting the impulse to pathologize women's problems and instead seek new avenues that explore deviance and difference as creative force.

TREES AND GENOGRAMS

The genogram as proposed by Bowen (1990) is modeled on the traditional family tree. The family tree in turn is modeled on the arborescent structure that sustains the systems of dominance. "The tree in western thought according to Deleuze and Guattari (1987) is premised on "the oldest and weariest kind of thought" (p. 5). That is to say, "the tree or root as an image, endlessly develops the law of the one that becomes two then the two that become four…Binary logic is the spiritual reality of the root tree" (p. 5). In this, we recognize from the previous discussion of modernity with its dualisms and binary constructions of this and that (man/woman, adult/child, right/wrong, and so on), that the logic of the tree is that of a hierarchy and totalizing principles. The tree is also teleological in the sense that it starts from a root, which splits into a trunk, with splits into branches that go higher and higher, and extend out into binary formations that become smaller and smaller.

The genogram contains this structure upside down. That is to say, the root is at the top and the binary splits occur as the chart descends down the page. The genogram as a tree structure is premised in the normative family structures of heterosexual reproduction and centres on male/female binaries that produce children who produce binaries that produce children who produce binaries, and so on. According to Bowen, various forms of pathology flow down this structure over succeeding generations with ever-greater intensity. The genogram is rooted in the idea that "in order to arrive at two…it must assume a strong principle unity" (p. 5). Similarly, in order to read a genogram, one must have an overarching system of representation that allows one to act as though things such as family structure and psychopathology are uniform across time and generations with the only variation being the ways these forms are conformed to or deviated from. As Deleuze and Guattari (1987) point out, this ignores the possibility of the multiplicity. If we are to think about this in a different way, we can provide a new model to think about lineage and the transmission of power.

CHAPTER 8

A VISION OF DIFFERENCE: A GENOGRAM OF FLIGHT

While in the throes of trying to describe what it is that I do when people come to consult with me; while I'm trying to tease apart what a therapeutic conversation might look like; while I'm trying to formulate a way to describe a family system via a line of flight and attempting to include the transformative possibilities of each family member living or dead, I take a break to go to Buffalo to a museum with some friends. We are there to see a particular artist named Petah Coyne. Her work is mesmerizing, ethereal, mystical, and spiritual. Her pieces use unusual mediums that attract and repulse, yet fit skillfully into her desire to communicate the contradictions of the human condition. She makes use of an unusual assortment of materials including wax, wire, car parts, religious statues, taxidermy, hair, and cast off or recycled objects. The effect of her work is beautiful and disturbing and seems to speak of the tragedy, complexity, and exquisiteness of life and death all at once. Many of the sculptures in this exhibit are Madonnas hidden beneath layers of wax flowers, ribbons, beads, twigs, wax covered leaves, and hair with the tiniest fragment of a face peering through as though refusing to be fully consumed by her circumstances. In other pieces, taxidermied birds lie buried under thickly webbed areas and, like the Madonna's faces, are barely visible. They seem to be captured in that moment of transition between life and death like the Phoenix that had been caught just before bursting into flames. The exhibit seemed to compel one to meditate on the ephemeral moments of our own lives and contemplate our own transformations, mystical or otherwise.

The piece that caught my breath was Coyne's family tree that she created after the untimely death of her brother. The piece is created out of braided horsehair that is frayed at the ends giving the effect of infinitude, of pointing toward endless possibilities in every which direction. The "tree" is flattened against the wall horizontally and the dark hair appears to be in flight while also resembling a rhizomatic configuration. The rhizomes attach themselves to various "nests," and in each nest rests a taxidermied bird. One nest is eerily empty and one can assume that it is that of her deceased brother. The empty nest is sad, yet also hopeful in that it remains a part of the rhizome and therefore continues to hold promise for the whole of the rhizomatic structure.

TOWARD A GENOGRAM OF FLIGHT

I have proposed the possibility of a new genogram that allows for a mapping (not a tracing) of power as creative force that pools or collects within bodies as sets of capacities that can only be expressed in the collision with other bodies that sets these capacities into flight in all directions at once. Deleuze and Guattari (1987) posit the form of the rhizome against the arborescent structure of the tree. They state that "…unlike trees or their roots, the rhizome connects any point with any other point, and none of its features necessarily refers to features of the same kind…" (p. 47). In other words the rhizome is not a binary structure, nor is it teleological. The rhizome according to Deleuze and Guattari (1987) runs under the surface and connects to all points at once. It "doesn't allow itself to be reduced to the one or the many" (p. 47). It is continuous and extensive, a multiplicity that goes in all directions at once.

If we are to think about a new form of genogram, which allows us to map the lived experience of women and other subjugated groups, I would argue that it is necessary to step aside from the old patriarchal tracings of linear hierarchy. As therapists it would be helpful to have maps that acknowledge the ongoing creative and complex interconnections between our lives, the lives we encounter in our work, and ourselves. Through new mappings, we may be able to find a way to flee our own rigid conceptions of the people we encounter as unities or predictable hierarchies of force. In other words, we could do with a mapping; not of boundaries and territories that capture our relations within webs of diagnosis and pathology, but one of lines of escape. In sort, we need what Deleuze and Guattari (1987) call a line of flight.

A line of flight cuts across the boundaries and territories of the social, de-territorializing all structures that it crosses. That is to say, it disrupts conventional sets of meanings and opens them to creative uncertainty. Coyne's family tree, which I found in the Buffalo museum that day, is evocative of just such a mapping of flight. Of course, any representation of our relations will be reductive and incomplete. At the same time, however, it has the capacity to make connections in all directions at once. These connections might include a vast array of possible objects and activities, which could include art, music, conversations, memories, and reflections. Each of these produces rhizomatic lines of flight that put creative force into play between us in our coming together within the counseling encounter.

LINEAGE OF STRONG WOMEN STANDING BEHIND ME

I remember a client I once saw who referenced as her source of strength "a line of women standing behind me." While working with Ana, she brought into our conversation the many contradictory voices of the women in her life. She was particularly confused by her desire to bring some sort of spirituality back into her "deviant" life. She seemed to me to be caught between the stories of women as the virginal Madonna (la Virgen de Guadalupe) and women as whores (La Malinche). Like the Steppenwolf in Hermann Hesse's novel by the same name, she had two selves doing battle with each other. She seemed to be attracted to the bourgeois world with its quiet respectability and saintliness, while at the same time being equally drawn toward the desires of the flesh and the attainment of momentary pleasure. Ana was struggling with the many dichotomies that she faced in her life. She, like me, had been brought up between worlds. She had been taught to reject her "non-white" self in order to be acceptable to the white world to which her father and her father's mother so desperately wanted to belong. At the same time, she was being encouraged to discover her Latina world, which to her, felt familiar and comfortable.

Obviously, given what I have described above as a genealogy of flight, these binary formations of either/or need to be exploded into a new rhizomatic proliferation of possibility. One way to begin this process is to have Ana speak with several of the people living, dead, and imaginary who have had an impact on her life. I would ask the reader to bear witness to a series of small conversations in which the women in Ana's life offer her a multitude of perspectives to which she responds. We might imagine ourselves watching Ana sitting in a circle of women, each passing a "talking stick" between Ana and themselves with each offering Ana a small gift to which she responds in kind.

THE CONVERSATIONS.

Mor Mor (maternal Norwegian grandmother): Ana, you must be a strong woman and take good care of your family. It is the duty of a good Norwegian woman to be industrious and productive. You must never allow yourself to become dependent upon anyone. Keep to yourself and don't draw attention to yourself and you will be safe.

Ana: Thank you, Mor Mor, for giving me the desire to be productive in my life. I will use this to become a strong and independent woman. I will take this further for you, mor mor, and show you, my friends, my sister, my mother, and other women that we are fully capable of caring for ourselves and supporting each other.

Abuela (paternal Latina grandmother): Model yourself after the Madonna. She is a kind and compassionate woman. She is strong and devoted. She is the mother of the orphans.

Ana: The Virgin is the consolation of the poor, the shield of the weak, the help of the oppressed. I appreciate that you helped me to understand why Mary has been so important to you. I understand now why you asked me to respect her and to be like her. Thank you Abuela, I will honour you by honouring her.

Chola: Yes, the Madonna. But not the alabaster faced Madonna that the nuns here teach us about. You have to learn about the Black Madonna. She helps women of all races and cultures to resist oppression and gives us the power of the feminine. This Madonna asks us to embrace our sexuality and be proud of who we are as women. Black Madonna is the great mother who presides not only over fertility but also over life and death. She wouldn't want us to sit back and be careful with our lives out of fear. She would want us to make our mark, to take up the cause of the oppressed and do something with the strength and compassion that we as women experience. She would not ask us to succumb to the voices of deceit, nor those that divide each of us from one another, but provides us a connection with the many.

Ana: Chola, you have given me the freedom to accept and explore my culture, my history and my desires. I have been trapped by the insistence on culturally defining the world by a rigid set of black/white, good/bad, clean/dirty divisions, versus the reality of individuality, uniqueness, and unlimited difference. Together we can make a difference in the lives of other women by raising their awareness of the oppressive nature of living under these strict double definitions. I will help you, Chola, to embrace the beauty of all that you are and stand up to those who would cast you in a critical light.

Catholic nun: Your grandmother is right; we do model ourselves after the Madonna. But I think that you misunderstand her significance to us. She is kind, compassionate, strong, and devoted, but not in a way that makes her subservient. She stands up for the weak, the oppressed, the sick, and the criminal. She sees the good in everyone and works very hard to help them see that in themselves.

Ana: This is what I want for people to understand! We don't have to submit ourselves to someone else's whims in order to be helpful. That we can use our compassion for more than simply dressing wounds, that we can be compassionate *and* political.

The activist: Then don't just sit on your ass. Do something! Political things—culture, community organizing, etc. Find a cause;

debunk the mythologies around Latina women. Help Latina men and women to find pride in who they are.

Ana: I see what you mean. It doesn't do any good to be angry about a situation. I can use that anger to organize and to bring together people with similar thinking. People who would otherwise roll over and let the situation win. There are too many misunderstandings about and within the Latino community that are getting in the way of our emancipation.

The student: But hey! Nobody is going to listen to a drop out; you need to find out about life and your passions from the inside out. Learn everything you can about the reasons and myths behind the lies that support the oppression of your people and you will be stronger that the other side.

Ana: My education can be my weapon. If I have knowledge of both sides, I will be a more effective advocate.

The drunk: It's too much; just drink your troubles away. No, that would be too easy wouldn't it? Simply to give in to a world of drunken misery and let everyone pity your sorry ass. Sometimes it does feel like too much, and you may need to take some time to stumble about in your pain. But don't let it be worthless. You can use that pain to move forward in your life. Devote yourself to climbing out of such a pit of despair by doing something about it. It is an amazing feeling to stand with the people you helped and together celebrate your liberation.

Ana: You're saying that I don't have to give up the celebratory aspect of drinking, or even the moodiness that sometimes comes with drinking. I need to understand that while I may need to feel the sorrow and misery that accompany life, I can acknowledge and grow with those experiences.

The gangsters: We need to come together as a community to prove to them that we are strong. They need to be afraid of us. We can use violence and weapons to get our point across. We are family and we stick together. I got your back; you got mine.

The chola: I agree with everything that you are saying except that we don't need to use violence. We can show our strength by supporting each other and taking on the enemy with our minds.

Ana: This is why I have found the gang to be so appealing. It's people my own age coming together and making a difference. It may not be the most productive difference, but I can understand how having a community can be a very empowering experience.

Mom: If you can hear anything that I tell you, hear this. Your family is right, your friends are right, even the drunk is right. But use what they say wisely. You have all of the power of each of these women and happen to be gifted with wisdom beyond your years. People pay attention to you in ways that they never did for me. I believe that you are capable of anything that you put your mind to. Like the drunk said, it is too much, but only if you go it alone. You have a vast assemblage of family and friends who will support you in your struggle.

Ana: Thank you mom, for never giving up on me. It seemed at times that you were the only one who didn't assume that I was inherently bad. You stood by and let me explore all of the possibilities within both of my cultures and let me sort it out. I have a much greater appreciation for, what seemed at times, your stoic strength.

Paternal Aunt: Your father is difficult and he doesn't know how to talk to you. He was raised never to question his parents' advice, to be obedient, and to expect that the women in the family would take care of the home while he went out and earned the family money. He has high expectations for you but also just wants you to be happy. He has grown up struggling against so much that he wants you simply to rise above it all and take advantage of the row he's hoed for you. He can't quite get his head around why you want to go back to the life he worked so hard to leave behind. He doesn't understand why it's so important for you to reclaim the history he's trying to forget.

Ana: Thank you, auntie, for helping me to better understand why my father seems to be so distant from me. I now have a better understanding of the struggle that he went through and what he denied in himself to try to make a better life for me. I realize now that some of the hardness that I feel in myself I learned from him. That hardness is something that can be useful when you need to push through life but my father lost his ability to be tender. I don't ever want to lose that ability.

MY REFLECTION

Of course the above scenario seems to put things into a package that is too neat and tidy. However, I have experienced such conversations with clients that have given insight into the difficulties between generations. I will always be grateful to that wise client who said, after a real time conversation with her grandmother, that she felt as if she had "a lineage of wise women standing behind [her]" understanding and transforming their struggles into a more powerful and fulfilling life for them all.

What is gleaned from exploring such conversations is the ability to move beyond the either/or experiences of modernity and into a both/and understanding of postmodernity. Ana seemed to be receiving conflicting information, not only from the maternal and paternal sides of her family, but from *within* each culture as well. The message that brought her into conflict with her mother and her Norwegian family was the stoicism and the training to remain below the radar, not to create waves. Ana viewed both her mother as well as her grandmother as weak and submissive for not standing up to the oppressive roles dictated to them by their culture. What Ana failed to see, initially, was that her mother's "friendly divorce" was an act of defiance against a gender based relationship with Ana's father. Ana's mother had made the decision to keep working in spite of her husband's protestations to the contrary, which was one of the reasons cited for getting divorced. Ana's grandmother instilled in all of her daughters and her granddaughters a sense of pride in being "industrious and independent." While Ana's grandmother acted out her independence within the boundaries of marriage, she supported her daughter's decision to assert her independence by divorcing Ana's father.

Ana's paternal grandmother provided Ana with access to her culture's fascination with the Madonna. Initially, Ana saw her grandmother's fixation with the Madonna as oppressive and manipulative on the part of the church and the community; a way to keep Mexican women "in their place" within the family. Ana came to understand through her grandmother's devotion to the Catholic faith and her own exploration of the Black Madonna, the strength and wisdom bestowed upon all Latina women. Ana began to see that her faith did not have to be an either/or proposition but a both/and possibility. By clearing away the binary formation of good versus evil within the Catholic community, Ana was able to align herself with the message of compassion and strength to be used as powerful lines of flight for all of the women in her family, both living and dead. She began to see each generation of women as moving forward and performing their own resistance each in accord with their moment in history. She stopped seeing her grandmother as weak and cowardly, but as a woman of fortitude and wisdom. She began to see that the Chola and the Drunk were not simply acting out in defiance, but taking up where her grandmothers and mother had left off. Once Ana was able to breakdown the binaries of the good/bad, virgin/whore, assertive/oppressed women in her life and accept all that was offered, she was able to take on the role of the feminist activist and reach out to other young women struggling to find their way within such a confusing moment in history. This was not only beneficial to Ana, but to her sister, her mother, her grandmothers, and her cousins, as they bore witness to the ways in which Ana was able to honour each of the worlds/cultures/women with whom she had contact.

Through Ana's story, we can see that feminine power is passed on by the ways in which each generation takes all of what came before them and transforms it into a line of force idiosyncratic to their own singular set of capacities and the demands of their own historical moment. The role of the therapist is to elicit this process, to support the client in finding such a rich resource without being caught in binary constructions of pathology/health, good/bad, and normal/abnormal behaviours.

To do this work well, however, we have to deconstruct the architecture of domination which we each carry within us—we must eschew the poisoned gifts of white privilege that separate us from one another. We, as therapists, counselors, and healers, can heal ourselves. Our "clients" can be great teachers in this work, if we let them. We have the opportunity to recognize that all our work is an auto-ethnography, a personal crucible of mutual transformation for everyone in the room of healing we call the therapy room. It is a political space, a revolutionary space, and a space through which to find the openings to new worlds.

Indeed, we must never forget the immense power of people in relation with one another.

Part III
Foucault and Power in Child Protection
Helen Gibbs

CHAPTER 9

BURNT OUT

> Good practitioners are uncomfortable about so much of the child protection agenda. But the bandwagon rolls on and the procedures manual gets fatter and fatter. And the good practitioners leave in their droves, frustrated, burnt out, but often without the language or the conceptual knowledge to challenge the very premise upon which the whole 'child protection' edifice is built. (Smith, 2003, p. 2)

After six years of employment at a child protection agency I was one of those workers who left frustrated with the system. One of my main complaints was that I could not reconcile the philosophical and ideological differences between the way that I thought families, children, and youth should be provided service and the service they actually received. On top of that, I was frustrated being "a cog in the wheel", with me being one of those who provided insufficient service. I was tired of seeing the "failures" (moving children from placement to placement, youth running away or being arrested) as my fault, and tired of criticizing myself for not having done more to "help".

In stepping away from the system and looking back at my experience, I wanted a conceptual tool that would assist me in putting the complaints I had in some context. I was aware that I was not alone in my frustration with the system. For years, the child welfare system has been under criticism from radical, socialist, Marxist, and feminist social workers regarding the way problems are identified and treated (de Montigny, 1995a). Even my fellow colleagues said numerous times that the system "may be broken but it is the only one we've got." It set me wondering what it is about the child protection system that creates such criticism and frustration.

There is little argument that the child protection system is under a great deal of pressure to keep children and youth safe from abuse. With limited financial resources and increased calls to investigate, workers in the child protection system are faced with a tremendously difficult job. It is not surprising, then, that staff turnover is often high within child protection agencies (Kammerman & Kahn, 1989). Research studies have identified the factors that contribute to staff turnover and burnout (see Baumann, Kern, McFadden, & Law, 1997; Figley, 1995; Fletcher, 1982; Fryer, Miyoshi & Thomas, 1989). It is important to note that there is a distinction made between turnover and burnout because some workers who are dissatisfied remain on the job (Rycraft, 1994). Within the literature, burnout is defined as "a syndrome of emotional exhaustion, depersonalization of clients, and feelings of reduced personal accomplishment" (Anderson, 2000, p. 840). Maslach and Jackson (1986) use a similar definition as the basis for the development of the Maslach Burnout Inventory (MBI), which has become the most widely used instrument for measuring burnout (Stalker & Harvey, 2002). Anderson (2000) reports that the following factors contribute to staff turnover and burnout: personal stressors experienced by the worker, such as trying to balance the demands of his/her own family's needs with the demands of the job; job requirements, such as dealing with the risk that a child on his/her caseload may get injured or neglected; and the work environment, such as dealing with a high number of cases and limited agency support.

Flower and Hughes (1973) suggest that understanding why workers remain in the job is equally, if not more important, than exploring why workers have left. I would suggest that greater emphasis within research is needed to examine how workers deal with the frustrations of the job. This is important because how workers view the agency and their own role has an impact on the quality of service they provide. For example, Maslach (1982) reports that if workers are frustrated they are unable to relate warmly or consistently to clients' needs.

A significant piece of research that described the struggles of doing child protection work was de Montigny's (1995a) book *Social Working: An Ethnography of Front-Line Practice*. Using Dorothy Smith's work, de Montigny examines people's lived worlds in a way that addresses socially organized practice, lived activities, and actual forms of work. Although de Montigny presents an exceptional description of the ways in which child protection workers are pressured to maintain discursive practices, such as writing documents that attempt to put coherence and order to chaotic and complex family situations, he does not spend much time addressing how and why both workers and clients resist these practices. Another critique of de Montigny's work is that there is little discussion on how the day-to-day interactions he had with his clients had an impact on him. Shulman (1985) states that this is important to consider as, "any attempt to understand practice would need to focus on the dynamic interaction between worker and client, each affecting and being affected by the other" (p. 276). He points out that "this complicated interaction" between worker and client does not occur in a "vacuum", but rather is situated within an agency setting and influenced by a number of factors. Shulman cites examples such as worker caseload, supervision and agency practices as having a powerful impact on the interactions between workers and clients. I would concur with Shulman that these factors play a role in shaping interactions between workers and clients. However, I would also add to this list the relationship of power.

CHAPTER 10

AUTHORITY AND POWER

There is very little research that addresses how child protection workers handle the power that is assigned to them due to their position. One study addresses the issue of power by distinguishing it from the concept of authority. Palmer (1983) argues that authority derives from power, but the two are not synonymous. Palmer uses McIver's definition of power, which is the capacity to control the behaviour of others, and authority, which is "the established right to make decisions on pertinent issues" (Palmer, 1983, p. 120), to suggest that authority requires the consent of the "other" in order for a helping relationship to be established (1983, p. 120). Palmer suggests that social workers must learn to use authority if they are to be effective and should encourage their clients to grant them authority. What Palmer fails to incorporate into this discussion is how "the established right" of social workers to have authority has been socially constructed and used so that the population can be regulated, managed, and controlled. So even though Palmer suggests that clients have the ability to choose whether or not they grant authority, it is not acknowledged that this choice has limits. For example, social workers are the "gatekeepers" to accessing resources (e.g., therapy and welfare allowances) or in the case of child protection, determine whether or not a family will be subject to certain types of intervention (e.g., apprehension of child). Palmer does not address what the implications are for clients who refuse to grant authority. Also Palmer does not address what it feels like for social workers to have to make decisions *on* clients versus *with* clients. What impact does this have on the worker? Does it have an impact on the workers' view of their jobs and their views on authority and in turn how they conduct their work with clients?

POWER AND THE CHILD WELFARE SYSTEM

When I explained to people that I was examining issues of power in the child welfare system, I heard time and time again a response like "Oh, you mean how the Children's Aid Society has the power and the clients don't?" At first, these comments were frustrating to me but I realized that there appears to be a general opinion about child welfare that the agency has all the power and the clients are dominated by a powerful, all- encompassing system. Research studies have reported that parents experienced the child protection system as *oppressive* (Wilford & Hetherington, 1997) or as the *enemy* (Callahan, Lumb, & Wharf, 1994) However, having been a worker within the system I came away with a different view of how power was exercised. In my view, the power relationship between the worker, the agency, and the client was much more complicated, complex, and interrelated. Here, Foucault's writings on power provide a theoretical framework to think about the child welfare system in a different way.

FOUCAULT AND POWER.

"Power," Foucault wrote, "is everywhere" (1978, p. 93). Foucault stresses that power should be understood as relational, in that it occurs *between* individuals and groups. This is in contrast to theories that view certain individuals and groups as having power—such as the ruling political party or police officers—while others do not. Foucault (1980 a, b) provides a framework of how to examine power relationships, which I follow for this project. First, Foucault stresses that notions of "truth" should be questioned. Rather than accepting dominant knowledge or discourses about concepts such as "youth," "family," and "child protection," Foucault emphasized that they be examined as historical constructs (Foucault, 1994). Second, we need to examine how the process of subjectification is inscribed upon individuals as well as how individuals take part in, use and resist their subjectivity. By engaging in this process, new forms of knowledge about “youth,” “family,” and “child protection” become available. Therefore this auto-ethnography is an examination into the power relationships to which I was subjected, by which I was constituted, and that I reproduced, as a worker in the child protection system.

CHAPTER 11

HISTORY OF THE FAMILY, YOUTH AND CHILD PROTECTION

The purpose of this chapter is to examine the development of perceptions about youth, families and the child protection system within a historical framework. By tracing the changes in these concepts we can begin to understand how current perceptions have become embedded in Western culture. There are two benefits to engaging in this process. First, by peeling away the layers of "fact" associated with youth, families, and child protection we can see that they are social constructions developed from the middle and upper class concerns about the state. Second, this process will determine that perceptions of youth, families, and child protection have not remained stagnant, as they are subject to changing societal, political, and economic environments.

The first part of the chapter will be divided into the following sections:

> 1) the creation of adolescence, which discusses how the period of adolescence became constructed as a distinct stage, controlled and supervised by various rules and institutions; 2) the creation of the family as an institution, which gives an overview of how families have been designated as the primary agent for looking after adolescents, with each member prescribed particular roles; and 3) the creation of the child protection system,

whereby social workers were designated as the "experts" to infiltrate family life and promote the expectations of appropriate parenting. The second part of this chapter consists of the theoretical underpinnings that are guiding this writing. Foucault's notion of governmentality and power relations will be explored with an emphasis on how these two concepts facilitate a critical analysis of my role as a social worker within a child protection system.

CREATION OF ADOLESCENCE

It needs to be acknowledged that outlining the history of youth is a complex task, since these experiences are shaped by numerous factors such as context, location, gender, class, and religion. As well, the terms children, childhood, youth, adolescence, and teenager are often used interchangeably. However, what these terms have in common is their distinction as separate from adult or adulthood. As Calvert (1998) suggests, it is important to look at why adolescence became so important, especially from the early twentieth century onward, for what purpose, and what have been the advantages and disadvantages.

YOUTH.

There has been a lengthy debate about the beginnings of childhood, youth, and adolescence. Much of this debate has stemmed from the ambiguity that has existed around the transition from childhood to adulthood. Some have argued that in medieval times, there was no distinction made between adults and children (Aries, 1962), in that they were in institutions together, "subject to the same disciplinary and supportive societal forces" (Tait, 2000, p. 25). Ackland (1995) states that prior to the modern period, the transition between childhood and adulthood was relatively quick and unremarkable. He states:

> The in-between stage of youth did not always exist as it does today. Phillipe Aries (1962) has shown that in Medieval Europe, the movement from child to adult was instantaneous. "Once he had passed the age of five or seven, the child was immediately absorbed into the world of adults: this concept of a brief childhood lasted for a long time in the lower classes". In the seventeenth century, "by the age of ten, girls were already little women: a precocity due in part to an upbringing which taught

> girls to behave very early in life like grown-ups." (Ackland, 1995, p. 26)

In contrast, Ross Beales (1975), for example, cites convincing evidence that Puritans in seventeenth century New England were well aware of developmental differences between infants, youth, and adults. Within the literature, there appears to be a fair bit of cross over between the beginnings of childhood and adolescence. Koops and Zuckerman (2003) indicate that the story of adolescence is the same as the one concerning childhood. It is not uncommon to find historians who refer to childhood but address this age group up and through what we now refer to as the teenage years. The approach that I have taken is to suggest that at first there was a distinction made between children and adults, and then a lengthening of the ages of childhood occurred. In order to explore how modern adolescence became defined as a period separate from adulthood, I first examine how childhood became separated. I then explore how the lengthening of childhood developed as the use of institutions (e.g., schools) responded to concerns about youth behaviour, especially working-class youth.

Several theorists have agreed that from the eighteenth century onward, the conceptualization of childhood, which was encapsulated in the middle-class or bourgeois family model as a period of dependency requiring moral and physical care within a family, informed child-rearing practices and reform initiatives (see Donzelot, 1979; Foucault, 1980b; Rooke & Schnell, 1982). Campaigns were implemented to prevent children from working, and focused on getting them in to systematic sex-specific schooling and monitoring their leisure activities (Fitz, 1981). However, by the late nineteenth century, although many middle-class children experienced childhood as a period of dependency, most working-class children did not. Despite the laws that had been put in place to regulate children's participation in work (e.g. Factory Acts), many children continued to labour in the unregulated areas of agriculture, domestic service, mining, and retail shops (Chunn, 2003). Attendance at school was still under parental discretion and the leisure time of working-class children was predominantly free from adult supervision.

Specifically in North America, it was during the late-nineteenth century that provincial statues and municipal by-laws were enacted and extended to prohibit child labour altogether in factories, mines, shops, and street trades (Houston, 1982). At the same time, compulsory attendance laws enforced that all children were required to participate in school up to a certain age and parents were subject to sanctions if they did not comply (Sutherland, 1976). Leisure activities of children and youth, particularly among the working classes, were also regulated. Vagrancy acts and curfews are just a few examples of how children and youth were monitored. The behaviour of girls, especially in relation to sexuality, was specifically targeted from the 1880s onward. Laws were enacted that both protected and controlled girls' behaviour. For example, in the 1892 Criminal Code, a number of wide-ranging categories of offences were added to protect girls from "male sexual predators" (Snell, 1983, p. 118). At the same time, laws were also put into place that made abortion and birth control illegal (McLaren, 1978).

Earlier I stated that once the distinction was made between children and adults, the period of childhood was systematically extended. This is very evident when the participation of children and youth in school is considered. In 1920, 28 percent of American youths between the ages of fourteen and seventeen were in high school; by 1930, 47 percent of this age group was attending high school (Spring, 1994). In the following section, I examine how the period of adolescence was lengthened in response to concerns raised by the psychological movement, as well as economic shifts and the creation of the welfare state.

ADOLESCENCE.

The burgeoning distinction between adolescence and adulthood became widespread during the early twentieth century and efforts were made to "universalize and to democratize the concept of adolescence" (Kett, 1977, p.215). The field of psychology played a significant role in distinguishing the characteristics and behaviours of this age group. The concern that adolescents were not in a position to make mature decisions was partly based on G. Stanley Hall's series of books. Hall (1916) viewed adolescents as "torn by dualisms which disrupted the harmony of childhood; hyperactivity and inertia, social sensibility and self-absorption, lofty intuitions and childish folly." In short, Hall professed that children and youth were not "ready for life, and that [he] had to be subjected to special treatment, a sort of quarantine, before he was allowed to join the adults" (p. 412).

However, not all of Hall's writings were supported by theorists of various persuasions who followed him (Adams, 1997). Whereas Hall (1916) suggested that adolescents should be "allowed free play, a full draining out or catharsis" (p. 411) and that adolescent faults should be viewed as instinctive urges and not placed under repression, the emphasis on controlling young people increased. Why was this ignored? One way to explore this is to examine the social context. Some sociologists and historians have argued that constructions of adolescence can be matched to parallel economic shifts. Enright and colleagues (1987) argue that in times of economic depression, theories that depicted adolescence as a period of immaturity requiring a prolonged period of separation from adult roles dominated. However, in wartime and during labour shortages, theories arose emphasizing the abilities and psychological competence of adolescents that negated the need for preparation.

Another way to examine how constructions of adolescence were developed is to consider the creation of the welfare state. The welfare state was concerned with the individual and social welfare of its citizens. Public institutions that managed children's lives, developmentally and educationally, and the emphasis on children's "best interests" served to change the way young people were treated (Goldson, 1997). Here, Kett's (1977) definition of adolescence as "the period after puberty during which a young person is institutionally segregated from casual contacts with a broad range of adults" (p. 36) reflects more accurately the experiences of young people aged 13 to 20. The types of settings and work in which young people were engaged became of great interest. The increase in factories and technology and the instituting of laws around work environments left many young people without work (Tanner, 2001). This resulted in further concerns as young people who had too much free time were considered to be a risk to society. Tanner (2001) argued that extending the age of attendance at school was a means to retain boys, especially, and keep them off the streets. The introduction and then later the enforcement of schooling for all children regardless of social class and gender, and the lengthening of school attendance to age 16, withdrew their full participation from the family but left them dependent on their families for longer periods of time. This had significant implications for some youth. For much of the nineteenth century, independence in youth, which was defined as a willingness to strike out on one's own, had been a precondition for success. However, "by 1900 such desires for independence and autonomy were viewed as prescriptions for failure" (Kett, 1977, p 36.)

Teenager.

With an increased number of adolescents out of the workforce and in the school system, adolescence became a "generation" recognized more by their common experience of age than by the class, racial or ethnicity-based differences that separated them (Knight Abowitz, & Rees, 2005). In this process, a youth culture began to form in America that included an increased emphasis on consumerism and the availability of information and recreation through the media (Danesi, 1994, p. 3). The symbolism of teenagers became closely connected with goods and services, as magazines, record shops, clothing, new dances, foods, and cars were carefully aimed to appeal to this age group (Palladino, 1996). Over the past fifty years, the success of young people as consumers has intensified the marketing towards this age group, such that, rather than having just a few styles to choose from, young people have a "smorgasbord" of styles that they can move within and between.

Even though youth in the twenty-first century have more access to information (especially through the World Wide Web) and choices, they continue to be bound by historical institutions. The mandatory attendance at school and the social demand of living within a family has not changed much over the past several decades. Rather, I would argue that youths' choices around where or how to spend their time are increasingly limited by policies and rules put into place by adults. Are the original purposes of these institutions still needed? Some would argue that they are needed more urgently than ever, as the demands for young people to achieve a high education and be responsible, personable people is the essence to obtaining a good job and a stable future. However, what about youth who do not agree with the school as a primary means of transition into employment? What about those youth who are unable to meet the growing requirements of academic expectations? I would argue that some of the previous strategies, specifically apprenticeships, are also needed and that their return could provide an opportunity for young people who may see themselves as having no options. Young people who feel they have no options can often be found in our jails and on our streets (Baron, 2001). Youth who do not comply with societal norms (e.g., schooling and/or working) are often defined as deviant. It is here that I want to examine how the creation of teenage deviancy has been formed and continues to have considerable influence on young people today. With this discussion, the ways in which these constructions of youth deviancy have provided the justification for programs and interventions that attempt to control and regulate youth are readily seen.

CREATION OF YOUTH AS DEVIANT

Prior to state intervention, the involvement of religious institutions in young people's lives played a significant role in defining appropriate behaviour. Taken from a document from the seventeenth century, a pastor was reported saying:

> Young people—unmarried boys and girls—behave very badly, both at night and during the day, meeting in taverns and other places reserved for the purpose; particularly scandalous and dangerous are visits to the girls, when they go walking in the streets or converse at windows, on Saturday, Sunday, and on holidays. (Schindler, 1997, p. 268)
>
> There are also documents that suggest that:
>
> The apprentice was represented as a rebellious adolescent who ditched his boss to run about the streets of the big city, blending into its sounds, absorbing its frustration, taking advantages of its resources, living on the fringe of legality, picking pockets, making hasty getaways, ever ready for riotous assemblies, demonstrations, fighting, or barricades. (Perrot in Levi & Schmitt, 1997, p. 68)

Adult fears, particularly among the middle class, of juvenile delinquency have driven much of the public debate since the late eighteenth century in Westernized nations (Hebidge, 1997). Particularly vulnerable to being viewed as delinquents were working class and poor youth. Kett (1977) suggests that the stereotyping of youth was no accident. He says:

> Adolescence was essentially a conception of behaviour imposed on youth rather than an empirical assessment of the way in which young people actually behaved. …A biological process of maturation became the basis of social definition of an entire age group. (pp. 215 & 243)

The notion that adolescence was a distinct developmental period can be traced back to the writings of G. Stanley Hall, the psychologist to whom I referred earlier as being the first to bring awareness of this age group. Influenced by the biological evolution of species, Hall argues that humans also passed through a series of stages in development.

Hall identifies adolescence as a period of “sturm und drang” (storm and stress), which he compares to the earlier unstable and tumultuous phase in the development of human civilization (Tanner, 2001, p. 30).

Hall's work suggests that there are biological causes for adolescent deviancy, evidenced by mood disruptions, a tendency to challenge parents, and adolescents' propensity to engage in reckless and antisocial behaviour (Arnett, 1999). Although Hall's theories have faced substantial criticism from other theorists, especially Mead (1928), who through her anthropological work demonstrated that storm and stress were not universal and biological, they remain "the mainstream view of the social and health scientists providing commentary to the media and to political authorities" (Males, 1996, p. 220).

At the same time, the idea of adolescence as a period of turmoil is often perpetuated within the general public. Arnett (1999) suggests that although there is no indication that most people in the American public see storm and stress as inevitable and universal, there is some support that adolescence is seen as the time of life when it is most likely to involve difficulties such as conflict with parents, risk behaviour, and mood disruptions. To describe this more clearly, I reflect on my own uses of adolescence as a period of turmoil and conflict. I can recall numerous occasions when I have made statements to parents or caregivers such as, "The teenage years are the hardest to get through," or "They have so much going on physically, hormonally, no wonder they are angry/moody." In examining why I made these statements, I can see that it was often to provide some "answer" as to why youth were not complying with certain requirements (e.g., attending school or observing curfew). Viewing the period of adolescence as a time of conflict, in some ways, normalized the youth. Stated differently, a youth's behaviour was not viewed as surprising or out of context. Although I used statements from a biological determinism perspective, they were not satisfactory to me. I felt that in many ways it took away from acknowledging the societal context in which Western youth have to live and thrive, e.g., schooling and professionalism.

THE SOCIOLOGY OF DEVIANCE

In contrast to theorists who look for reasons of deviancy within the individual, such as biological and genetic causes, sociologists look for explanations outside the individual. Specifically, sociologists examine social relations and how norms become defined and used to categorize behaviours as normal or deviant. There are several theories on deviance, which Schaefer (2001) puts into the following groups: a) the functionalist perspective (strain theory); b) the symbolic interactionist perspective (differential association theory, control theory); and c) the conflict perspective (conflict theory). Sociologists working from an interactionist perspective focus on how people label one another, how they relate to one another on the basis of these labels, and the consequences of these social relations (Rubington & Weinberg, 2002). For example, Bernberg (2003) suggests that youth who are formally labelled as deviant through the court system face exclusionary processes that have long-term negative consequences for life chances, such as educational attainment and employment opportunities.

Political economists and other conflict theorists have done a great job of demonstrating the link between how deviancy is defined and issues of power and inequality. For example, Richard Quinney's (1974) social reality theory of crime argues that political and class power factors are the root explanations of crime. Quinney's central thesis was that the politically powerful created one form of negative deviance—crime—as a means of social control:

> Criminal law is used by the state and the ruling class to secure the survival of thecapitalist system, and, as capitalist society is further threatened by its own contradiction, criminal law will be increasingly used in the attempt to maintain domestic order. (1974, p. 16)

Palmer and Humphrey (1995) state that while society professes to abhor certain forms of deviant behaviour in fact it contributes to the organization and perpetuation of society. It ensures that certain institutions are maintained, such as prisons. At the same time, it perpetuates the division between adults and youth. Researchers have found that there is differential treatment within the legal system towards youth, and especially towards minority youth. For example, Males (1996) reports on a 1993 California Department of Corrections study that found youth were consistently confined for 60 percent longer than adults for the same crimes (nearly a year longer). In regards to discrimination based on class, James (1998) found that social class, as well as gender and race, played a significant role in determining whether the police treated youth more harshly. Within the court system, Leiber and Stairs (1999) found differential treatment for African American youth, particularly those charged with drug offenses, compared to White youth. Specifically, African American youth were more likely than White youth to receive a more severe sentence and less likely to be admitted into diversionary options.

Despite the evidence that has shown most crimes are committed by adult males (Statistic Canada), there continues to be public fears about youth delinquency. Tyyska (2001) suggests that in Canada there is a persistent myth about the dramatically increasing youth crime, violence, and gang activity. Focusing on young people as deviant removes the possibility of re-examining stereotypes and attitudes towards youth. The displacement of social anxiety onto young people has created them as "a convenient scapegoat group" (Hall & Jefferson, 1976, p. 72). Scapegoating young people allows us to avoid admitting that we (meaning society as a whole) have backed young people into a corner, offering few options other than to conform to societal norms or be considered deviant. As Furstenberg (2000) argued,

> to a great degree, the problematic features of adolescence and the transition to adulthood are structurally created and maintained by social institutions that isolate youth from adults; ironically, this is done to prepare them for future roles. (p. 3)

I think it is important to acknowledge how much of a role institutions, especially those geared toward youth, have played in vilifying youth.

AGENCY AND INDUSTRY SELF-INTEREST

Males (1996) reports that a considerable amount of evidence has been amassed that agency and industry self-interest in North America, not the true conditions of teenagers, have driven the "epidemic" of youth problems (p. 29). He provides the following examples:

> At the 1986 National Conference on Drug and Alcohol Abuse Prevention, the NIAAA and the National Institute on Drug Abuse painted mid-1980s teen drug abuse at 'epidemic proportions', justifying expanded programming and agency funding. (p. 29)

and,

> The American Medical Association and National Association of State Boards of Education…unabashedly doubled the number of teenage unwed births and claimed a widely embellished 30-fold increase in youth crime since 1950. (p. 30)

During the 1990s, youth across North America were up to six more times likely to have contact with some sort of private professional organization (e.g., psychiatric wards, drug and alcohol treatment programs, and counseling) than in the 1980s. That is a very profitable business. However, despite all these interventions the rates of youth homicide, violent crime, suicide, drug deaths and teenage pregnancies rose dramatically (Males, 1996). Coontz (1995) argues that this has occurred because the long-term structural changes that underlie many of the problems were ignored. Issues such as poverty, abuse, and adult behaviours (violence) on teenagers often receive very little attention in the political arena (Males, 1996).

In a later section, I discuss how the development of the "risk society" was in response to social concerns around uncertainty and control. The language of risk has become quite popular especially within youth studies. Understanding how risk is defined and used to regulate the behaviour of youth is important since it has provoked a number of practices and regulations that have the potential to have a negative impact on youth. But first, I want to examine how the family has been constructed as a mechanism to reproduce middle class norms. I then explore how interventions (e.g., Children's Aid Societies) into families' lives, especially those who are not conforming to social norms, have been justified.

CREATION OF FAMILY

> "The family" is not only a product of the larger society, but also its producer and reproducer. Any adequate historical understanding of family must acknowledge its central role in social and political as well as personal relationships, in societal as well as biological reproduction. 'The family" may be classified as a "natural" or biological unit, a "traditional", divinely ordained, and universal entity, but it also very much a social construction. It is whatever we need it to be, at once the source of all good and of all evil. (Comacchio, 1999, p. 6)

A government machine?

It is interesting to note that it was not until the period of modernity that the family, as a unit, became of interest to the state. Foucault (1978) indicated that previously, the sovereign was not concerned about the state of affairs within families or their health and well-being. However, in order to benefit the sovereign, it was concluded that through the "art of government", which involved making the head of the household responsible for all aspects of the family's life, the needs of the sovereign could be achieved (Tait, 2000). Therefore, the family's designation as a governing unit became emphasized.

Similar to Foucault's writings, Aries (1967) argued that in the fourteenth century, the modern family began to take shape. The system of power changed from the sovereign as overseer of the population to that of patriarchy, where males were identified as the dominant force within each family. Therefore, "a value was attributed to the family which had previously been attributed to the line. It became the social cell, the basis of the State, the foundation of the monarchy" (Aries, 1967, p. 367).

The significant piece here is that the family served a specific function for the sovereign that elevated the importance of families and precipitated the beginning of its manipulation by outside forces. Donzelot (1979) in his book, *The Policing of Families*, argued that the central role of the family became the production and government of good children. This production was overseen by "medical, educational, and psychological experts who successfully bridged the gap between the inner workings of the family unit and the broadest objectives of government" (Tait, 2000, p. 69).

Comacchio (1999) identifies how the concept of family has become so encompassing and enduring when she says:

> Much of the family's symbolic power comes from the religious, moral and ideological forces that have sustained it in the face of continued threats, real and imagined. Add to these the power of law, education, science and the state, and it is clear why the family's institutional basis is so durable. A pervasive ideology of "familism" has left few social relations untouched. (p. 147)

Comacchio highlights a number of key points. The family has been subjected to religious and political forces that have strengthened its purpose and argued its usefulness. Any "attack" on the "ideal" family is often matched with activism from people or groups who promote religious ideology. Significantly, the family has also functioned as a means to teach appropriate conduct to future generations (Tait, 2000). Middle class norms have been promoted and perpetuated, either through families incorporating these norms into their daily lives or by its use as a baseline to judge families who do things differently. Those families who fail to meet the "norms" are often labelled as deviant or dysfunctional. In this next section, I will examine how this identification of deviancy has enabled the state to intervene into families and place expectations on parents that meet middle-class standards.

CREATION OF THE "DYSFUNCTIONAL FAMILY".

> To protect their society and the families as its base, reformers asserted rules for proper family relations, and encouraged public surveillance of families to see that they were followed. The crisis that they identified hinged on the great divide between their own middle-class families and those of other Canadians. Yet it was just as much about the gap between the ideal family—the family as it ought to be—and families as they actually existed. Convinced that the social problems were increasing at an alarming rate, reformers blamed pathological families, directly linking "broken homes", sexual immorality, juvenile delinquency, and violence. (Comacchio, 1999, p. 49)

Coontz (1992) argued that many of our "memories" about family life are myths and that families have never lived up to nostalgic notions about "the way things used to be" (p. 2). Despite this recognition, these myths continue to hold a lot of power in the way that families, especially families that break from traditional values, are talked about and treated. For example, the notion that youth are more problematic today because of the breakdown of families and family values continues to be cited as the cause of increasing crime rates (Woodson, 2001).

Blaming the family for the behaviour of the children has served a number of purposes. Scraton (1997) argued that the creation of the dysfunctional family has served to disguise the reality that adult power is a problem in *all* families. By focusing on those families who either use their power beyond the limit (e.g., child abuse) or fail to use it (e.g. parental neglect) we can ignore that power imbalances exist in every family. Scraton (1997) adds that, "the routine ordinariness of adult power and violence within the family is diminished by theoretical assumptions and professional practices which contribute causation to deviant, dangerous or pathological individuals and families" (p. 70). Hence, over the years, we have collected a plethora of scientific data that has served to reassure us that deviancy can be explained by looking at the individual and their family background.

The creation of the dysfunctional family has also served to create an explanation for, and a solution to, several categories of problems (Dimmock, 2004). The identification of problems as existing within families has encouraged development and implementation of programs that target "at risk" families. Through focusing on families as the locus of change, we have been able to avoid seriously addressing the systemic and economic imbalances that have plagued families throughout history. For example, rather than addressing increased youth unemployment because of the emphasis on credentials and the elimination of apprenticeship programs, youth are said to lack qualifications because they fail to succeed at school due to limited parental supervision (Dimmock, 2004). Placing the blame on families has treated social problems as identifiable, manageable, and treatable. By examining how the child protection system has been developed, we can see that it has been complicit in attempting to manage the population.

CHILD PROTECTION.

One of the significant systems of intervention that has had a profound impact on family life is child protection. Foucault (1980b) described how during the eighteenth and nineteenth centuries, family lifestyle (especially the conduct of sex) was subject to social controls. Along with the fields of medicine, psychology, and criminal justice, social work served as a tool to monitor families. Foucault stated that the purveyors of social controls,

> screened the sexuality of couples, parents, and children, dangerous and endangered adolescents—undertaking to protect, separate and forewarn, signaling perils everywhere, awakening people's attentions, calling for diagnoses, piling up reports, organizing therapies. (p. 31)

Mariana Valverde (1991), in her book, *The Age of Light, Water and Soap*, studies the "social purity movement" that began at the turn of the twentieth century in Canada. The social purity movement was an informal network of organizations and individuals, mostly church people, educators, doctors, and those we would now describe as community and social workers, whose goal was to "raise the moral tone" of Canadian society (p.17). Of particular interest to this group were the urban working class communities. Promoting sexual morality, prohibition, and Sunday observance were the key issues of the social purity movement and they were thought to solve the problems of poverty, crime, and vice. Valverde pays particular attention to the philanthropic organizations and individuals who championed these campaigns. She highlights how the state played a secondary role, either as supplementing private initiatives or acting like a philanthropic organization. What Valverde stresses is that the state did not have the monopoly on moral regulation, but rather private organizations—notably the medial and legal professions and the philanthropic groups—have played a crucial leadership role in establishing the social norms. To extrapolate this to the world of child protection, the state has not necessarily dictated how this type of work should be conducted: rather we must examine how professions such as social work have played a part in setting up the system.

In North America, an increase in child protection cases occurred during the late nineteenth century, when social reformers widened their definition of needy children to include those who suffered from parental neglect or cruelty (Bullen, 1991). The growing interest in childhood as a distinct stage requiring special attention combined with the notion that the future of the society was linked to the welfare of children; there was great concern, predominantly in the middle and upper classes, about the future of these children and thus began what has been referred to as the "first wave of the child rescue movement" (Tomison, 2001, p. 47). At first, it was run by volunteers. However, in order to address the increasing need for intervention, the introduction and training of paid social workers occurred (Bullen, 1991).

Intervention into families began as a means to model appropriate behaviour to parents who were deemed to be lacking. However, the growing belief in the influence of the environment led to reformers insisting that the only means to "save" these children, who were living in urban poor communities, was to remove them and place them in a rural family setting (Peikoff & Brickey, 1991). There was a strong belief that rural life, which consisted of being involved in agricultural labour, was the means to instill morality and responsibility in children. This approach was also used with adolescents. During the late 1800s, a New York child protection agency conducted a very controversial program that involved being a "placing agency" for both voluntary and non-voluntary youth. It involved moving young people who were either living on the streets (referred to as waifs or strays), or young people living at home but finding it difficult to locate work, into rural families who needed labourers (Gish, 1999). Finn (2001) indicated that this program was based on both pity for, and condemnation of, thc poor, and a fear of the potential political and social force of this group as they aged.

Toward the end of the nineteenth century, laws that supported state intervention were introduced. This legalization of intervention into family life legitimized the role of social work and served as a means to threaten families who were resisting involvement (McGillivrary, 1997). Social workers were able to approach the courts to get permission to remove children. Over the next two decades, the state considerably increased the conditions under which it could apprehend children. Previously, preventing infanticide and severe physical abuse had been the main interests. However, with its growing authority, the state became involved in monitoring the health care and educational needs of children (Piekoff & Brickey, 1991).

Over the past several decades there has continued to be an expansion of child protection services. In Canada, one of the groups significantly affected by this state intervention into children's care has been the Aboriginal community. "The Sixties Scoop" is a term that Patrick Johnston (1983), author of *Native Children and the Child*

Welfare System, coined to describe the mass removal of Aboriginal children from their communities and placement into foster care or into white adoptive families. While the authorities at the time considered these apprehensions in the "best of the interest of the child," Aboriginal activists from the beginning condemned this practice and labelled them as actions from the Federal and Provincial governments to force assimilation and cultural genocide (The Aboriginal Justice Implementation Committee, 1999). The Aboriginal parents who did not follow what was considered to be appropriate, Westernized ways of raising children, found their parenting styles misunderstood and unvalued by non-Aboriginal social workers. As a result, between 1971 and 1981 alone, over 3,400 Aboriginal children were shipped away to adoptive parents in other societies, and sometimes in other countries (Johnston, 1983).

Mack (2000), in her critique of child protection, suggested that all families are at risk of a "parentectomy", as the system is hypersensitive to parental behaviour that may cause harm to children. She cites incidents of children being removed from their families due to "spanking, grounding, for home schooling, and even for no reason other than a suspicion…that while conditions in the home are at present stable, they may be conducive to neglect or abuse in the future" (p. 59). We cannot dismiss Mack's statements as an over-exaggeration of the situation, as the statistics support the argument that there has been an increase in the number of investigations of families and in the number of children admitted into care. As stated in the Ontario Children's Aid Society annual report, from March of 1998 to March of 2003, there had been a 47% increase in the number of investigations conducted and a 58% increase in the number of children admitted into care.

One way to explain the increase in child protection cases is to examine the development of the risk society. Beck (1992), in his exploration of the nature of modernity, wrote that a shift had occurred from the "class" society to a "risk" society. He wrote:

> In the transition from class to risk society, the *quality* of community begins to change…Class societies remain related

> to the ideal of *equality* in their developmental dynamics…not so the risk society. Its normative counter-project, which is its basis and motive force, is safety…Basically, one is no longer concerned with attaining something "good" but rather with *preventing* the worst.
>
> (Emphasis in original, p. 49)

In short, Beck argued that instead of using the past to determine the present, society has become more concerned about predicting the future in order to prevent or take precautions against the problems and crises of tomorrow. Mayerfield and Bell (1999) argue that this influx of interest in risk is a modern conceptual language that, when taken apart, is really about the historical problems of uncertainty and control. The language of risk is very appealing, as it has provided a means to deal with the uncertainty that human life faces as well as a tool to exert control. Mayerfield and Bell (1999) warned that the problem with risk is that it is highly rationalistic. They said, "risk explains uncertainty, and it also explains it away. It gives control and it takes control, and therefore we often feel trapped in an iron cage of risk" (p. 1). I argue that this notion of being "trapped" by risk seems reflective of the way that risk is dialogued in today's society. For example, parents see their children at greater risk of harm from outside influences than when they were young. The language of risk has spread throughout the population such that it has become a collective state of mind rather than an objective reality (Smith, 2004). In order to cope with this risk, all sorts of assessment and management tools have been established which attempt to predict and prevent risk.

Smith (2003) stated that over the past decade the child protection system has been placed under pressure to investigate and manage risk. Smith argued that this is an impossible task, one in which the social work profession has been complicit, since its main promise to protect children is one on which it cannot deliver. Unfortunately, the time spent trying to manage risk has come at the expense of the overall concern for the welfare of children. He described how he saw the shift in social work, "where there was once dialogue there is now dogma; where there was practice wisdom, there is now prescription; where there was once assessment there is now investigation (and the ubiquitous "risk assessment") (2003, p. 2). Although Smith makes some credible statements about how the system has changed, he seems to idealize the past and fails to acknowledge how the child protection system has served, from its very beginning, as a "front" for the government to manage the conduct of the population. Just as families have been held responsible for the conduct of their children and youth, the child protection system has been held responsible for the failure to protect. By placing the blame onto these institutions, a critical examination of the distribution of power, the role of government, and the reproduction of power by institutions such as the child protection system has been avoided. It is here that I turn to the work of Foucault, whose arguments have been influential in examining the modern exercise of governmental power.

CHAPTER 12

THEORETICAL UNDERPINNINGS: FOUCAULT AND GOVERNMENTALITY

GOVERNMENTALITY

In his early work, *Discipline and Punish*, Foucault (1977) described a shift during the sixteenth to nineteenth century in the way the sovereign treated the population. What was different about this style of government was that it sought to cover the entire social body. By ensuring the docility and utility of his/her subjects, the sovereign ensured his/her principality, even in the face of threats to his rule from inside and outside his territory (Tait, 2000). Several new techniques were employed which included: 1) treatment of the body as an individual rather than as a collective, "indissociable body"; 2) interest in the person as a whole, their movements, their attitudes, and their language; and 3) managing people's time, space and movement such that they were never free from the "uninterrupted, constant coercion," and control which sought to supervise "the processes of the activity rather than its result" (Foucault, 1977, p. 137). Foucault later referred to this as governmentality or "the art of government", whereby power is exercised from innumerable points. However, it would be a misreading of Foucault's argument if it were purported that the state has the monopoly on moral regulation. Rather, Foucault stresses that every individual plays a role in reproducing power in that the individual internalizes the norms of their particular social group and becomes his own overseer (Foucault, 1977). In the following sections I consider how the use of "experts" has allowed the state to "govern from a distance", how we as individuals are engaged in regulating ourselves, and how these two concepts have shaped my approach to conducting an examination of my role as a child protection worker.

POWER OVER POPULATION

Through the use of disciplines, such as education, medicine, and social work, the population has been observed and regulated. Tait (2000) uses this conceptual framework to examine how the sexual behaviour of youth has been managed. Tait (2000) argues that the government has managed sexual behaviour of youth by making it the object of a number of governmental programs. Through the implementation of these programs onto the population, the state has been able to maintain its position as being an objective "overseer". The employment of experts to address the "problem" has firmly located youth sexuality as deviant and needing to be contained. Families and schools have been pinpointed as the institutions responsible for preventing sexual behaviour. However, these institutions are not free to determine how to manage young people's sexuality. Through the norms that have been promoted by the experts and the family internalizing the expectations and assuming responsibility, the state is able to govern from a distance.

Kelly (2000) used Foucault's work on disciplinary, sovereign, and governmental forms of power as a generative framework to analyze institutionalized mistrust, surveillance, and regulation of youth. Kelly (2000) argued that the use of experts has served an important purpose. Pathologizing individuals and subcultures as dangerous allows the exercising of power over "dangerous" youth as well as providing a reason to subject all youth to surveillance and regulation. More than that, Kelly added, it suggests that this type of management is absolutely necessary and in the population's best interest. What it does allow, but fails to acknowledge, is that the focus is then shifted away from looking at how institutions have played a part in shaping all youth. Rather, the increased anxiety about "dangerous" youth provides support for the idea that these institutions are necessary.

POWER AS RELATIONSHIP

Tait's (2000) and Kelly's (2000) work on analyzing interventions that involve youth is important. However, what is missing is an understanding of how youth engage in, react to, or resist these interventions. The field of youth studies has a plethora of research that identifies how youth are subject to institutions and interventions that attempt to regulate youth behaviours (Tait, 2000). What this has created is a top-down understanding of power and its effects on youth. Said differently, it has continued to reinforce the notion that adults have all the power and youth have no power and are passive recipients. I argue that this is limiting and not reflective of how power is experienced.

Foucault's work suggests a different way to conceptualize power, in that it is "exercised from innumerable points and should be analyzed as something that circulates throughout a complex of social techniques, practices and routines" (Tait, 2000, p. 58). Hence, power comes through us, around us, and over us. We are all subject to power but we are also reproducers of power. We are not passive recipients of power but rather "we are involved in accepting or resisting the normative constraints placed upon us...Whether accepting or rejecting it, though, [we] are all actively engaged in the process" (Butin, 2001, p. 162).

Foucault also stressed that it was imperative that the exercise of power be viewed as productive and organizational rather than oppressive. He said, "[t]he individual is an effect of power, and at the same time or precisely to the extent which it is that effect, it is the element of its articulation" (Foucault, 1980 a, p. 98). Hence, we are created by power. The very exercise of power draws us into existence and produces our subjectivities, implying that it gives us a name to call ourselves and others. By the very nature of calling oneself woman, White, daughter, and so on, it places the multiplicity of other subjects such as man, Asian, father, in contrast. Power, from a Foucauldian perspective, is not necessarily about who has it and who does not. Power is "a machine in which everyone is caught, those who exercise power just as much as those whom it is exercised" (Foucault, 1980, p. 156). Indeed, for Foucault (1980b), power "reaches into the very grain of individuals, touches their bodies and inserts itself into their actions and attitudes, their discourses and every-day lives" (p. 39).

Foucault also stressed that power does not exist in some abstract sense but is embedded in the relations among individuals and groups. Relations of power become identifiable and analyzable through individuals (and groups) engaging with each other (Butin, 2001). As well, resistance also occurs within relationships. At the moment of domination by another, there is a space of resistance that is created. Resistance may take the form of seizing the practices imposed by another and transforming them. It may also occur in more subtle ways such as the use of humour or passivity (Scott, 1990). Therefore, if we want to examine how power and resistance are taken up and used then we have to explore the relationships in which we are engaged.

Some research studies have used this approach to examine the role of "experts" in the provision of services to clients. Peckover (2002) draws on the notion of disciplinary power to explore the role of British Health visiting (referred to as Public Health Nurses in Canada) and whether it can be understood in terms of support or surveillance. Peckover uses interviews with Health visitors, examining how they view their role as exercising disciplinary practices. Findings suggest tensions in the health worker's role between welfare and surveillance. One of the limitations of Peckover's (2002) work is that it fails to identify what could be possible for both workers and clients amidst this tension.

However, Keenan's (2001) analysis of her role as a psychotherapist and her relationship with her client takes some steps in this direction. Keenan (2001), using Foucault's notion of power relations, identifies how spaces of resistance developed for both her and her client within and because of their relationship. Keenan (2001) identifies one of the key aspects of resistance, which is the notion of struggle. As Keenan struggled and addressed her own feelings of anxiety and tension about her client's suicide attempts, it opened up the possibility for new areas of discussion to occur with her client. I argue that this is an example of Keenan resisting disciplinary practices. Due to her status as a therapist and therein her responsibility to ensure her patient's safety, Keenan could have recommended and/or sought out hospitalization for her client in order to minimize her anxiety about her client's suicide attempts. Instead Keenan acknowledged her feelings of anxiety and tension as her own and used the counseling sessions to focus on the key themes behind her client's behaviour such as grief, guilt, and fear. Keenan's work illustrates well what could be possible if we take a look at the complexities within relationships and acknowledge the uncertainty and tension that exists and how this can shape social work practice with clients. Butin (2001) argues that within this uncertainty, "a greater opportunity exists for transformation" (p. 171).

In the present auto-ethnography, I am interested in exploring the tensions that are created within a relationship between child protection worker and youth client. What spaces of resistance are created for both worker and youth based on this relationship? How do youth play a part in taking up, negotiating, and resisting this relationship? Also, in keeping with Foucault's position that disciplinary practices need to be exposed, I am interested in examining the practices with which workers are faced that, I would argue, suppress the feelings of uncertainty, as well as identify the consequences to both worker and youth when these practices are successful. What might be gained (and lost) in recognizing young people as competent and critical actors, capable of meaningful participation in the decisions that affect their lives? How might reflecting on the youths' perceptions of the child protection system help me and others modify practices to work collaboratively with young people? And having engaged in an auto-ethnography that situates my lived experiences as part of the research "data", what did I learn about myself as a worker, as a researcher, and as a human being?

CHAPTER 13

AUTO-ETHNOGRAPHY: FILLING THE GAP

In the present research, I was specifically interested in examining youths' experiences of a child protection agency. I argue that if child protection workers are to service the youth population well, a greater awareness about how youth see and understand the system is important. But the present research was more than exploring "others'" experiences. I felt it was necessary as a researcher and as a child and youth worker to, as Ellis and Bochner (2000) describe, "reflexively bend back on self and look more deeply at self/other interactions" (p. 740).

For four years, I was an "insider" to the culture of one specific child protection agency. My experiences within the child protection agency left me with the conclusion that as a worker I played a significant role in the determination of intervention with youth and their families. I also came away with the notion that if I wanted to precipitate change in how this population was served, I had to begin with myself. Therefore, I went into this project not only interested in exploring the experiences of youth but also to reflect on my own role, either positive or negative, within these interactions. This fits with the theoretical arguments made earlier that in order to understand "others" better, we must also come to understand our "self."

There are a number of benefits to engaging in this inquiry. First, there is very little research on the experiences of young people who are at risk of coming into care. Much of the research on child protection services falls into one of the following categories: a) examining the causes of admission to care (e.g. percentage of abuse, neglect cases); b) critiquing the foster care system; and c) examining the experiences of children and youth who have spent a number of years living in care. Fine, Palmer, and Coady (2001), in preparing for their research on clients' views on child welfare services, completed a chart that consolidated the findings of existing research. In reviewing this chart and seeking out additional research, I found that there have been only a handful of studies that have looked at the perceptions of parents. For example, Callahan, Lamb and Wharf (1994), Maiter, Palmer, and Manji (2003), and McCallum (1995) interviewed parents who were receiving services from a child protection agency. Research that examined youth perspectives predominantly involved interviewing youth already in care or emancipated from care and asking them to reflect back on these experiences (see Chalmers, 1996; Leslie & Hare, 2000; Raychaba, 1993). I could identify no research that looked at perceptions of youth who were involved with a child protection service and at risk of being admitted into care. Nor was there research that examined child protection workers' reflections on their work with children or youth. Therefore, the present research adds considerably to the field.

Using a reflexive approach allowed for the documentation of my journey of transformation and may encourage other professionals to participate in a similar exploration. The benefits of self-reflection within the helping professions are numerous. One of the important benefits is the increased likelihood that workers will search for new ways to interact with others and seek new possibilities within the relationships (Miehls & Moffat, 2000).

METHOD

Due to an existing relationship with one particular child protection agency, I approached the Senior Management about the possibility of conducting this research. During my seven years of employment and a previous research study that I had conducted with this particular agency, a level of credibility had been established with them. After gaining the agency's consent to conduct the project and approval form the Brock University Research Ethics Board, I attended a meeting at the Children's Aid office to present my project to 15 Family Services Workers. During that meeting I explained the purpose and intent of the project and asked them to think about their caseload and whether they had youth/families who would consider participating. The criteria I had for participants included:

a) the young person in the family is between the ages of 13 and 15;
b) the young person is at risk of coming into care due to safety concerns either from the young person's behaviour or the parent's behavior;
c) the young person had never been in care;
d) the young person would not be placed at higher risk by participating in this study.

PARTICIPANTS.

Participants were obtained based on purposeful and nomination methods (Morse, 1994). Workers who identified a potential participant were provided with a telephone script and a recruitment letter for both parent and youth. In order to protect the identity of the families, the Family Services Worker approached the nominated family with an outline of the project and an invitation to participate. If the youth/family were interested they provided verbal consent to their worker to release their name and telephone number. I then followed up with a telephone call.

In total, eleven youth were invited to participate. However, only three youth were interviewed. Eight youth declined to participate for varying reasons. The Family Services Workers reported the following as reasons for the youths turning down the request: three youth declined because their involvement with the Children's Aid was coming to an end and they did not want to have any more meetings; one youth declined because, according to the worker, she did not want to do anything that would "help" her social worker; one youth was interested in participating, but due to conflict between the youth and father, the father did not consent. The small sample size was appropriate, as I was not attempting to determine common characteristics or make generalizations about any group. Two of the three participants were female. All three participants identified themselves as Caucasian and raised in Canada. All three participants were living in single, female-headed families. Their involvement with the child protection agency varied from six months to 1 year. For one youth, this was her third involvement with a child protection agency. For the other two youth the current involvement had been their first.

PROCEDURE.

I began by conducting individual, audiotaped, semi-structured interviews with youths. My choice to conduct standard ethnographic interviews with youths is unusual for a study that purports to be an auto-ethnography. However, I chose to conduct these interviews with youths for two reasons: first, to initiate a discussion with the youths around how they saw power relations operating in order to draw comparisons between their perceptions and my own; and second, to be "in the moment". Although I could have used a method where I recalled my interactions with clients, it seemed much more effective if I was going *into* the interviews with youth cognizant about identifying and analyzing power relations. I feel that this approach was beneficial as there were times that I found myself surprised about how I handled myself in these interviews. It is likely that this would not have occurred had I only used my memories and recollections of past interviews.

A second source of data was my journals. Berg (2004) indicated that though conceptually recognized as a means of data collection by Allport (1942) and Denzin (1978), journalling remains an under-utilized method in research. There are several advantages to using journals (see Courtright, 1994). Most importantly, journalling provided an opportunity for me to reflect on my own performance and interactions with others. Hence, I wrote in my journals before and after the interviews with youths to reflect on their answers to the interview questions as well as examine my performance.

In addition to journalling about the interviews with the youths, I also wrote about my previous experiences as a worker. To assist with recalling some of these experiences, I visited the Children's Aid office where I used to work, sat at my old desk, and talked with some of the staff. Using systematic sociological introspection (Ellis, 1991), which means paying attention to the physical feelings, thoughts, and emotions, I wrote about this experience. Ronai and Ellis (1989) used this approach to conduct a retrospective account of her experience as an exotic dancer.

Lastly, I used my journals to chronicle my research experience, in that I wrote about what I had learned about myself, what had transformed my thinking, and how I could use this to consider a new way of working collaboratively with youth. Using a reflexive approach allowed for the documentation of my journey of transformation and may encourage other professionals to participate in a similar exploration.

DATA ANALYSIS.

One week after the final interview was completed, I began the process of analyzing the data. I started with transcribing the tapes of the youth interviews. Lapadat and Lindsay (1999) argue that the transcription process is not an objective activity but rather involves the researcher making choices that have an impact on the interpretations that can be drawn from the data. Hence, Lapadat and Lindsay (1999) stressed the importance of outlining how the transcription process was approached. I approached the process with the question that Kvale (1996) suggested that researchers use, which is "What is a useful transcription for my research purposes?" (p. 166). Rather than aiming for completeness, which Kvale states is not achievable, I created a transcript that was in keeping with the purpose of this project. Hence, the transcript consisted of the youths' responses to the interview questions, with specific emphasis on statements that I identified as highlighting issues of power relations and resistance as well as statements that resonated with my own experiences of the child welfare system. In order to avoid missing important statements made by each youth, I listened to each of the tapes on two separate occasions.

After the transcripts were written, I read through each transcript three times in order to code the data into categories (Coffey &

Atkinson, 1996). The first read involved looking specifically for quotations that addressed the issue of power relations. The second read involved looking for quotations that addressed how the youth and I interacted with, took up, and used power relationships. The third read involved pulling out quotations that resonated with my own experiences of being part of the child welfare system. I then turned to my journals and completed the same steps as described above. Laying out all the quotations obtained from the transcripts and my journals, I then examined them according to Foucault's writings on power relations. Foucault (1994) indicated that when analyzing power relations a certain number of points needed to be established:

1) *The system of differentiations*—identify the differences that are in place that permits one to act upon the actions of others, e.g., the designation of social worker as being an "expert";
2) *The types of objectives*—identify what those who act upon the actions of others, e.g., the maintenance of boundaries between worker and clients, are pursuing;
3) *Instrumental modes*—identify how power is exercised, what methods are used to act upon others, e.g., the use of home visits and documentation;
4) *The degrees of rationalization*—identify how power is adjusted, elaborated, transformed, such that its instruments can better ensure the desired outcomes, e.g., the introduction of the Risk Assessment Model.

I categorized quotations pulled from the transcripts and my journals based on the above four points. I also incorporated existing literature on youth, workers, and power relations to compare and reflect on the points that I identified.

Lastly, I examined the research process, not only as a researcher but as a participant as well. This allowed me actively to explore my own lived experiences and reflect on the process as a whole. I pooled all of the collected data, and examined what I had learned about myself through the research process. I also considered what new possibilities became available in regards to working collaboratively with youth.

CHAPTER 14

POWER AND THE CHILD PROTECTION WORKER

In the seventeenth and eighteenth centuries, a form of power came into being that exercised itself through social production and social service. Foucault (1980b) referred to this as disciplinary power. Disciplinary power sought to obtain productivity from individuals and did so by gaining access to the bodies of individuals, to their actions, attitudes and behaviours. Hence, the introduction of methods such as school discipline that served to make children subject to manipulation and conditioning. Foucault (1980b) described this new power as "a web" that permeated all of society (p. 39). The population was now subject to "a whole set of instruments, techniques, procedures, levels of application" (Foucault, 1977, p. 202) that were intended to manage its conduct.

Although Foucault's discussion on disciplinary power appeared to suggest that power is about domination and control, he went on to argue that power should not be viewed as oppressive and negative but rather as productive and organizational. For example, one of the ways we have come to know ourselves is through our interactions with specific institutions such as husband/wife, parent/child, and teacher/student.

Foucault was less interested in looking at *why* someone dominates another but rather interested in *how* subjects are constituted to operate in certain ways. Foucault identifies that when analyzing power relationships, it is not necessary to search for their foundation or source, but rather to examine how power relationships are used, rationalized, and internalized.

> Foucault's approach to analyzing power is not to study [i]ts origin, its principles, or its legitimate limits, but to study the methods and techniques used in different institutional contexts

> that act upon the behaviour of individuals taken separately or in a group, so as to shape, direct, and modify their way of conducting themselves, to impose ends on their inaction, or to fit into overall strategies. ((1994b, p. 4)

Therefore, in the next sections, I will examine the practices and instruments within a child protection institution that serve to constitute and objectify both workers and clients. At the same time, I will incorporate into these sections what was evoked for me about my experiences as a child protection worker and some reflections on how both the youth and I took up, used, and resisted our subjectivities. I also incorporate the suggestions that postmodernists have made about how to do social work differently, such that power relations between workers and clients are acknowledged and adjusted.

THE SYSTEM OF DIFFERENTIATIONS

Foucault (1994b) stated that "every relationship of powcr puts into operation differences that are, at the same time, its conditions and its results" (p. 344). Hence, relationships between clients and child protection workers are based on a set of defined differences that are used to manage the relationship. From the youth interviews and my journal entries, I found the following examples of differences between clients and child protection workers.

"I'M THE WORKER/YOU'RE THE CLIENT".

While conducting the interviews, I had an opportunity to examine how the notion of child protection worker can go uncontested by clients. For example, one youth responded to a question about the legitimacy of the worker's involvement with him by saying "there's got to a purpose if they're here." However, he goes on to say "I just don't know what that purpose is." This statement is very revealing of the notion that clients, and especially youth clients, may not question the legitimacy of the Children's Aid Society's (CAS) involvement. One possible explanation that clients may not question the intentions or motivations of their workers is that they have internalized the notion that the social work profession is a legitimate field that holds truths, scientific knowledge and technical expertise. A study conducted by Van Nijnatten and colleagues (2000) found that youth who were involved with a child protection agency ascribed authority to their worker on the basis of their "supposed expertise" (p. 465). The youth indicated that they based their obedience to the worker on professional grounds, as they felt their worker knew what was best (p. 466).

Throughout the interviews I conducted, my "expertise" was never put into question. Despite the fact that the parents and youth heard about me only from their social worker, they did not challenge my "status" as a worker or as a researcher. For example, the parents and youth did not ask about my qualifications, my training, or my experience. Rather, they engaged with me in ways that served to reinforce my role as a social worker. For example, within the first ten minutes of being in the home of one of the participants, the youth's mother advised me of the psychiatric diagnoses she was struggling with, some of the past abuse she had experienced, and her concerns about her child's behaviour, both in the home and out in the community. She also expressed her hope that my discussion with her child might result in a change in behaviour. So, during this very brief interaction, the youth's mother identified me as someone who was entitled to hear very personal information and had knowledge and abilities to create change.

The youths also constituted me as a social worker who was entitled to hear personal information about their lives. Despite statements I made that I was not seeking to hear why they were receiving services from a child protection agency, invariably the interviews turned to this discussion. The youths shared with me some of their experiences of dealing with a parent who was ill, their use of drugs, and family conflict.

During the interviews, there were times when I found myself reinforcing my role as a worker. In re-reading the transcript of one of the interviews, I found that after a youth had revealed some information about drug use, I had followed up with questions that attempted to explore this further, such as why did they use, how often, et cetera. As well, in my post-interview journal entry I had written: "I'm trying to figure him out, what makes him tick, why does he do the things he does?" The desire to "know" this youth has come from my training as a worker/helper. I have been taught that to understand and attempt to "help" my clients, I have to ask questions to seek out their understanding of their behaviour. The emphasis in the worker/client relationship is based on getting to know the client through interviewing, helping them to see the origins of their difficulties, and to give them assistance to change (Trevithick, 2000). In the following section, I will examine how the relationship between worker and client is distinguished by the inequality of how information is collected and shared.

"Tell me more/but don't expect anything back".

Another difference noted between clients and child protection workers was the imbalance of sharing personal information. As child protection workers providing intervention, we expect clients to share very personal information with us, often before a relationship has been formed. As one youth reported: "It took me a long time to get used to them, 'cause they were asking me all these personal stuff and they don't really know you." However, there is not the same expectation on the worker to share themselves *fully* with clients; rather, it is "discouraged" within the social work profession and in the institution to share much personal information. Self-disclosure is considered a "hot topic"; as Reamer (2003) reports, it can have mixed results in that it "may be both helpful and harmful to the same client—helpful in that the client feels more 'connected' to the social worker, and harmful in that the self-disclosure undermines the client's confidence in the social worker" (p. 123). Within in the social work field there is a degree of self-disclosure that is considered "therapeutic" (Anderson & Mandell, 1989), in order to develop the relationship with the client. Roberts (2005) outlines the various theories on self-disclosure in therapeutic relationships that range from Haley's position of tight boundaries to narrative viewpoints that suggest that therapists should be transparent about values and life experiences that inform their practices. However, what is not clear is how child protection workers who are in dual roles (as investigator and helper) make decisions about what to share and what not to share, what influences their decisions about what to share, and how they judge whether their self-disclosure was "therapeutic" or not.

I experienced this ambiguity about self-disclosure multiple times as a child protection worker. I especially struggled with disclosing my concerns and frustrations with the system, as I was worried that I was crossing the professional boundary line. Put differently, I was worried that if I shared too much about myself, the focus was on *my* issues and not those of the clients. During the interviews with the youths, I found that self-disclosure was something that I deemed important but it also created in me a sense of uncertainty. After one particular interview I wrote in my journal:

> I'm talking to J. about how workers don't share personal stuff but when I shared about my own struggles with being a child protection worker, I felt uncomfortable. I had a physical reaction during the discussion; my speech became muddled, I struggled to find words, and my heart beat faster. I had this nagging voice in my head that was questioning my intentions and warning me that I might be crossing a line. But I also saw that the more I shared with J. the more she shared back.

I recognized that there was a struggle for me between wanting to be reciprocal in sharing personal information and using it to develop rapport with my client and the "ingrained" notion that self-disclosure is a practice that should be used only to "help" the client. There is no simple answer to how much information is too much or when and how self-disclosure should be used. Rather, what I want to emphasize is that as child protection workers we need to keep in mind that we have the privilege of being able to select what we can and do share. Compared to clients, workers are not faced with strategies (such as interviews) whereby our personal information is sought and interrogated. One youth commented about how social workers are not faced with personal questions: "They probably wouldn't like it if they were asked those types of questions."

In completing the analyses of the interviews I noticed that not only was there an imbalance of sharing of personal information but there also appeared to be an imbalance about how much the youths and the worker knew about the system. In the next section, I examine how "cases" are handled such that workers are constituted as in control.

"I'M IN CONTROL".

Throughout the three interviews, the youths each raised areas over which they felt they had little control. They all indicated that it was the social worker who called and set up the home visits, without directly speaking to them to determine their availability. Home visits were arranged between the social worker and their mothers, and all three youths reported that they were frustrated that they received very little notice that the worker was coming. Another area that they felt they had no control over was when the worker would close the case. None of the youths could identify what it would take for the worker to stop visiting and they were unclear about what the "goals" were. All three youths expressed some uncertainty around how decisions were made. For example, one youth reported: "I think they read what we said and then make their own decisions." Another youth stated that she was not sure how decisions got made because "…they don't tell me." The notion that youth are often left out, ignored, and disrespected by the child protection system has been reported in several research studies. Youth report that when dealing with the child protection system they have felt powerless because they were not given important information about plans or decisions about their lives (Callahan et al, 2000; Chalmers, 1996; Fine, Palmer & Coady, 2001; Gove, 1995).

I suggest that there are some important benefits to providing youth with more information about how the child protection system works, the expectations which workers have to meet, and so on. It appears that the youth who participated in the present research also saw some benefit to knowing more. For example, when one youth learned about the legal requirements her social worker had regarding the number of visits, she stated that it changed her perception of the worker. She said, "Now I understand why he comes so much." It made me wonder why it is that youth report knowing little about how the system works. My initial reaction was to blame the workers for not taking the time to explain the system. However, it came out in the interviews with the youths that there was no consensus whether or not *all* youth wanted more information about the system. In one interview, the youth clearly stated that she was not interested in learning about how the system worked. This comment challenged my view that as workers we need to be educating *all* youth about the system. Rather, it left me a dilemma: how do workers who recognize that youth feel powerless within the system work with youth who express no interest in learning more about how the system operates? At the same time, my belief that educating youth about the system was important came into question. Although I thought it was important, what was the value to the youth of knowing more? Could this in fact deepen their governance? These questions raise important issues that could benefit from further research. For example, what kind of impact does awareness of the system have on youth's behaviour and view of the system? Is not being interested in the system a form of resistance?

During the interviews with the youths there also arose some discussion about what type of information and how much information they could "handle". One youth indicated that she was not aware of many of the details of her family's involvement with the Children's Aid because she was told "…it wasn't my thing to worry about." From my experience, I found that there was a different form of information sharing with adult clients versus youth clients. Youth clients were often left out of or excluded from certain pieces of information, such as the treatment needs of their parent(s). I am curious if constructions of adolescence such as "not quite an adult" have an impact on how information is shared with youth. Do workers limit what they share with youth based on a "belief" that youth are too vulnerable, and therefore not capable of managing sensitive information? Do child protection workers assume the role of "gatekeeper" when it comes to deciding how much information youth know about the system, their reason for involvement, and so on?

THE TYPES OF OBJECTIVES

Foucault wrote that when analyzing power relations it was important to examine what was being pursued by those who act upon the actions of others. In this next section, I approach this question by examining what child protection workers are often looking for in their work with clients.

MAINTENANCE OF PRIVILEGE.

In the previous section, I discussed how the assigning of roles (client/worker) is often unquestioned and reproduced. I explored how parents and youth took my status as a social worker at face value. Here, I want to examine further how I as a social worker also wanted to reproduce these roles such that I could fulfill my duties as a worker.

de Montigny (1995a) states that "the art of producing a professional identity allows a person to insert him or herself into discursively organized and warranted relations of power and authority" (p. 48). I want to explore this statement by examining what occurred for me during the process of interviewing for the present research. I distinctly recall the anxiety and nervousness I felt while setting up, driving to, and just prior to, the first face-to-face contact with the participants. I remember wondering: "What gives me the right to go into this family and ask questions about their experiences?" I remember feeling a need to be rid of the anxiety, as it was overwhelming. This experience of battling uncertainty was not new. During my years as a child protection worker, I was frequently faced with situations where I was entering into new relationships with families. Every time I was given a new case it meant that there was a new relationship that had to be established. In looking back at how I handled this anxiety when I was a worker, I recall how I drew on my "sense of entitlement" as a child protection worker. The privilege of being a "child protection worker" provided me with the "justification" to enter into the families' worlds, especially since some would argue that I was involved for the right reasons, such as trying to prevent children and youth from being harmed. However, this feeling of entitlement was not satisfactory. It was not something that I could "buy into" because rather than addressing my concerns, it just covered them up. At the same time, by putting aside my anxiety it prevented an opportunity for the client and me to discuss openly and challenge the roles that were assigned to us as worker and client.

In the past several years, some social workers have argued that there are benefits to addressing our uncertainty and social tensions rather than trying to suppress them. Miehls and Moffat (2000) suggest that being open to our feelings of anxiety is necessary if we want to be sensitive to the experiences of others. For example, being aware of my own anxiety about meeting new clients, I can imagine (but not assume) how clients might feel anxious about me showing up at their door. By acknowledging my own anxiety and uncertainty with the client, I can build a mutual relationship that suggests that both the client and I are open to being altered by the relationship. Stated differently, by viewing the relationship as fluid rather than fixed, in that the worker is the expert and the client is the recipient of service, there is potential for both the worker and client to be transformed by the relationship.

Sharing some of the concerns that the clients have about the system can be a space of resistance for both the client and the worker. At the same time, by joining together to address these concerns it can be a source of empowerment for both worker and client. For example, I recall a young woman who was 15 years old and wanting to leave care to live with her boyfriend who was several years older than she was. I knew that the agency (meaning the supervisor and Director of Services) would be against the idea because of her age. However, in conjunction with the youth, we met with the supervisor and Director of Services to explain the reasons why we both thought it was a good idea (e.g., for stability, as the youth had been subjected to numerous placements within the system). This was after the youth and I talked about the reasons that the supervisor and Director of Services would be against the idea and my own struggle with how the supervisor and Director of Services would view my support of this plan. As expected, the supervisor and Director of Services had concerns about the idea but because the youth and I presented a united front and had solid reasons for the decision, they agreed. This scenario could have played out very differently if I as the worker had bought into the supervisor's and Director of Services' beliefs about what was appropriate for a teenager.

AVOIDING THE "GAZE".

Foucault (1977) uses the notion of the ideal prison, the Panopticon, as developed by Bentham, to describe how individuals have become subject to mechanisms of power that make them visible and cause them to act upon themselves. The principle of the panopticon was this: "at the periphery, an annular building; at the centre, a tower" (p. 200). The building consisted of individual cells with wide windows and black lighting that enabled those in the tower to have an unobstructed view of each person in their cell. The advantage of the panopticon is that it "made perfect the exercise of power" (p. 206). It is efficient, as it requires only a small number of people to observe a large number of subjects. At the same time, by always being subjected to the outside gaze of another, it causes individuals to act upon themselves (p. 206). Foucault (1977) said:

> He who is subjected to a field of visibility and who knows it, assumes responsibility for the constraints of power, he makes them play spontaneously upon himself, he inscribes in himself the power relation in which he simultaneously plays both roles; he becomes the principle of his own subjection. (p. 202)

Foucault takes the principle of the panopticon and describes how it transferred into the management of the entire population, not just those in jails. It became used in education, social work, and in the army. Foucault wrote that "the panopticon has become a transparent building in which the exercise of power may be supervised by society as a whole" (p. 207), which Foucault refers to as the "disciplinary society" (p. 209). This subtle form of observing, analyzing, and reforming individuals was used to increase the possible utility of individuals. For example, Christian schools during the seventeenth century were used to "reform" the children of the poor and prepare them for a future in some form of work; to give them "an observant eye, a sure hand and prompt habits" (Foucault, 1977, p. 211).

In using the panopticon to examine child protection services, I would suggest that this principle explains how the worker has been prescribed as the "watcher" or "inspector" and the client as the subject. Rather than individual cells, families are monitored in their homes. Rather than wide windows that clearly look into the home, the community has become complicit in watching. But it is more than how clients are observed. In order to ensure the automatic functioning of power, clients are caught up in a power situation in which they are themselves the bearers. Because clients know they are visible, and also because they are never sure whether they are being observed, they have to think that they may always be watched. However, not only are the clients subject to this gaze, the employees of institutions are also subject to this visibility (Foucault, 1975). In the case of child protection workers, we are subject to supervision both within and outside of the agency. In a later section, I examine more closely how workers are subject to methods within the institution, such as regular meetings with the supervisor, to monitor the workers' performances. Here, I want to address how child protection workers are supervised by methods outside of the agency.

Child protection workers are sensitive to the fact that they are subject to unfair representation in the media (Morris, 2005). Media reports on child protection work predominantly focus on were the system has failed, such as a child's death or serious injury. Research has shown that the risk of being identified in the media and facing legal liability has a significant impact on workers' views of themselves. As one participant in Morris's (2005) qualitative study on child protection workers states:

> ...the public has a negative perception of what the Department does...the public is only informed of things which go wrong, not the good things that happen on a daily basis. Due to this, many employees feel that they are undervalued and often leave the Department due to scrutiny from the public and the media. (p. 142)

Considering the risk to one's reputation, job status, and personal wellbeing if something goes wrong on a case, as workers, we try to avoid being in the gaze. How do we do this? By putting the youth/family into the spotlight and defining their problems as abnormal. To explore this, I turn to the work of Edward Said in *Orientalism* (1979). Said's central thesis is that the Orient has been constructed from the imagination of the West. He addresses the creation of "Whiteness" in relation to the colonial project. Said argues that the construction of the Orient followed along the same lines as the construction of delinquents, the insane, women, and the poor. These groups were identified as "problems to be solved or confined...or taken over" (Said, 1979, p. 207). It is Said's contention that the "Orient" was constructed as the "Other" in order to obscure indigenous histories, knowledges, and possibilities. To extrapolate Said's arguments to the work of child protection, I would assert that having workers label families as abnormal constitutes the worker as "normal". This dichotomy provides a clear division, meaning that the worker has nothing in common with the family, and establishes the worker in a position of privilege. To look at families from this privileged position provides a singular view in which the family can be seen, but makes the workers become invisible. In Said's terms, it is to become White, meaning to become invisible to oneself as a construction of colonization. This privilege ensures that workers focus their attention on "fixing" families, rather than examining the disciplinary practices that have shaped them into workers.

EXERCISING AUTHORITY.

As a child protection worker, I was never able to separate from the authority I had over my clients. Even if I had wanted to engage in a helping, mutually supportive relationship with a client, there was always the risk that I would have to step in and enforce a rule or policy. There was also the risk that I would have to take more serious action, in that I could remove their child or take them to court if they failed to meet expectations. Although there has been some development in understanding how workers are faced with dual roles, as helper and investigator, in the field of health visiting (Peckover, 2002), there is a shortage of research that has examined how child protection workers negotiate these two roles. More specifically, I could find only one research article that addressed how child protection workers should deal with their authority. As previously discussed, Palmer (1983) makes a distinction between authority and power and presents a positive view of authority. Palmer argues that authority is inherent in every form of social work practice and that social workers must learn to use authority if they are to be effective. Rather than attempting to shed or cover up the authority that is assigned to us as child protection workers, constructive use of authority can strengthen the worker-client relationship (Palmer, 1983).

I can see the appeal to Palmer's argument that client-worker relationships would be more "comfortable" if the client grants authority to the worker. If the client views the worker in a position of authority there is less likely to be conflict about case decisions. From my experience, dealing with conflict was one of the most stressful parts of the job. I strongly disliked having to argue with the clients. However, my view is that without these arguments, how would clients be able to assert their power? At the same time, if there were no concerns about clients challenging the worker, it would allow workers not to think about their privilege of power.

During the interviews with the youths, a number of examples were provided on how child protection workers exercise authority. One youth described how the worker had set up parameters regarding the type and frequency of contact with her mother. Another youth talked about how the worker was getting him into counseling for his drug use, even though he did not view his drug use as problematic. This youth felt that he had no choice but to attend, as he believed that other methods would be used (such as being put into care) if he refused. Through the analyses of the interviews, it occurred to me how social work interventions are privileged as the "answer" to client problems. If a youth has drug problems, have them go to addiction services; if a youth has experienced abuse, have them go to counseling so they can talk about it. However, what gets missed is how clients view the problem, whether they see themselves as having a problem, whether they want to change, and if the prescribed intervention is something in which they want to participate. This tension between what the client wants and what the worker thinks was particularly evident in one youth's interview. This youth described how her child protection worker repeatedly made requests of her to go to individual counseling despite her statements that she found talking about her problems ineffective. This youth articulated that she found ways to deal with her issues through artwork and journalling. Despite this youth finding coping strategies that she found effective, she continued to be faced with requests to participate in counseling.

Thinking about this scenario from the worker's perspective, I suggest that having clients participate in social work interventions is connected to looking effective as a worker. When it comes to reporting on the case to the supervisor, having clients registered or participating in services (e.g., counseling and anger management) is seen as a sign of accomplishment. However, referring clients to other social work interventions is merely moving individuals from one disciplinary apparatus to another (Foucault, 1975, p. 226). I was left wondering if privileging the methods that clients use to cope is a space of resistance for me as a child protection worker. Rather than reproducing the value of certain social work interventions, I could advocate to my supervisor that clients find varied ways to manage the crises in their lives.

In the analysis of the youth interviews, it also became clear that though they were subject to authority, the youths found ways to resist. For example, the youth who had limits placed on her contact with her mother ignored the restrictions and visited her mother when she wanted to. The youth who was asked to go to counseling for addictions agreed to attend, but then added stipulations about where the counseling would take place. The youth who was faced with repeated requests to go to counseling remained firm in her statement that she would not attend. These are just a few examples of how clients exercised their own power in moments of domination. Foucault's writing on resistance suggests that it is "both a precondition for power relations and a manifest response to ongoing relations of power" (Butin, 2001, p. 169). My authority as a child protection worker only exists because clients "as the subjects are free" (Foucault, 1994b, p. 292). It is because clients are involved in accepting and rejecting the constraints placed upon them that the need for my role as an authority exists. If all of our clients did what we asked them to do, then the need to assume an authoritative/dominating role would be negated.

INSTRUMENTAL MODES

As mentioned earlier, when examining power relations, Foucault (1977) suggests that it is crucial to identify which methods are used to act on the actions of others. In his writings on disciplinary power, Foucault discusses the instruments of hierarchal observation, normalizing judgment, and documentation (p. 170). Although they were initially used to place prisoners more efficiently under surveillance, Foucault found that the same principles applied to disciplines such as education, medicine, and psychiatry. Here, I examine how these instruments are used within the child protection system.

HIERARCHICAL OBSERVATION.

As suggested by the name “hierarchical”, there are levels of supervision, monitoring, and surveillance that occur within a child protection agency. First, we have the family who is monitored through the use of home visits, telephone calls, and contact with service providers, e.g., doctors, day care providers, and schools. The very idea of being investigated/supervised by a child protection system is a very powerful instrument. It imposes on the family “a principle of compulsory visibility” (Foucault, 1977, p. 187), meaning that they are asked to expose themselves, e.g., their practices and their thoughts. Foucault stated that the population’s visibility assured the hold of power that is exercised over them. He said, “…it is the fact of being constantly seen, of being able always to be seen, that maintains the disciplined individual in his subjection” (p. 187). This has a significant impact, as parents report feeling intimated, threatened, and/or controlled at least part of the time during their involvement with a child protection agency (McCallum, 1995).

As identified earlier through the principle of the panopticon, the child protection worker is also under observation and surveillance by the child protection system. Here, I want to outline the instruments used to monitor and control workers’ performance. First, workers are faced with agency guidelines such as norms for client contact and compliance with paperwork. Second, workers are expected to consult with their supervisor on a regular basis regarding decision making and case planning. Also, supervision sessions, where a worker reviews some or all of their cases to advise the supervisor of the status of the cases, ensure that the supervisor is aware of what is happening but also finds out the type of contact and quality of contact the worker is having with the family. For example, workers are asked to report if they have not completed the required number of home visits set out by the agency’s guidelines. Galper (1975) suggested that these types of controls are intended to “foster discipline in workers, encourage the acceptance of hierarchical and authoritarian structures, and create passivity and disengagement from others” (p. 56).

NORMALIZING JUDGMENT.

Foucault (1977) stated that normalizing judgment operates through a classification system that polarizes good and bad behaviour. Individual acts are compared to:

> …a whole and to one another in a hierarchal, value-laden construction that outlines an average, and defines the bounds of the external limits. Healthy behaviours become defined in opposition to the forbidden, the shameful and the abnormal. (Keenan, 2001, p. 213)

Referrals made to the child protection agency are often based on community or family members suggesting that a parent's behaviour is not "normal". Determining whether a case will be opened for service or closed is based on the identification of problems that require intervention. Although normalizing judgment plays a significant role in the world of child protection, it receives very little attention. Social workers are trained to be non-judgmental but the hypocrisy of this notion is rarely challenged. How can social workers be non-judgmental when it is required of them to label families as having problems such that intervention into their lives can be justified?

I assert that there are some benefits to the social work profession by not addressing the role of normalizing judgment. One of the outcomes of the normalizing judgment is that it allows for individual behaviour to be measured without the requirement of considering and incorporating contextual and historical circumstances. For example, parental behaviour, such as substance abuse, can be individualized rather than considering how substance abuse has been constituted as a "deviant" behaviour. By keeping substance abuse as an individual problem it means that a solution to the problem is possible, especially since social work treatments are seen as a means to overcome addictions. Another outcome is that by treating individual families and their behaviour as the problem, the notion of intervening in their lives, as an issue of power, is made invisible. The child protection worker is justified to enter into the family's world because they have been identified as having a "problem". The need to "fix" the problem overrides the family's right to privacy and self-determination. In summary, by not addressing the role of normalizing judgment in social work, professionals get to keep their positions of authority.

DOCUMENTATION.

During home visits and other contacts with the family, the worker is expected to write notes. Foucault (1977) stated that the use of documentation serves to constitute the person as "a describable, analyzable object" (p. 190). de Montigny (1995a) argues that the practice of writing professional reports is a subtle and less visible exercise of power. He wrote, "power is realized as social workers construct their accounts about clients' lives and thereby appropriate for themselves the right to tell the story and to decide what gets counted as relevant" (p. 219). Little (1998) points out that the subjects of case files rarely have an opportunity to submit their own words into the case file. Instead, the worker's voice is privileged as they recount and interpret their experiences.

Documents are very powerful, especially in child protection cases. Richardson (2003) wrote about her own experience of being investigated by a child protection agency. She argues that once something is written in a file it becomes "almost indistinguishable from fact and it is never removed or changed even in the light of 'further reflection' or new evidence" (p. 125). This is quite significant considering that many of these documents are used in court to determine whether a parent will lose their parental rights. I would assert that there is not enough emphasis within the child protection field that documents are never a complete synopsis of events and happenings. Rather, as a worker I recall being pressured to ensure that the documents were complete, especially by the lawyers who would be using this information in their presentation to the court. In a later section, I discuss the struggles I experienced dealing with the practice of documentation.

Throughout the present research, I found that the youths were aware of how much power there was in documentation and how vulnerable they were if information was reported incorrectly. All three youths stated seeing their social worker taking notes during home visits. They appeared to recognize the significance of these notes as they all made comments about it. For example, one youth said, "I'd watch him write the notes…I would glance over and look at the notes. I don't want them to write the wrong thing or mixing it up." This suggests that the youths recognize that workers are susceptible to documenting information in a different manner than what the youths intended. At the same time, the youths also appear to recognize the power of the written document. The youths' concern that they may be misquoted suggests that they recognize the permanence of the written document. Once something they said was in writing, they had no control over how it would be interpreted and used.

As a worker, writing notes was one of the most difficult parts of the job for two reasons. First, I found that trying to write notes during interviews interfered with my ability to be "present". Second, I found that my notes were never complete in describing the interaction and/or events upon which I was reporting. I recall that some of my notes would include half-finished sentences, or individual words that were supposed to jog my memory at a later time. However, when it would be time to write up a report, my notes were often difficult to decipher or missed information. This is important considering that in the child protection system, these notes carry a great deal of significance, especially for those cases that go to court.

While conducting the present research, I was given the opportunity to review some of the previous reports that I had written about children and youth. In looking at the reports I became aware of how much "sense making" in which I attempted to engage. In writing a report that was to describe a child's life for the past 30 days or 90 days, I felt that it had to make sense. If a child was acting out for a period of time, I had to incorporate information or suggestions about why this would occur. For example, "Johnny's temper tantrums were very difficult to deal with over the month of July. It is speculated by this worker that having no school to attend meant that he had no regular routine to follow and therefore he felt confused." I would then make suggestions on how we were trying to improve the situation to stop the disruptive or difficult behaviours. de Montigny (1995b) stated that social workers are expected to enter into the good sense and cogency of their work. Through the use of written documents, social workers are engaged in constructing a reality that can be ordered, regulated, and administered. This is just one example of many where I was called upon to try to put coherence to children's behaviours.

I would suggest that there is an approach to writing these reports whereby engaging in sense making is not the primary goal. Rather, the emphasis is on reporting the worker's experiences and presenting multiple interpretations, rather than one single view of the situation, and thereby incorporating multiple voices in the document to present various viewpoints, such as the youths', the foster parents', the biological parents', and the service providers'. This might mean sharing the report writing. Predominantly, reports are written by the social worker. However, Richardson (2003) reports that parents and professionals may have very different perceptions of events and happenings. Richardson advocates that these varying perspectives should be added to reports even if it means that professionals have to relinquish some degree of power and control over the documents.

Through the youth interviews, I also became aware of how the reports that we write are not shared with them. All three youth reported that they had never seen any written reports from their worker. Where is the youth's voice in the reports? What if he or she disagrees with what is written? How do we incorporate their views into these reports? These are important questions that have to be addressed if we want to engage in social work that works *with* youth rather than *on* youth.

THE DEGREES OF RATIONALIZATION

Foucault suggested that because the field of possibilities of how individuals act is extensive, the exercise of power is connected to the effectiveness of its instruments. When instruments do not work, or do not achieve the desired outcome, changes are made in order to increase the likelihood of their results. Within the child protection system, we can see how instruments have changed in order to try and improve the outcomes, where outcomes are defined as protecting all children from harm. Predominantly, these changes are precipitated due to an inquest into a child's death, which is viewed as the ultimate failure of the system. For example, the Gove (1995) inquiry into child protection in British Columbia has brought about a number of changes in practice, such as mandatory 20-week training for new staff before they begin carrying cases.

At the same time, child protection has changed over the years due to greater pressure to investigate, assess, and manage risk (Smith, 2003). One of the most significant tools that has been introduced is the Risk Assessment Model. This model was promoted as a means to provide a systematic method of assessing risk such that consistency among workers would occur. However, it has been argued that there may be another agenda behind the use of the Risk Assessment beyond trying to protect children. Goddard, Saunders, and Stanley (1999) argued that,

> under the guise of protecting children, risk assessment instruments may essentially be devices designed to be used by bureaucratic, managerialist organizations in attempts to protect themselves from blame when tragedies occur. With risk assessment procedures in place, organizations are better placed to shift responsibility to individual workers when mistakes are made. (p. 258)

This is quite duplicitous, considering that the forms, in the first place, remove much of the worker's ability to consider various decision options, define the boundaries of their work, and minimize their discretion (Jones & May, 1992).

The Risk Assessment Model (RAM) incorporates many of the disciplinary functions that I have described above. First, risk factors used in the RAM forms are based on research information on various behaviours that have been identified as predictive of abuse or re-abuse, despite the fact that much of this research is plagued with "doubtful validity"(Goddard et al. 1999, p. 255). Second, although the RAM is intended to evaluate the family, it inherently individualizes clients because each adult is rated separately. At the same time, problems are individualized, such as a person's limited financial resources, rather than addressing social issues such as poverty. Third, the RAM enables workers to be easily monitored by the supervisor, as the supervisor has access to tracking forms that notify them when reports are being completed on time or not. Fourth and finally, the RAM is a professional document that engages the worker in compiling evidence that either supports the designation of a level of risk or not. The RAM is set up according to a rating scale—1 being no risk and 5 being high risk. If a family is rated as a 1, the file is closed. However if a family is rated as a 5, then the worker is expected to take evasive action, e.g., remove the child from the home. The RAM is set up to draw more attention to the risks than the strengths of the family, and thus allows for the possibility for more intrusive measures to be taken with families. For example, at the end of the RAM, all of the categories that are rated as a three or higher are brought together. However, none of the strengths are brought forward. This could lead to unnecessary actions toward the family. Consider the following case example. A father is identified as using cocaine on a regular basis and having a mental health issue. There are concerns because there is a five-year old child in the home. If the worker were to base her decision on the risk factors alone, the strengths or protective factors would be missed. For example, in this case, the child's grandmother also lives in the home and never allows the child to be alone in the presence of her father and intervenes if the father is not in good mental health.

The limitations of the RAM have been identified by a number of researchers. Therefore, it is not surprising that more changes to how child protection work is done are planned. The Ontario Association of Children's Aid Societies (OACAS) recently presented a position paper (March 8, 2005) outlining their recommendations for amendments to the Child and Family Services Act (CFSA). The OACAS wants a more "flexible" system of child welfare, which would reach beyond the limits of risk-based practice. One of these amendments is to move to a model called "Differential Service Response". In short, the Differential Response model advocates for a broadened screening system, which would incorporate both protection and assessment processes. Cases that were determined to be low-risk would no longer be subject to a full protection investigation but would be diverted to other agencies were services would be available. Although this model suggests that low-risk families would move through the child protection system more swiftly, critics of the model argue that intervention would be more extensive. Specifically, Pelton (2000) argues that the broadening screening system the differential service model promotes would mean that more families would be identified and the involvement from services would be more extensive. At the same time, Pelton argues that by referring clients to community agencies, these agencies would be enlisted as coercive social control agents. The community agencies would be responsible to report back to the child protection system about the family's participation, in case further intervention from the child protection agency was required. So, although families would be dealing with a community agency, the child protection system still has some control over the family. Pelton (2000), concerned with the direction that child protection is heading, argues that,

> it is time to re-examine the deeper issues that CPS (child protection services) terminology and statistics tend to obscure. The level of explicit discussion must shift to that of underlying values, political philosophy, attitudes towards the poor, the political meaning of authority, the nature of social justice, and what we mean by social services and social work. If it does not, the future of child protection is dim, indeed. (p. 187)

CHAPTER 15

NEVER WITHOUT POWER

This writing has taken some initial steps in examining the child protection system from a position that is rarely discussed. Specifically, I have explored how Foucault's concept of disciplinary power can be used to understand how power operates within the client/worker relationship that occurs within the child protection system. This relationship is shown to be quite complex, with power flowing bi-directionally rather than top-down. Instead of viewing power imbalances as a function of state control, I have come to see how the client/worker relationship is constituted by the worker, the client, and the social body. How clients and workers are defined comes from the process of subjectification in which we all engage in accepting or resisting. By calling myself a child protection worker, I clearly distinguish myself as different from a client. At the same time, by making the client the "Other" and portraying his/her life as problematic, I make myself invisible. The cost to this invisibility is that it obscures the privilege of power that has been assigned to professions, such as child protection work.

While the fields of medicine, psychiatry, and health visiting have used Foucault's work to examine how the profession develops "regimes of truth" that privilege their knowledge, the child protection system has been slow to examine how the practices that they use (e.g., home visits and risk assessment) serve to constitute clients as "abnormal" or a "problem" and the child protection worker as the "expert". With the shift toward postmodernism in social work (Hartman, 1991), I would assert that the child protection system is being provided a theoretical tool to challenge the accepted "truths" about how best to serve children and families. It is possible that by viewing clients' worlds as consisting of a web of meanings, created and sustained by both the client and the worker, different approaches to make intervention beneficial to all involved might become available.

A benefit of using Foucault's work is that the child protection system is viewed within the context of the social body. We can see how child protection has become a privileged field, such that it has been given the authority and mandate to monitor, subject to intervention, label, and treat children and families. As a former worker in this system, it is important for me to place my frustrations with the system into this larger framework. Rather than personalizing my frustrations, such as "I never have enough time" or "I'm not cut out for this type of work," I can see how the instruments and practices that I was required to use reproduced power. Stated differently, it was not that I lacked certain qualities in order to do the job effectively and in a manner that respected my clients, but that as a child protection worker, I was operating in an environment where certain techniques (e.g., supervision and documentation) were exercised that ensured that I maintained power over my clients.

It is important to acknowledge how complex the power relationship is between workers and clients and between the worker and the agency. Although there is a view that the worker has all the power, this auto-ethnography has shown that the power relationship is fluid and unstable. Both workers and clients are subject to disciplinary practices that define the boundaries of the relationship. For example, I have discussed how ingrained notions of limiting self-disclosure by the worker serve to keep up barriers between the worker and the client. However, within the power relationships between workers and clients and the worker and the system, there are also acts of resistance. Foucault points out that the very act of dominating another creates a space for resistance. This auto-ethnography showed that in the child protection system there are spaces of resistance that exist, and are often used, by both workers and youth. At the same time, I also introduced some possible ways that workers can resist some of the disciplinary practices within the child welfare system. For example, I discussed the possibility of incorporating clients' voices into the documentation.

Further research is needed to identify the impact of these types of resistance strategies on the worker, on the client, and on the system.

I am left wondering if it is possible to operate from a power-sharing model within the child protection system. Given the number and breadth of disciplinary practices that are involved, and the importance of maintaining these practices in order to sustain the social work profession, it is questionable whether a shift in practice is possible. Although I have suggested ways to adjust current practices, Margolin (1997) argues that "tinkering" may only further mask the hidden agendas of control that are now are part of social work practice. Unless the fabric of the profession changes its training, theory, and practical application of theory, the fundamental issues of power and control will continue.

Given that the child protection field is constantly shifting and changing in order to improve its ability to safeguard children, a greater emphasis is required on examining how workers operate within this complex, overwhelming, and multi-dimensional world. For instance, there are several reasons to be concerned about the number and type of documents child protection workers are expected to complete. Administrative paperwork and case recording consume fifty per cent or more of workers' time (Esposito & Fine, 1985). Keenan (2000) identifies that there is great risk to having the worker be overwhelmed with paperwork. Keenan suggests that in these circumstances, workers are more likely to implement disciplinary practices and be less open to examining the social dynamics of their relationships. Further research could provide more insight into the factors that facilitate workers to engage in reflexively examining their position of power.

REFLECTIONS ON PROCESS

The present research was focused on the issues of power relationships. Therefore, to have reported on other peoples' experiences without reflecting on myself would have contravened what I was attempting to accomplish. My intent was not to create knowledge—e.g., about how the child protection system works—but, rather, to promote dialogue. Through describing some of my conversations with the youth participants and the conversations I had with myself through my journal entries, I demonstrated my struggle to make sense of my experience as a child protection worker. Using a postmodern auto-ethnography allowed me to get "personal" with the subject matter. Actually, what I experienced was that it demanded that I be close to the subject matter. Looking back, I can see how important that was. If I am advocating that workers be open to examining the social dynamics of their relationships with clients, how could this have any significance if I had not engaged in the process myself?

The limitation to using auto-ethnography is that it cannot be generalized to all workers in child protection. Some workers may view their power differently, in that they have no problem using their power because they see it as acting in the best interests of the child. Although my experience may not be the same as that of other child protection workers, the one thing we have in common is our position of power over clients. How we see and use our power is important if we want to work *with* clients and not *on* them.

There are some researchers and scholars who may view the present research as self-indulgent. The field of auto-ethnography has been criticized for being narcissistic (Coffey, 1999). There were times during this process that I was concerned about how my voice was privileged over the voices of the youths who participated in the research. At times, I felt that it was more important to write about the youths' experiences rather than my own. However, I also believe that the voices of workers have been marginalized, which is supported by how little research I could find on this subject, and saw this as an opportunity to present my experience as a worker. Moreover, I believe I am a better worker for having completed this process. I am now aware of the many instruments and practices to which I was subjected, but that I also reproduced with clients. I am also aware of how I resisted these practices and have identified some other approaches that I can use to work in a more power-balanced relationship with my clients. Although a shift in social work practice may be a long way off, there are some strategies that I can now use to be more inclusive of clients' power.

WHAT HAVE I LEARNED?

Throughout this research process, there have been some very trying times for me. Undertaking this auto-ethnography has brought up very personal issues about power. Although in my research I was focused on addressing power from a Foucauldian perspective, there were times that I referenced power as something I owned. In examining why this occurred, I recognized that although power was something with which I was uncomfortable, it was also something I did not necessarily want to give away or view as something that was assigned to me. It took work for me to step out of viewing power as something I owned, and this process opened up some very painful emotional wounds. It was safer to look out at the world viewing myself as a person with inherent power, rather than as a person struggling with coming to terms with how power was assigned to me as a White woman, as well as how I took up and used power.

Consequently, there were many occasions in the research process when I ended up in tears, protesting that it was too hard and that I wanted to run away. I felt trapped, helpless, overwhelmed, and exhausted. I was actually quite surprised by how those feelings were very similar to the frustrations I experienced as a child protection worker. My advisor observed in our discussions that it was not surprising that studying the topic of power also brought up my own issues with power.

What Foucault's writing on power has shown me is that my feelings of powerlessness are not fact. I am never without power. Although my subjectivity may be inscribed by my relationship with certain institutions (e.g., family and work), it is never complete. There is always room to move, to resist, and to create change. This is an important concept that I can incorporate into my work with youth and their families. Just as I am never without power, neither are the youth and their families.

REFERENCES

Aapola, S., Gonick, M., & Harris, A. (2005). *Young femininity. Girlhood, power and social change.* Basingstoke: Palgrave.

Acker, S. (2000). In/out/side: Positioning the researcher in feminist qualitative research. *Resources for Feminist Research, 28*(1&2), 189–208.

Ackland, C. R. (1995). *Youth, murder, spectacle: The cultural politics of "youth in crisis".* Boulder, CO: Westview Press.

Adams, M. (1997). *The trouble with normal: Postwar youth and the making of heterosexuality.* Toronto: University of Toronto Press.

Allen, J. R., & Allen, B. A. (1995). Narrative theory, redecision therapy, and postmodernism. *Transactional Analysis Journal, 25*(4), 327–334.

Allport, G. (1942). *The use of personal documents in psychological science.* New York: Social Science Council.

Anderson, D. G. (2000). Coping strategies and burnout among Veteran child protection workers. *Child Abuse & Neglect, 24*(6), 839–848.

Anderson, S., & Mandell, D. (1989). The use of self-disclosure by professional social workers. *Social Casework, 70,* 259–267.

Aries, P. (1962). *Centuries of childhood: A social history of family life.* New York: Vintage Books.

Arnett, J. J. (1999). Adolescent storm and stress, reconsidered. *American Psychologist, 54*(5), 317–326.

Bhabha, H. K. (1994). *The location of culture.* New York: Routledge.

Baker, M. (1995). *Canadian family policies: Cross-national comparisons.* Toronto: University of Toronto Press.

Bandura, A. (1977). *Social learning theory.* Englewood Cliffs, NJ: Prentice Hall.

Baron, S. W. (2001). Street youth labour market experiences and crime. *Canadian Review of Sociology and Anthropology, 38,* 189–215.

Basaglia, F. (1987). *Psychiatry inside out: Selected writings of Franco Basaglia* (N. Scheper-Hughes & A. M. Lovell, Eds., A. M. Lovell & T. Shtob, Trans.). New York: Columbia University Press.

Bateson, G., Wilder-Mott, C., Weakland, J. H., International Communication Association, Speech Communication Association, & San Francisco State University. (1981). *Rigor & imagination: Essays from the legacy of Gregory Bateson.* New York: Praeger.

Baumann, D. J., Kern, H., McFadden, T., & Law, J. R. (1997). *Individual and organizational factors in burnout and turnover: A decision making ecology approach.* Texas: Texas Department of Protective and Regulatory Services.

Beales, R. W., Jr. (1975). In search of the historical child: Miniature adulthood and youth in Colonial New England. *American Quarterly, 27,* 379–398.

Beck, A. T. (1967). *Depression: Clinical, experimental, and theoretical aspects.* New York: Hoeber Medical Division, Harper & Row.

Beck, A. T. (1999). *Prisoners of hate: The cognitive basis of anger, hostility, and violence* (1st ed.). New York: HarperCollins.

Beck, U. (1992). *Risk society: Towards a new modernity.* London: Sage.

Berg, I. K. (1994). *Family based services: A solution-focused approach.* New York: W.W. Norton.

Berg, B. L. (2004). *Qualitative research methods for the social sciences* (5th ed). San Fransisco: Pearson.

Bernberg, J. G. (2003). State reaction, life-course outcomes, and structural disadvantage: A study of the impact of formal criminal labeling on the transition to adulthood. *Dissertation Abstracts International, A: The Humanities and Social Sciences, 63*(7), 2702-A.

Best, S., & Kellner, D. (1997). *The postmodern turn.* New York: Guilford Press.

Blakemore, S. J. C., S. (2006). Development of the adolescent brain: Implications for executive function and social cognition. *Journal of Child Psychology and Child Psychiatry, 47*(3–4), 296–312.

REFERENCES

Bochner, A. P. (2000). Criteria against ourselves. *Qualitative Inquiry, 6*(2), 266–272.

Bochner, A. P., & Ellis, C. (2002). *Ethnographically speaking: Autoethnography, literature and aesthetics*. Walnut Creek, CA: Alta Mira Press.

Bourke, A. (1999). *The burning of Bridget cleary: A true story*. London: Pimlico.

Bowen, M. (1990). *Family therapy in clinical practice*. New York: J. Aronson.

Bullen, J. (1991). J.J. Kelso and the 'New' Child-Savers: The genesis of the children's aid movement in Ontario. In R. Smandych, G. Dodds, & A. Esau (Eds.), *Dimensions of childhood: Essays on the history of children and youth in Canada*. Manitoba, Canada: Legal Research Institution.

Burman, E. (1998). *Deconstructing feminist psychology*. London, Thousand Oaks, Calif.: SAGE Publications.

Burman, E. (2008). *Deconstructing developmental psychology* (2nd ed.). Hove, New York: Routledge.

Butin, D. W. (2001). If this is resistance I would hate to see domination: Retrieving Foucault's notion of resistance within educational research. *Educational Studies, 32*(2), 157–176.

Caelli, K., Ray, L., & Mill, J. (2003). 'Clear as mud': Toward greater clarity in generic qualitative research. *International Journal of Qualitative Methods, 2*(2), 1–24.

Callahan, M., Lumb, C., & Wharf, B. (1994). *Strengthening families by empowering women: A joint project of the Ministry of social services and the school of social work*. Victoria, BC: University of Victoria, Ministry of Social Services.

Calvert, K. (1998). Children in the house: The material culture of early childhood. In H. Jenkins (Ed.), *The children's culture reader* (pp. 67–80). New York: New York University Press.

Canadian Broadcasting Company. (2005). *News indepth: Same sex rights, where the parties stand.* Found here: http://www.cbc.ca/news/background/samesexrights/parties-positions.html

Canadian Broadcasting Company. (2007). *Married people outnumbered for first time: Census.* Found here: http://www.cbc.ca/canada/story/2007/09/12/census-families.html

Canadian Human Rights Commission. (2004). *Legislation and policies: Submission of the Canadian human rights commission to the standing committee on justice and human rights on same sex marriages.* Found here: http://www.chrc-ccdp.ca/legislation_policies/submission_marriage-en.asp#Bona%20Fide

CAS Annual report April 1, 2002 – March 31, 2003. Ontario Association of Children's Aid Societies. Retrieved on February 26, 2004 from www.oacas.ca

Castaneda, C. (1971). *A separate reality: Further conversations with Don Juan*. New York: Simon & Schuster.

Chalmers, M. L. (1996). Voices of wisdom: Minnesota youth talk about their experiences in out-of-home care. *Community Alternatives: International Journal of Family Care, 8*(1), 95–121.

Chunn, D. E. (2003). Boys will be Men, Girls will be Mothers: The legal regulation of childhood in Toronto and Vancouver. In N. Janovicek & J. Parr (Eds.), *Histories of Canadian children and youth*. Don Mills: Oxford University Press.

Clark/Keefe, K. A. (2006). Degrees of separation: An ourstory about working-class and poverty-class academic identity. *Qualitative Inquiry, 12*(6), 1180–1197.

Coffey, A., & Atkinson, P. (1996). Concepts and coding. In A. Coffey & P. Atkinson (Eds.), *Making sense of qualitative data: Complementary research strategies* (pp. 32–42). Thousand Oaks, CA: Sage.

Coffey, P. (1999). *The ethnographic self.* London: Sage.

Collier, A. (1977). *R.D. Laing: The philosophy and politics of psychotherapy*. England: The Harvester Press.

Comacchio, C. R. (1999). *The infinite bonds of family: Domesticity in Canada, 1850–1940*. Toronto: University of Toronto Press.

Coontz, S. (1995). The American family and the nostalgia trap. *Phi Delta Kappan*, K1–K20.

Courtright, K. E. (1994). *An overview of the use and potential advantages of the diary method.* Paper presented at the annual meeting of the Academy of Criminal Justice Sciences, Boston.

Danesi, M. (1994). The signs and meanings of adolescence. Toronto: University of Toronto Press.

De Montigny, G. A. J. (1995a). *Social working: An ethnography of front-line practice*. Toronto: University of Toronto Press.

De Montigny, G. A. J. (1995b). The power of being professional. In M. Campbell & A. Manicom (Eds.), *Knowledge, experience, and ruling relations: Studies in the social organization of knowledge*. Toronto: University of Toronto Press.

De Shazer, S. (1985). *Keys to solution in brief therapy* (1st ed.). New York: W.W. Norton.

Deleuze, G., & Guattari, F. (1987). *A thousand plateaus: Capitalism and schizophrenia* (B. Massumi, Trans.). London: Athlone Press.

Deleuze, G. G., & Felix. (1983). *On the line* (J. Johnston, Trans.). New York: Semiotext(e).

Delgado, R., & Stefancic, J. (1997). *Critical white studies: Looking behind the mirror*. Philadelphia: Temple University Press.

Denzin, N. K. (1978). *The Research Act*. New York: McGraw-Hill.

Denzin, N. K., & Lincoln, Y. S. (1994). *Handbook of qualitative research*. Thousand Oaks, CA: Sage Publications.

Denzin, N. K., & Lincoln, Y. S. (2000). *The handbook of qualitative research*. Thousand Oaks, California: Sage Publications.

Denzin, N. K. (2006). Analytic autoethnography, or déjà vu all over again. *Journal of Contemporary Ethnography*, *35*(4), 419–428.

Derrida, J. (2005). *Writing and difference*. London: Routledge.

Descartes, R. (1990). *Meditations on first philosophy = Meditationes de prima philosophia* (Bilingual, Ed.). Notre Dame, Ind.: University of Notre Dame Press.

Dimmock, B. (2004). Young people and family life: Apocalypse now or business as usual? In J. Roche, S. Tucker, R. Thomson, & R. Flynn (Eds.), *Youth in society* (2nd ed.). California, USA: Sage Publications.

Diner, H. R., & Johns Hopkins University. (1983). *Erin's daughters in America: Irish immigrant women in the nineteenth century*. Baltimore: Johns Hopkins University Press.

Dobson, J. (1983). *Love must be tough: New hope for families in crisis*. London: Word Publishing.

Donzelot, J. (1979). *The policing of families*. New York: Pantheon Books.

Ellis, A., & Dryden, W. (1997). *The practice of rational emotive behavior therapy* (2nd ed.). New York: Springer Pub. Co.

Ellis, C. (1991). Sociological introspection and emotional experience. *Symbolic Interaction*, *14*(1), 23–50.

Ellis, C. (2004). *The ethnograhic I: A methodological novel about auto-ethnography*. Walnut Creek, CA: Alta Mira Press.

Ellis, C., & Flaherty, M. G. (Eds.). (1992). *Investigating subjectivity: Research on lived experience*. Newbury Park, California: Sage.

Ellis, C., & Bochner, A. P. (2006). Communication as autoethnography. In J. St. John & T. Striphas (Eds.), *Communication as . . . perspectives on theory*. Thousand Oaks, CA: Sage Publications.

Ellis, C., & Bochner, A. P. (2000). Autoethnography, personal narrative, reflexivity: Researcher as subject. In N. K. Denzin & Y. S. Lincoln (Eds.), *Handbook of qualitative research* (2nd ed., pp. 733–768). California, USA: Sage Publications.

Enright, R., Levy, V., Jr., Harris, D., & Lapsley, D. (1987). Do economic conditions influence how theorists view adolescents? *Journal of Youth and Adolescence*, *16*, 541–559.

Erera, P. I. (2002). *Family diversity: Continuity and change in the contemporary family*. London: Sage Publications.

Erikson, E. H. (1963). *Childhood and society* (2nd ed.).

Erikson, E. H. (1980). *Identity and the life cycle*. New York: Norton.

Erikson, E. H., & Frye, N. (1968). *Identity, youth, and crisis* (1st ed.). New York: W.W. Norton.

Esposito, B., & Fine, M. (1985). The field of child welfare as a world of work. In J. Laird & A. Hartman (Eds.), *A handbook of child welfare*. New York: Free Press.

Etch-A-Sketch. (2008). Etch-a-sketch: Wikipedia. Found here: http://en.wikipedia.org/wiki/Etch_A_Sketch

Figley, C. R. (1995). Compassion fatigue as secondary trauma disorder: An overview. In C. R. Figley (Ed.), *Compassion fatigue: Coping with secondary traumatic stress disorder in those who treat the traumatized*. New York: Brunner/Mazel.

REFERENCES

Fine, M., Palmer, S., & Coady, N. (2001). *Service participant voices in child welfare, children's mental health and psychotherapy*. Partnerships for Children and Families Project. Retrieved July 13, 2004, from http://www.wlu.ca/fsw/cura/pdf/theme_papers/pdf

Finn, J. L. (2001). Text and turbulence: Representing adolescence as pathology in the human services. *Childhood, 8*(2), 167–190.

Fisch, R., Segal, L., & Weakland, J. H. (1982). *The tactics of change: Doing therapy briefly* (1st ed.). San Francisco: Jossey-Bass.

Fitz, J. (1981). The child as a legal subject. In R. Dale, G. Esland, R. Fergusson, & M. MacDonald (Eds.), *Education and the State: Politics, patriarchy and practice* (Vol. 2). Milton Keynes: Open University Press.

Fletcher, L. (1982). Battered professionals. In K. Oates (Ed.), *Child abuse: A community concern* (pp. 239–245). London: Butterworths.

Flower, V. S., & Hughes, C. L. (1973). Why employees stay. *Harvard Business Review, 51*(4), 49–60.

Foa, E. B., & Rothbaum, B. O. (1998). *Treating the trauma of rape: Cognitive-behavioral therapy for PTSD*. New York: Guilford Press.

Foucault, M. (1972). *The archaeology of knowledge and the discourse on language*. New York: Pantheon Books.

Foucault, M. (1977). *Discipline and punish: The birth of the prison* (1st Vintage Books, Ed.). New York: Vintage Books.

Foucault, M. (1978). *The history of sexuality: Volume 1, An introduction*. New York: Vintage.

Foucault, M. (1980a). Two lectures. In *Power/knowledge: Selected interviews and other writing, 1972–1977*. New York: Pantheon.

FOUCAULT, M. (1980B). HISTORY OF SEXUALITY – VOLUME 1: AN INTRODUCTION. NEW YORK: VINTAGE BOOKS.

Foucault, M. (1988). *Madness and civilization: A history of insanity in the age of reason*. New York: Vintage Books.

Foucault, M. (1991). Governmentality. In *The Foucault effect: Studies in governmentality* (G. Burchell, C. Gordon & P. Miller, Eds.). London: Harvester Wheatsheaf.

Foucault, M. (1994). On the archaeology of the sciences: Response to the epistemology circle. In P. Rabinow & N. Rose (Eds.), *The essential Foucault: Selections from the essential works of Foucault 1954–1984*. New York: The New Press.

Foucault, M. (2002). *Archaeology of knowledge*. London, New York: Routledge.

Foucault, M. (2008). *The birth of biopolitics. Michel Foucault: Lectures at the College De France*. New York: Palgrave Macmillan.

Freedman, J., & Combs, G. (1996). *Narrative therapy: The social construction of preferred realities*. New York: W.W. Norton.

Freud, S., Brill, A. A., & Frye, N. (1938). *The basic writings of Sigmund Freud*. New York: The Modern Library.

Freud, S., & Strachey, J. (1991). *Introductory lectures on psychoanalysis*. England: Penguin Books.

Fryer, G. E., Jr., Miyoshi, T. J., & Thomas, P. J. (1989). The relationship of child protection worker attitudes to attrition from the field. *Child Abuse & Neglect, 13*, 345–350.

Furstenberg, F. E. (2000). The sociology of adolescence and youth in the 1990s: A critical commentary. *Journal of Marriage & the Family, 62*(4), 896–911.

Gabriel, J. (2000). Whiteness: Endangered knowledges, endangered species? In G. Lee-Traweek & S. Linkogle (Eds.), *Danger in the field: Risk and ethics in social research* (pp. 168–180). London: Routledge.

Galper, J. H. (1975). *The politics of social services*. Englewoods Cliff, NJ: Prentice-Hall.

Garcia-Preto, N. (1998). Latinas in the United States: Bridging two worlds. In M. McGoldrick (Ed.), *Revisioning family therapy: Race, culture, and gender in clinical practice*. New York: The Guilford Press.

Gergen, K. J. (2001). Psychological science in a postmodern context. *The American Psychologist, 56*(10), 803–813.

Gergen, K. J., Lightfoot, C., & Sydow, L. (2004). Social construction: Vistas in clinical child and adolescent psychology. *Journal of Clinical Child and Adolescent Psychology, 33*(2), 389–399.
Gergen, K. (1992). The postmodern adventure. *Family Therapy Networker, 16*(5), 56–57.
Gilligan, C. (1982). *In a different voice: Psychological theory and women's development.* Cambridge, Mass.: Harvard University Press.
Gilligan, C. (1993). *In a different voice: Psychological theory and women's development.* Cambridge, Mass.: Harvard University Press.
Gillis, J. R. (1996). *A world of their own making: Myth, ritual, and the quest for family values.* New York: HarperCollins Publishers, Inc.
Ginorio, A. B., Guterrez, L., Cauce, A. M., & Acosta, M. (1995). Psychological issues for Latinas. In H. Landrine (Ed.), *Bringing cultural diversity to feminist psychology: Theory, reseach, and practice* (pp. 241–263). Washington, DC: American Psychological Association.
Gish, C. (1999). Rescuing the 'waifs and strays' of the city: The western emigration program of the Children's Aid Society. *Journal of Social History, 33*(1), 121–141.
Giroux, H. A. (1996). *Fugitive cultures: Race, violence, and youth.* New York: Routledge.
Giroux, H. A. (2000). *Stealing innocence: Youth, corporate power, and the politics of culture* (1st ed.). New York: St. Martin's Press.
Giroux, H. A. (2005). *Border crossings: Cultural workers and the politics of education* (2nd ed.). New York: Routledge.
Gjerde, J., & Qualey, C. C. (2002). *Norwegians in Minnesota.* St. Paul: Minnesota Historical Society Press: Published in cooperation with the Norwegian-American Historical Association.
Gleason, M. (1999). *Normalizing the ideal: Psychology, schooling, and the family in postwar Canada.* Toronto: University of Toronto Press.
Goddard, C. R., Saunders, B. J., & Stanley, J. R. (1999). Structured risk assessment procedures: Instruments of abuse? *Child Abuse Review, 8,* 251–263.
Goldenberg, I., & Goldenberg, H. (1996). *Family therapy: An overview.* New York: Brooks-Cole.
Goldson, B. (1997). 'Childhood': An introduction to historical and theoretical analyses. In P. Scraton (Ed.), *"'Childhood' in 'Crisis'?* London: UCL Press.
Good, M. (2003). While we were hunting rabbits [Recorded by Matthew Good]. On *Avalanche* [CD]. Canada: Universal Music.
Goodley, D. (2007). Becoming rhizomatic parents: Deleuze, guattari and disabled babies. *Disability & Society, 22*(2), 145–160.
Gove, The Honorable Judge Thomas J. (1995). *Executive summary: Report of the Gove inquiry into child protection in British Columbia.* Retrieved September 23, 2005, from http://www.qp.gov.bc.ca/gove/
Guattari, F. (1984). *Molecular revolution: Psychiatry and politics.* New York City: Puffin.
Guattari, F. (2000). *The three ecologies.* London: The Athlone Press.
Haley, J. (1978). *Problem-solving therapy: [new strategies for effective family therapy].* New York: Harper & Row.
Hall, G. S. (1904). *Adolescence: Its psychology and its relations to physiology, anthropology, sociology, sex, crime, relition and education.* New York: Appleton and Company.
Hall, G. S. (1916). *Adolescence* (Vols. 2). New York: Appleton.
Hall, S., & Jefferson, T. (Eds.). (1976). *Resistance through Rituals: Youth subcultures in Post-War Britain.* London: Hutchinson.
Hardt, M., & Negri, V. (2000). *Empire.* Cambridge, Mass.: Harvard University Press.
Hare-Mustin, R. T. (1978). A feminist approach to family therapy. *Family Process, 17,* 181–194.
Hartman, A. (1991). Words create worlds. *Social Work, 36,* 275–276.
Hebdige, D. (1991). *Subculture: The meaning of style.* London, New York: Routledge.
Hebidge, D. (1997). Posing...threats, Striking...poses: Youth surveillance, and display. In K. Gelder & S. Thornton (Eds.), *The subcultures reader.* New York: Routledge.
Hendrix, K. G. (2001). Mama told me...: Exploring chilhood lessons tat laid a foundation for my "endarkened" epistemology. *Qualitative Inquiry, 7*(5), 559–577.

REFERENCES

Hoffman, L. (2000). A communal perspective for relational therapies. In M. E. Olson (Ed.), *Feminism, community and communication*. Binghamton, NY: Haworth.
Holt, N. L. (2003). Representation, legitimation, and autoethnography: An autoethnographic writing story. *International Journal of Qualitative Methods, 2*(1), 1–22.
Hook, (2001). Discourse, knowledge, materiality, history: Foucault and discourse analysis. *Theory & Psychology, 11*(4), 521–547.
Houston, S. E. (1982). The "Waifs and Strays" of a Late Victorian City: Juvenile deliquents in Toronto. In J. Parr (Ed.), *Childhood and family in Canadian history* (pp. 129–142). Toronto: McClelland and Stewart.
Ignatiev, N. (1995). *How the Irish became white*. New York: Routledge.
Irigaray, L., & Whitford, M. (1993). *The irigaray reader*. Cambridge, Mass.: Basil Blackwell.
James, C. E. (1998). "Up to no good": Black on the streets and encountering police. In V. Satzewitch (Ed.), *Racism and social inequality in Canada: Concepts, controversies and strategies of resistance*. Toronto: Thompson Educational Publishing Inc.
Johnson, P. (1983). *Native children and the child welfare system*. Toronto: James Lorimer.
Johnson, N. G., Roberts, M. C., & Worell, J. (Eds.). (1999). *Beyond apperance: A new look at adolescent girls*. Washington, DC: American Psychological Association.
Jones, A., & May, J. (1992). *Working in human service organisations: A critical introduction*. Melbourne: Longman Chesire.
Kammerman, S. B., & Kahn, A. J. (1989). *Social services for children, youth and families in the United States*. Baltimore, Maryland: Annie E. Casey Foundation.
Kaufmann, J. (2005). Autotheory: An autoehtnographic reading of Foucault. *Qualitative Inquiry, 11*(4), 576–587.
Kelly, P. (2000). The dangerousness of youth-at-risk: The possibilities of surveillance and intervention in uncertain times. *Journal of Adolescence, 23*, 463–476.
Kett, J. F. (1977). *Rites of passage: Adolescence in America 1790 to present*. New York: Basic Books, Inc.
King Keenan, E. (2001). Using Foucault's "Disciplinary Power" and "Resistance" in Cross-Cultural Psychotherapy. *Clinical Social Work Journal, 29*(3), 211–227.
Knight Abowitz, K., & Rees, R. (2005). *What is a teenager?* Obtained on September 24, 2005, from http://www.units.muohio.edu/eap/departments/edl/eduleadership/courses/334/334_What_is_teen?.html
Kohlberg, L. (1984). *The psychology of moral development: The nature and validity of moral stages /Lawrence Kohlberg* (1st ed.). San Francisco: Harper & Row.
Kogan, S. M., & Gale, J. E. (1997). Decentering therapy: Textual analysis of a narrative therapy session. *Family Process, 36*(2), 101–126.
Kochanska, G., & Askan, N. (2006). Children's conscience and self regulation. *Journal of Personality, 74*(6), 1587–1618.
Koops, W., & Zuckerman, M. (2003). Introduction: A historical developmental approach to adolescence. *The History of the Family, 8*(3), 345–354.
Kozol, J. (2005). *The shame of the nation: The restoration of apartheid schooling in America* (1st ed.). New York: Crown Publishers.
Kvale, S. (1996). *InterViews: An introduction to qualitative research interviewing*. Thousand Oaks, CA: Sage.
Laing, R. D. (1961). *Self and others*. London: Tavistock Publications.
Laing, R. D. (1965). Mystification, confusion and conflict. In I. Boszormenyi-Nagy & J. L. Framo (Eds.), *Intensive family therapy*. New York: Harper & Row. Found here: http://laingsociety.org/biblio/mystification.htm
Laing, R. D. (1967). *The politics of experience and the bird of paradise*. London: Penguin.
Laing, R. D. (1969). *The politics of the family and other essays*. New York: Pantheon Books.
Landrine, H. (1995). *Bringing cultural diversity to feminist psychology: Theory, research, and practice*. Washington, DC: American Psychological Association.
Lapadat, J. C., & Lindsay, A. C. (1999). Transcription in research and practice: From standardization of technique to interpretive positionings. *Qualitative Inquiry, 5*(1), 64–86.

Lee, J. (1997). Women re-authoring their lives through feminist narrative therapy. *Women and Therapy, 20*(3), 1–22.
Leiber, M. J., & Stairs, J. M. (1999). Race, contexts, and the use of intake diversion. *Journal of Research in Crime and Deliquency, 36*(1), 56–86.
Leslie, B., & Hare, F. (2000). *Improving the outcomes of youth in transition from care*. Toronto, Ontario: Report of Working Group, Children's Aid Society of Toronto.
Lesko, J. (1996). Denaturalizing adolescence: The politics of contemporary representations. *Youth and Society, 28*(2), 139–161.
Lesko, N. (2001). *Act your age!: A cultural construction of adolescence*. New York: Routledge Falmer.
Levy-Warren, M. (1996). *The adolescent journey: Development, identity formation, and psychotherapy*. London: Jason Aronson Inc.
Little, M. H. (1998). Ontario's mothers allowance case files as a site of contestation. In F. Iacouetta & W. Mitchinson (Eds.), *On the case: Explorations in social history* (pp. 227–240). Toronto: University of Toronto Press.
Lovell, A. M., & Scheper-Hughes, N. (1987). *Psychiatry inside out: Selected writings of Franco Basaglia*. New York: Columbia University Press.
Lyotard, J. F. (1984). *The postmodern condition: A report on knowledge*. Minneapolis: University of Minnesota Press.
Lyotard, J. F. (1984). *The postmodern condition: A report on knowledge*. Minneapolis: University of Minnesota Press.
Maccoby, E. F. (2007). Historical overview of socialization research and theory. In J. E. Grusec & P. D. Hastings (Eds.), *Handbook of socialization: Theory and research*. New York: Guilford Press.
Malinowski, B. (1964). *Argonauts of the Western Pacific; an account of native enterprise and adventure in the archipelagoes of Melanesian New Guinea. With a pref. by Sir James George Frazer*. London: Routledge & K. Paul.
Map Navigation. (n.d.). *Maps definition*. Found here: http://www.mapnavigation.net/maps-definition
Mack, D. (2000). *The assault on parenthood: How our culture undermines the family*. New York: Simon & Schuster.
Magnet, S. (2006). Protesting privilege: An ethnographic look at whiteness. *Qualitative Inquiry, 12*(4), 736–749.
Maiter, S., Palmer, S., & Manji, S. (2003). *Invisible lives: A qualitative study of 61 parents receiving child protective services. A partnerships of children and families project*. Retrieved January 07, 2005, from http://info.wlu.ca/~wwwfsw/cura/pdf/finding_a_fit/ ILTEoPRCPS_summary.pdf#search='Maiter%2C%20Palmer%20%26%20Manji%20%282003%29'
Males, M. A. (1996). *The scapegoat generation: America's War on adolescents*. Monroe, ME: Common Courage Press.
Margolin, L. (1997). *Under the cover of kindness: The invention of social work*. London: University Press of Virginia.
Marx, K., Engels, F., Engels, F., Marx, K., & Tucker, R. C. (1978). *The Marx-Engels reader* (2nd ed.). New York: Norton.
Maslach, C. (1982). *Burnout: The cost of caring*. Englewood Cliffs, NJ: Prentice-Hall.
Maslach, C., & Jackson, S. E. (1986). *The Maslach burnout inventory manual* (2nd ed.). Palo Alto, CA: Consulting Psychologists Press.
Mayerfeld Bell, M., & Bell Mayerfeld, D. (1999). *The rationalization of risk*. Obtained September 16, 2004, from http://socserver.soc.iastate.edu/sapp/Risk.html
McCallum, S. (1995). *Safe families: A model of child protection intervention based on parental voice and wisdom*. DSW Dissertation, Wilfred Laurier University, Waterloo, ON.
McGillivrary, A. (Ed.). (1997). *Governing childhood*. Vermont, USA: Darmouth Publishing Company Ltd.
McGoldrick, M. (1998). *Re-visioning family therapy: Race, culture, and gender in clinical practice*. New York: Guilford Press.
McGoldrick, M., & Gerson, R. (1985). *Genograms in family assessment* (1st ed.). New York: Norton.

McGoldrick, M., Gerson, R., McGoldrick, M., & Shellenberger, S. (1999). *Genograms: Assessment and intervention* (2nd ed.). New York: W.W. Norton.
McGoldrick, M., Giordano, J., & Garcia-Preto, N. (2005). *Ethnicity and family therapy* (3rd ed.). New York: Guilford Press.
McGraw, P. (2004). *Family first: Your step-by-step plan for creating a phenomenal family*. London: Free Press.
McKinnon, S. (2007). Mirrored asylum: Reflections on naming home and subjectivity in Ireland. *Limnalities: A Journal of Performance Studies, 3*(1).
McLaren, A. (1978). Birth control and abortion in Canada, 1870–1920. *Canadian Historical Review, 59*, 319–340.
Mead, M. (1928). *Coming of age in Samoa*. New York: Morrow.
Miehls, D., & Moffat, K. (2000). Constructing social work identity based on the reflexive self. *British Journal of Social Work, 30*, 339–348.
Minuchin, S. (1974). *Families and family therapy*. Cambridge, MA: Harvard University Press.
Mitterauer, M. (1992). *A history of youth*. Oxford, UK: Blackwell.
Mølbak, R. L. (2007). A life of variable speeds: on constructing a Deleuzian psychotherapy. *Theory & Psychology, 17*(3), 473–488.
Moradi. (2005). Advancing womanist identity development: Where we are and where we need to go. *The Counseling Psychologist, 33*(2), 225–253.
Morris, J. (2005). For the children: Accounting for careers in child protective services. *Journal of Sociology and Social Welfare, 32*(2), 131–146.
Morse, J. M. (1994). *Critical issues in qualitative research methods*. Thousand Oaks, CA: Sage.
Nichols, M. P., & Schwartz, R. C. (1995). *Family therapy: Concepts and methods*. Needhamheights, MA: Simon and Schuster.
Nederveen Pieterse, J. (1995). *The decolonization of imagination: Culture, knowledge, and power*. London, Atlantic Highlands, NJ: Zed Books.
Norman B. Leventhal Map Centre. (n.d.). *The cartographer*. Found here: http://maps.bpl.org/ex/activity/guide5/
Noy, C. (2003). The write of passage: Reflections on writing a dissertation narrative methodology. *Forum: Qualitative Social Research, 4*(2). Retrieved January 30, 2004, from http://www.qualitative-research.net/fgs/-texte/2-03/2-03noy-e.htm
OACAS CFSA/FLR Committee. (2005). *Proposed Child and Family Services Act Amendments*. A position Paper of the Ontario Association of Children's Aid Societies. Retrieved October 03, 2005, from http://www.oacas.org/whatsnew/announcements/cfsapositionpaper05march8.pdf
Ontario Human Rights Commission. (2007). *Policy and guidelines on discrimination because of family status*. Found here: http://www.ohrc.on.ca/en/resources/Policies/fampolicy/pdf
Palmer, S. E. (1983). Authority: An essential part of practice. *Social Work, 28*(2), 120–125.
Palmer, S., & Humphrey, J. A. (1995). *Deviant behaviour: Patterns, sources, and control*. New York: Plenum Press.
Palladino, G. (1996). *Teenagers: An American History*. New York: Basic Books.
Pardeck, J. T., Murphy, J. W., & Choi, J. M. (1994). Some implications of postmodernism for social work practice. *Social Work, 39*(4), 343–346.
Paré, D. A. (1996). Culture and meaning: Expanding the metaphorical repertoire of family therapy. *Family Process, 35*(1), 21–42.
Parekh, B. (1995). Liberalism and colonialism: A critique of Locke and Mill. In J. N. Pieterse & J. P. B. Parekh (Eds.), *The decolonization of the imagination, culture, knowledge and power*. London: Zed Books.
Parker, I. (1997). *Psychoanalytic culture: Psychoanalytic discourse in western society*. London: Sage Publications.
Parker, I. (2005). *Qualitative psychology: Introducing radical research*. New York: Open University Press.
Parker, I. (2007). *Revolution in psychology: Alienation to emancipation*. Pluto Press: London.

Parker, I. (2008). Psychoanalytic theory and psychology: Conditions of possibility for clinical and cultural practice. *Theory & Psychology, 18*(2), 147–165.
Parker, I., Georgaca, E., Harper, D., McLaughlin, T., & Stowell-Smith, M. (1995). *Deconstructing psychopathology*. London: Sage Publications.
Parry, A., & Doan, R. E. (1994). *Story re-visions: Narrative therapy in the postmodern world*. New York: The Guilford Press.
Peckover, S. (2002). Supporting and policing mothers: An analysis of the disciplinary practices of health visiting. *Journal of Advanced Nursing, 38*(4), 369–377.
Peikoff, T., & Brickey, S. (1991). Creating precious children and glorified mothers: A theoretical assessment of the transformation of childhood. In R. Smandych, G. Dodds, & A. Esau (Eds.), *Dimensions in childhood: Essays on the history of children and youth in Canada* (pp. 29–51). Winnipeg: Legal Research Institute of the University of Manitoba.
Pelton, L. H. (2000). The future of child protection (Book Review). *Journal of Sociology & Social Welfare, 27*(1), 184–188.
Perrot, M. (1997). Worker youth: From the workshop to the factory. In G. Levi & J. C. Schmitt (Eds.), *A History of Young People in the West* (pp. 61–73). Cambridge, Mass.: The Belknap Press of Harvard University Press.
Philaretou, A. G., & Allen, K. R. (2006). Researching sensitive topics through autoethnographic means. *The Journal of Men's Studies, 14*(1), 65–78.
Philp, M. (1985). Michele Foucault. In Q. Skinner (Ed.), *Return of grand theory in the human sciences* (pp. 65–82). New York: Press Syndicate of the University of Cambridge.
Piaget, J. (1968). *The moral judgment of the child*. London: Routledge & Kegan Paul.
Quinney, R. (1974). *Critique of the legal order*. Boston, Mass.: Little, Brown.
Raby, R. C. (2002). A tangle of discourses: Girls negotiationg adolescence. *Journal of Youth Studies, 5*(4), 425–448.
Raby, R.C. (2005). Polite, well dressed and on time: Secondary school conduct codes and the production of docile bodies. *Canadian review of sociology, 42*(1), 71–91.
Raychaba, B. (1993). *Pain lots of pain: Family violence and abuses in the lives of young people growing up in care*. Ottawa: Youth in Care Network.
Reamer, T. G. (2003). Boundary issues in social work: Managing dual relationships. *Social Work, 48*(1), 121–134.
Reed-Danahay, D. (1997). *Auto/ethnography: Rewriting the self and the social*. New York: Berg.
Richardson, L. (2000). New writing practices in qualitative research. *Sociology of Sport Journal, 17*, 5–20.
Richardson, L. (2005). Writing: A method of inquiry. In N. Denzin & Y. Lincoln (Eds.), *Handbook of Qualitative Research* (3rd ed.). Thousand Oaks, Ca: Sage.
Richardson, M. (2003). A personal reflective account: The impact of the collation and sharing of information during the course of a child protection investigation. *Child and Family Social Work, 8*, 123–132.
Roberts, J. (2005). Transparency and self-disclosure. *Family Processes, 44*(1), 45–64.
Roediger, D. R. (1991). *The wages of whiteness: Race and the making of the American working class*. London, New York: Verso.
Ronai, C. R., & Ellis, C. (1989). Turn-Ons for money: Interactional strategies of the table dancer. *Journal of Contemporary Ethnography, 18*(3), 271–298.
Rooke, P. T., & Schnell, R. L. (1982). *Studies in childhood history*. Calgary, Alberta: Detselig Enterprises Ltd.
Rorty, R. (1982). *Consequences of pragmatism*. Minneapolis: University of Minnesota Press.
Rose, P. C., & Suzanne, I. (1978). The imposter phenomenon in high achieving women: Dynamics and therapeutic intervention. *Psychotherapy Theory, Research and Practice, 15*(3), 241–247.
Rubington, E., & Weinberg, M. S. (2002). *Deviance: The interactionist perspective* (8th ed.). Toronto: Allyn and Bacon.
Rycraft, J. R. (1994). The party isn't over: The agency role in the retention of public child welfare caseworkers. *Social Work, 39*(1), 75–80.

Sandelowski, M., & Barroso, J. (2002). Reading qualitative studies. *International Journal of Qualitative Methods, 1*(1), Article 5. Retrieved September 19, 2005, from http://www.ualberta.ca/~ijqum/
Said, E. W. (1979). *Orientalism* (Vintage Books ed.). New York: Vintage Books.
Sangari, K. (1987). The politics of the possible. *Cultural Critique, 7*, 157–186.
Satir, V. (1972). *Peoplemaking*. Palo Alto, Calif.: Science and Behavior Books.
Schaefer, R. T. (2001). *Sociology* (7th ed.) New York: McGraw-Hill Book Company.
Schlessinger, L. (2000). *Parenthood by proxy: Don't have them if you won't raise them*. New York: HarperCollins Publications.
Schlessinger, L. (2008). *About Dr. Laura*. Retrieved from: http://www.drlaura.com/faq/
Schindler, N. (1997). Guardians of disorder: Rituals of youthful culture at the Dawn of the modern age. In G. Levi & J. C. Schmitt (Eds.), *Ancient and medieval rites of passage: A history of young people in the West* (pp. 259–273). London: The Belknap Press of Harvard University Press.
Scott, J. C. (1990). *Domination and the arts of resistance: Hidden transcripts*. New Haven: Yale University Press.
Scott, J. W. (1992). Experience. In J. Butler & J. W. Scott (Eds.), *Feminists theorize the political* (pp. 22–40). New York: Routledge.
Scraton, P. (Ed.). (1997). *'Childhood' in crisis?* London: UCL Press.
Shulman, L. (1985). The dynamics of child welfare: A report of a study in progress. In K. C. Levitt & B. Wharf (Eds.), *The challenge of child welfare* (pp. 276–290). Vancouver: University of B.C. Press.
Skott-Myhre, H. A. (2005). Towards a minoritarian psychology of immanence and a psychotherapy of flight: Meditations on the society of control. *Parallax: A Journal of Metadiscursive Theory and Cultural Practices, 11*(2), 44–59.
Skott-Myhre, H. A., Skott-Myhre, J. D., Skott Myhre, K. S. G., & Harris R. (2004). Radical youth work: Creating and becoming everyone. In T. Strong & D. Pare (Eds.), *Furthering talk: Advances in the discursive therapies*. Hingham, MA: Kluwer Academic Press.
Skott-Myhre, H. A., & Skott-Myhre, K. S. G. (2008). Radical youthwork: Love and community. *Journal of Relational Child and Youth Care Practice, 20*(3), 48–57.
Skott-Myhre, K. S. G. (2005). Aliens and adolescence. *International Youth and Childcare Network, December*(83).
Skott-Myhre, K. S. G. (2007). Learning my mother's magic: Mothers, daughters, youthwork and power. *Scottish Youth Issues Journal, 10*(Autumn), 29–40.
Smith, M. (2003). Questioning 'child protection' – 1. The International Child and Youth Care Network. Issue 58. Retrieved January 13, 2005, from http://www.cyc-net.org/cyc-online/cycol-1103-smith.html
Snell, J. (1983). The white life for two: The defence of marriage and sexual morality in Canada, 1800–1914. *Histore Social, 16*(31), 111–128.
Spiro, M. E. (1993). *Oedipus in the Trobriands*. New Brunswick, USA: Transaction Publishers.
Spring, J. (1994). *The American School, 1642–1993* (3rd ed.). New York: McGraw-Hill, Inc.
Stalker, C., & Harvey, C. (2002). *Professional burnout: A review of theory, research, and prevention. Partnerships for children and families project*. Retrieved September 12, 2005, from http://info.wlu.ca/pcfproject/pdf/theme_papers/PB.pdf#search='burnout%20in%20social%20work'
Statistics Canada. (2006a). *Definitions of concepts and variables: Census family*. 2006 Census. Version updated July 3, 2006. http://www.statcan.ca/english/concepts/definitions/cen-family.htm
Statistics Canada. (2006b). Population and housing census short form. 2006 Census. Found here: http://unstats.un.org/unsd/demographic/sources/census/quest/CAN/CAN2006enS.pdf
Stoler, A. L. (1995). *Race and the education of desire: Foucault's History of sexuality and the colonial order of things*. Durham: Duke University Press.
Sutherland, N. (1997). *Growing up: Childhood in English Canada from the great war to the age of television*. Toronto, Ontario: University of Toronto Press.
Sutherland, N. (1976). *Children in English-Canadian society: Framing the twentieth-century consensus*. Toronto, Ontario: University of Toronto Press.
Tait, G. (2000). *Youth, sex & government*. New York: Peter Lang.

Tanner, J. (2001). *Teenage troubles: Youth and deviance in Canada*. Scarborough, ON: Thomas Canada Ltd..

The Aboriginal Justice Implementation Committee. (1999). *Report of the aboriginal justice inquiry of Manitoba*. Retrieved September 29, 2005, from http://www.ajic.mb.ca/volume.html

Tierney, W. G. (2001). The autonomy of knowledge and the decline of the subject: Postmodernism and the reformulation of the University. *Higher Education, 41*(4), 353–372.

Tomison, A. M. (2001). A history of child protection: Back to the future? *Family Matters, 60*, 46–57.

Toulmin, S. E. (1969). *The uses of argument*. Cambridge, England: Cambridge University Press.

Trevithick, P. (2000). *Social work skills: A practice handbook*. London: Open University Press.

Tyler, S. A. (1986). Post-modern ethnography: From document of the occult to occult document. In J. Clifford & G. E. Marcus (Eds.), *Writing culture: The poetics and politics of ethnography*. London: University of California Press.

Tyyska, V. (2001). *Long and winding road: Adolescents and youth in Canada today*. Toronto, Ontario: Canadian Scholars Press.

United Nations Statistical Division. (1998). *Principles and recommendations for population and housing censuses, revision 1*. New York: United Nations publication. Found here: http://unstats.un.org/unsd/publication/SeriesM/SeriesM_67rev1E.pdf

United Nations Statistical Division. (2001). *Principles and recommendations for a vital statistics system, revision 2*. New York: United Nations publication. Found here: http://unstats.un.org/unsd/publication/SeriesM/SeriesM_19rev2E.pdf

United Nations Statistical Division. (2007a). *2010 world population and housing census programme*. New York: United Nations publication. Found here: http://unstats.un.org/unsd/demographic/sources/census/2010_PHC/more.htm

United Nations Statistical Division. (2007b). *Principles governing international statistical activities*. New York: United Nations publication. Found here: http://unstats.un.org/unsd/methods/statorg/Principles_stat_activities/principles_stat_activities.pdf

University of Wisconsin Cartography Laboratory. (2006). *What is a map?* Found here: http://www.geography.wisc.edu/cartography/maps.htm

Valverde, M. (1991). *The age of light, water and soap: Moral reform in English Canada, 1885–1925*. Toronto: McLelland & Stewart.

Van Nijnatten, C., van den Ackerveken, M., & Slaats, M. (2000). Conceptions of professional authority in child protection. *Youth & Society, 31*(4), 456–468.

Wall, S. (2006). An autoethnography on learning about autoethnography. *International Journal of Qualitative Methods, 5*(2), 1–12.

Watzlawick, P., Fisch, R., & Weakland, J. H. (1974). *Change; principles of problem formation and problem resolution* (1st ed.). New York: Norton.

Weakland, J. H., & Ray, W. A. (1995). *Propagations: Thirty years of influence from the Mental Research Institute*. New York: Haworth Press.

Weeks, K. (2007). Life wihin and against work: Affective labor, feminist critique, and post fordist politics. *Ephemera: Theory and plotics in organization, 7*(1), 233–249.

Weingarten, K. (1998). The small and the ordinary: The daily practice of a postmodern narrative therapy. *Family Process, 37*(1), 3–15.

Wilford, G., & Hetherington, R. (1997). *Families ask for help: Parental perceptions of child welfare and child protection services in an Anglo-German study*. London, UK: Centre for Comparative Social Work Studies, Brunel University.

White, M., & Epston, D. (1990). *Narrative means to therapeutic ends* (1st ed.). New York: Norton.

Wolfe, D. A., & Mash, E. J. (2005). Behavioral and emotional problems in adolescents: Overviews and issues. In D. A. Wolfe & E. J. Mash (Eds.), *Behavioral and emotional disorders in adolescents: Nature, assessment and treatment*. New York: Guilford Press.

Woodson, R. L. (2001). Breaking the cycle of family breakdown: Against all odds. *The World and I Online*. Retrieved March 03, 2005, from http://www.worldandi.com/public/2001/June/woodson.html

Wylie, B. J. (1997). *Family: An exploration*. Canada: Northstone Publishing Inc.

REFERENCES

Zempel, S. (1991). *In their own words: Letters from Norwegian immigrants.* Minneapolis, Minn.: University of Minnesota Press.

NOTES

[1] A "Body without Organs" (BwO) is "made in such a way that it can be occupied, populated only by intensities", and is therefore a kind of "matter that occupies space to a given degree – to the degree corresponding to the intensities produced" (Deleuze & Guattari, 1987, p. 153).

[2] The BwO "is the *field of immanence* of desire, the *plane of consistency* specific to desire" (Deleuze & Guattari, 1987, p. 154).

[3] Deleuze and Guattari (1987) define desire as "a process of production without reference to any exterior agency, whether it be a lack that hollows it out or a pleasure that fills it" (p. 154).

[1] The term chola generally refers to a young latina woman who is closely afflilated with a latino gang. A chola is not simply the girlfriend of a gang member but is as "tough" as the male members of the gang and will defend her barrio and anyone affiliated with her gang.

Lightning Source UK Ltd.
Milton Keynes UK
UKOW050717141012

200547UK00006B/15/P

9 789460 917479